Building Resilient Migration Systems in the Mediterranean Region

Building Resilient Migration Systems in the Mediterranean Region

Lessons from COVID-19

Mauro Testaverde and
Jacquelyn Pavilon

WORLD BANK GROUP

Contents

Boxes

Figures

Maps

Tables

Foreword

For thousands of years, migration has been a source of social and economic well-being for people living on different shores of the Mediterranean Sea. Whether through higher earnings for migrants, access to labor for receiving countries, or remittances for sending communities, migration has been an important driver of development in the Mediterranean region. Economic disparities, diverging population dynamics, conflict, and climate change have all led people in the region to cross national borders and will likely continue to play roles in the future.

The diversity of the migration paths, stories, and experiences of people moving across the Mediterranean is unique. The southern and eastern shores of the Mediterranean are home to both large sending countries such as Algeria, the Arab Republic of Egypt, Morocco, and Tunisia and to important destinations such as the Gulf Cooperation Council states. Jordan, Lebanon, and Turkey currently host and, in some cases, are transit points for large numbers of refugees while also being important senders of economic migrants. Several North African countries are also transit hubs and at times hosts of many migrants from Sub-Saharan Africa. On the northern Mediterranean shores, many European countries have large immigrant populations while at the same time sending migrants within and outside the region.

The COVID-19 (coronavirus) pandemic has severely disrupted this complex web of movements across the Mediterranean, raising questions about whether migration will continue to be an important driver of the region's well-being. To contain the spread of the virus, countries imposed strict mobility restrictions in early 2020. However, as time passed, the economic costs of these measures have become increasingly apparent, including via channels that directly affected not only migrants but also their receiving and sending countries. It also became clear that the drivers of migration in the Mediterranean region are so strong that mobility restrictions can only reduce movements, not halt them entirely.

As discussed in *Building Resilient Migration Systems in the Mediterranean Region: Lessons from COVID-19*, the lessons learned during the COVID-19 pandemic provide key insights that can inform the response to future shocks. While some of the challenges that emerged during the pandemic are specific to public health crises, others are common to different types of shocks, including those related to economic, conflict, or climate-related factors. Ukraine's ongoing crisis with its large refugee inflows into Eastern European countries is a tragic reminder that migration and forced displacement will remain relevant issues for the region for years to come. This book also shows that the COVID-19 crisis has exacerbated problems with the Mediterranean migration regime that predate the pandemic. Delays in admitting migrant workers in receiving countries and only partial access to key services in both source and destination countries are examples of challenges that limit the developmental impact of migration even in the absence of shocks.

This book also suggests that countries in the region were able to adapt their migration systems to address some of the challenges created by the COVID-19 pandemic. Mobility restrictions were lifted, new health protocols established, migration procedures fast-tracked, and coverage of basic services expanded. These efforts show that mobility in the Mediterranean region can and should continue safely in the wake of large shocks. However, although these actions were key to addressing the pandemic's immediate impacts, this book highlights the importance of more systematic reforms to better respond to future shocks. To inform this reform process, it suggests a set of actions that can help Mediterranean countries maximize the benefits of migration for *all* people living in the region while at the same time ensuring the sustainability of migration flows. The COVID-19 pandemic has created momentum for policy reforms. Mediterranean countries cannot miss the unique opportunity to write a new chapter in the region's history of migration.

Asli Demirgüç-Kunt
Chief Economist
Europe and Central Asia
The World Bank

Roberta Gatti
Chief Economist
Middle East and North Africa
The World Bank

Acknowledgments

This book was prepared by a team drawn from the Social Protection and Jobs Global Practice and the Development Economics Research Group of the World Bank, in partnership with the Center for Mediterranean Integration and under the joint guidance of the World Bank's Europe and Central Asia and Middle East and North Africa Chief Economist Offices. The authors of the book are Mauro Testaverde and Jacquelyn Pavilon. Gael de Moraes and Janis Kreuder provided excellent research assistance. The authors benefited from background analyses provided by Philippe Fargues, Giulia Marchesini, Sandra Rozo, and Jackline Wahba.

The authors thank Quy-Toan Do and Çağlar Özden, task team leaders, for their guidance during the various stages of this work; Daniel Lederman and Michael Lokshin for their detailed comments and support; and Giulia Marchesini for her key contributions to the overall task. The book benefited from discussions with representatives from the Agence Française de Développement, the European Bank for Reconstruction and Development, the European Commission, the Organisation for Economic Co-operation and Development, the International Organization for Migration, and the Policy Center for the New South as well as with participants from policy and academic institutions in Europe and North Africa during consultations held in Marseille and virtually at the initial and final stages of this work, respectively. Special thanks to Amal El Ouassif, Francesco Fusaro, and Caterina Francesca Guidi for their insightful comments during the virtual consultation held in December 2021. The contributions of the Center for Mediterranean Integration were key for the success of these events.

During the preparation of this book, the team received insightful comments and useful material from Anush Bezhanyan, Kevin Carey, Philippe Fargues, Daniel Garrote Sanchez, Johannes Koettl, Anna Maria Mayda, David McKenzie, Cem Mete, Harry Moroz, Ganesh Seshan, and Jackline Wahba.

The work was conducted under the general guidance and intellectual leadership of Asli Demirgüç-Kunt, Roberta Gatti, and Blanca Moreno-Dodson. The team is grateful for the excellent advice provided by the following peer reviewers at the concept note and decision review stages: Xavier Devictor, Roberta Gatti, Anna Maria Mayda, Truman Packard, Dilip Ratha, and Federica Saliola. We thank Heran Getachew Negatu, Swati Raychaudhuri, and Suzette Dahlia Samms-Lindsay for providing excellent administrative support.

About the Authors

Jacquelyn Pavilon is the deputy director of the Center for Migration Studies of New York. She is a labor economist whose research focuses on migration, forced displacement, and immigration policy. In addition to working on various projects at the World Bank, Jacquelyn previously worked for the Georgetown University Initiative on Innovation, Development, and Evaluation on several randomized control trials to study digital financial inclusion in East Africa; as the international communications coordinator for Jesuit Refugee Service International in Rome; and as a mathematician for Chicago-based WMS Gaming Inc. She obtained her doctorate in economics from Georgetown University.

Mauro Testaverde is a senior economist in the Social Protection and Jobs Global Practice of the World Bank. Mauro's work focuses on labor markets, human capital development, and migration policies. His research on these topics has been published in economic journals including the *Scandinavian Journal of Economics* and *The World Bank Economic Review*. Since 2012, Mauro has been part of and led World Bank teams providing technical and analytical assistance in the areas of labor policy, migration, and refugee integration in Europe and Southeast Asia. Before joining the World Bank, Mauro was part of the migration research team at the University of Southampton (UK), where he earned a doctorate in economics and a master's degree in econometrics.

Abbreviations

3RP	Regional Refugee and Resilience Plan
ADBI	Asian Development Bank Institute
AU	African Union
COVID-19	Coronavirus Disease 2019
EC	European Commission
ECOWAS	Economic Community of West African States
ESSN	Emergency Social Safety Net
EU	European Union
EU-LFS	European Union Labour Force Survey
FAO	Food and Agriculture Organization of the United Nations
Frontex	European Border and Coast Guard Agency
GCC	Gulf Cooperation Council
GDP	gross domestic product
GFMD	Global Forum on Migration and Development
GIZ	German Agency for International Cooperation (Deutsche Gesellschaft für Internationale Zusammenarbeit)
IBC	International Blue Crescent
ICT	information and communication technology
ICU	intensive care unit
IFRC	International Federation of Red Cross and Red Crescent Societies
ILO	International Labour Organization
IMISCOE	International Migration, Integration and Social Cohesion in Europe
INPS	National Institute for Social Security (Italy) (Istituto Nazionale della Previdenza Sociale)
IOM	International Organization for Migration

ISCO	International Standard Classification of Occupations
IT	information technology
KNOMAD	Global Knowledge Partnership on Migration and Development
MMC	Mixed Migration Centre
MoMRA	Ministry of Municipalities and Rural Affairs (Saudi Arabia)
NGO	nongovernmental organization
NUTS	Nomenclature of Territorial Units for Statistics
OAMDI	Open Access Micro Data Initiative
OCHA	United Nations Office for the Coordination of Humanitarian Affairs
OECD	Organisation for Economic Co-operation and Development
O*NET	Occupational Information Network
PCR	polymerase chain reaction
PISA	Programme for International Student Assessment
SIM	Subscriber Identity Module
SVR	Expert Council of German Foundations on Integration and Migration
TRC	Turkish Red Crescent Society
UAE	United Arab Emirates
UK	United Kingdom
UN	United Nations
UN DESA	United Nations Department of Economic and Social Affairs
UNDP	United Nations Development Programme
UN ESCWA	United Nations Economic and Social Commission for Western Asia
UNHCR	United Nations High Commissioner for Refugees
UNICEF	United Nations Children's Fund
UNODC	United Nations Office on Drugs and Crime
US	United States
WFP	World Food Programme
WHO	World Health Organization

Overview

Introduction

This report presents evidence on the effects of the COVID-19 pandemic on mobility in the Mediterranean region to inform policy responses that can help countries restart migration safely and better respond to future shocks. Given its unique position connecting Africa, Asia, and Europe, the Mediterranean Sea has been a bridge between different cultures throughout human history. The flows of people across its shores date back to at least ancient Greek civilization and have continued in different forms since then. The COVID-19 pandemic has been a large and unforeseen public health shock that triggered immediate policy responses aimed at protecting people from the spread of the virus, including by limiting mobility within and across borders.

Given the important role of migration in the economic and social well-being of the people living in Mediterranean countries and economies,[1] this report presents evidence on the pandemic's short- and long-term impacts on the region's migrants and on their receiving and sending communities. States in the Gulf Cooperation Council (GCC) are also included in the discussions given their important role as destinations of Mediterranean migrants.[2] Distinguishing between new challenges posed by the COVID-19 crisis and preexisting issues exacerbated by the pandemic, the report not only proposes policies for restarting migration safely amid the ongoing public health crisis; it also recommends ways to better respond to future shocks and ensure the sustainability of migration flows. While some of the proposed policy actions focus on challenges typically arising in the context of public health shocks, other actions are suitable to respond to a broader set of shocks, including those related to economic, conflict, or climate-related factors.

Main findings

The report shows that the COVID-19 crisis significantly disrupted mobility in the extended Mediterranean region. Of all the world's immigrants, one in every four lives in the extended Mediterranean region, which includes Mediterranean and GCC countries and economies. Almost one in every six emigrants in the world is from this region. But since the beginning of the COVID-19 outbreak in early 2020, all of the region's countries and economies have imposed mobility restrictions of some type to contain the unforeseen public health crisis (figure O.1). The result has been a significant decline in mobility, as several examples illustrate:

- In France and Spain, permanent migration decreased by 21 percent and 38 percent, respectively, between 2019 and 2020 (OECD 2021).
- In Saudi Arabia, the number of work visas in the second half of 2020 declined by 91 percent relative to the same period in 2019 (Baruah et al. 2021).
- New asylum applications throughout the European Union (EU) Mediterranean countries dropped significantly in 2020.[3]

Figure O.1   Share of Mediterranean and GCC countries and economies with mobility restrictions, by type, 2020–21

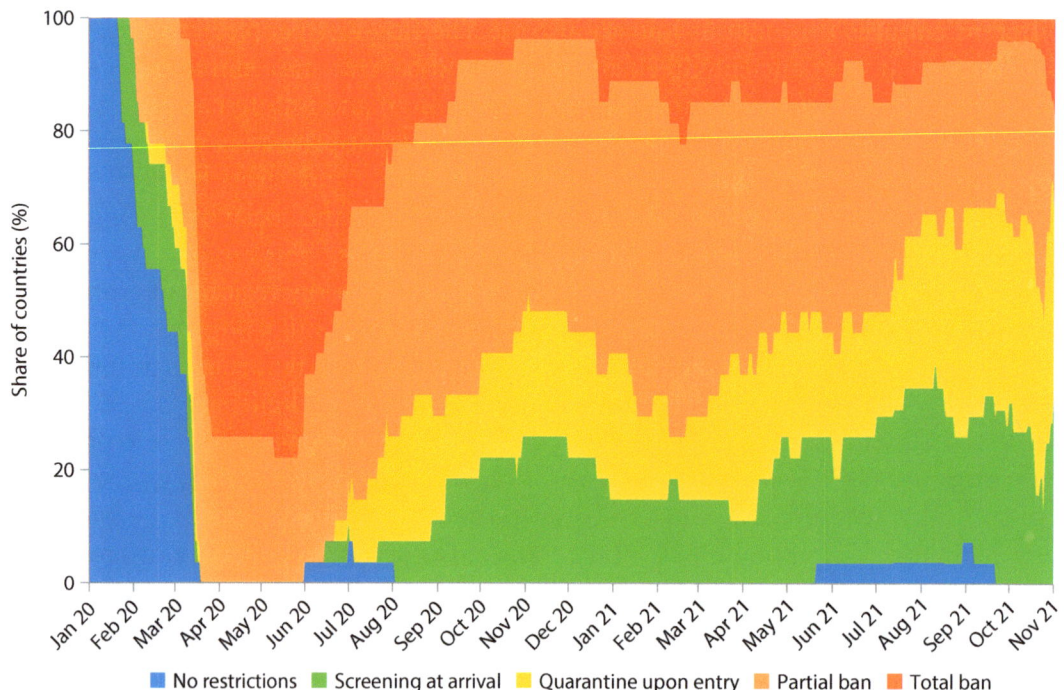

Source: Hale et al. 2021.
Note: The data cover 21 Mediterranean countries and economies as well as the Gulf Cooperation Council (GCC) countries: Bahrain, Kuwait, Oman, Qatar, Saudi Arabia, and the United Arab Emirates. Data for Montenegro were unavailable.

Mobility restrictions reshaped migration flows but did not halt them entirely. Migration in the region is driven by economic motivations, forced displacement, and often a combination of the two. These drivers persisted despite the restrictions and migrants' potential concerns about their own health, as demonstrated by the persistence of mobility flows to some countries during the pandemic. For instance, although arrivals of asylum seekers to Greece dipped at the beginning of the pandemic in March 2020 and never rebounded throughout 2020 and 2021, arrivals to Spain were higher for most of 2020 than in 2019 and even higher in 2021. Arrivals to Italy were also consistently higher for most of 2020 than in 2019 and substantially higher throughout 2021 than in each of the two previous years (figure O.2).

Figure O.2   Land and sea arrivals of migrants at the EU's main points of entry and in selected Mediterranean countries, 2019–21

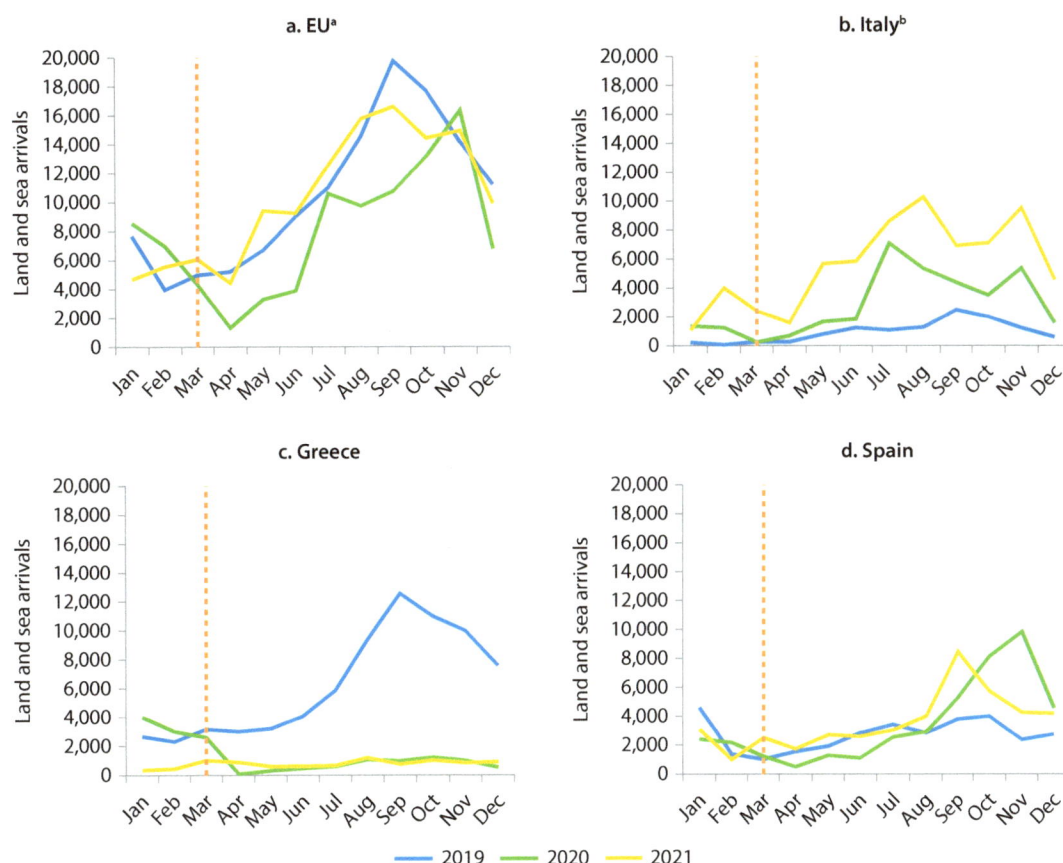

Source: United Nations High Commissioner for Refugees (UNHCR) Operational Data Portal on Refugee Situations, Mediterranean Situation monthly data (https://data2.unhcr.org/en/situations/mediterranean).
Note: The vertical line designates the onset of the COVID-19 pandemic in March 2020 and the subsequent one-year mark in March 2021.
a. Panel a encompasses the main points of entry to the European Union (EU), as defined by the UNHCR data: (1) sea arrivals to Cyprus, Greece, Italy, Malta, and Spain; and (2) land arrivals to Greece and Spain.
b. Only sea arrivals to Italy are documented.

Those who moved during the pandemic—partial closures notwithstanding—faced significant risk. More dangerous routes were more frequently used. For instance, more than 2.5 times more people used the deadliest route to Europe—from North Africa to Italy—in 2020 than in 2019.[4] An increase in arrivals to Europe via the Canary Islands resulted in a doubling of fatalities in the first eight months of 2021 compared with the same period in 2020 (IOM 2021). Migrants in West and North Africa also reported a greater reliance on smugglers, higher smuggling fees, and smugglers taking more dangerous routes (MMC 2020), as shown in figure O.3. Vulnerabilities to risks including domestic violence and economic exploitation were particularly severe for women.

Even the partial disruption to mobility had economic consequences. Migrants fill labor shortages across the region in both high- and low-skill jobs. Before the pandemic, there was a positive correlation between the share of foreigners in an occupation and the share of European countries that reported labor shortages in that occupation, with the most extreme shortage being for nursing professionals (figure O.4). Migrants account for the majority of the workforce in every GCC country (De Bel-Air 2017, 2018a, 2018b, 2018c, 2019a, 2019b). They also play important roles in critical supply chains. In Turkey, for example, 20 percent of agricultural workers were refugees in 2019 (3RP 2020). In Italy, approximately 27 percent of the formal agricultural workforce are foreigners (EPRS 2021).

Once the COVID-19 pandemic began, whether migrants continued to work in essential jobs or endured their own employment disruptions, they faced challenges in protecting themselves from the health risks of the crisis, with spillover effects for source and destination communities. Migrants faced greater COVID-19–related health impacts than native-born populations—with more infections, hospital admissions, intensive care unit (ICU) treatments, and deaths per capita while already experiencing significant unmet health needs before the crisis (figure O.5). Migrants' living conditions, such as overcrowded housing, employment in frontline occupations, and limited or lack of access to adequate health care, help explain these greater impacts.

Infections among migrant populations also put local populations at risk. In Saudi Arabia, for instance, most COVID-19 cases were among migrants at the beginning of the pandemic (Sorkar 2020), drawing attention to the importance of ensuring health protection for everyone if the spread of the virus is to be limited effectively. Return migrants can also be vectors of contagion if health protocols to ensure safe returns are not established. This was the case in some countries outside of the Mediterranean region in the early months of the crisis (Barker et al. 2020).

Migrants also faced significant employment disruptions, which were compounded by limited access to social welfare programs. Especially in 2020, employment rates dropped more among migrants than natives, particularly in Cyprus, Greece, Italy, and Spain (figure O.6). In other receiving countries and economies in the extended Mediterranean, the pandemic was particularly disruptive to migrants who were

Figure O.3 Changes in migrant smuggling from West and North Africa since the start of the COVID-19 pandemic

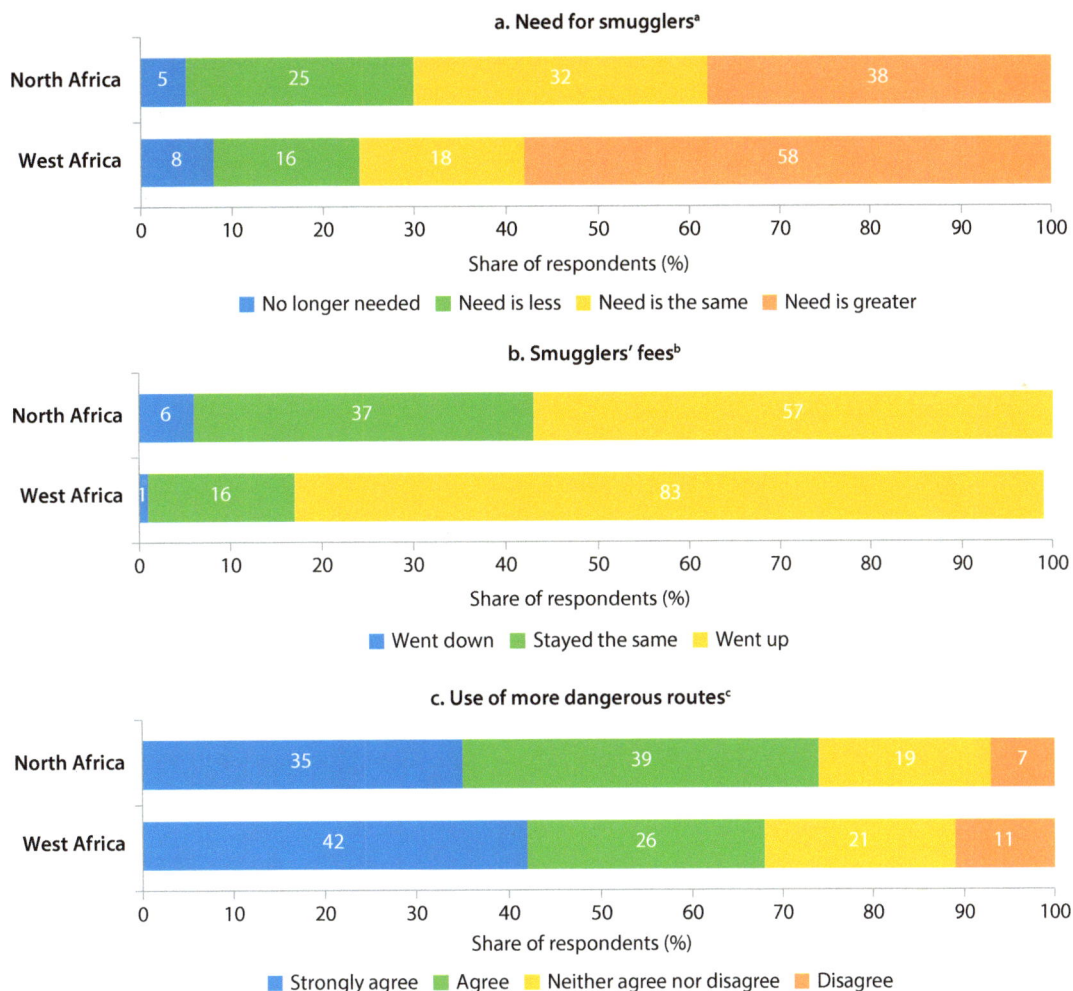

a. Need for smugglers[a]

North Africa	5 / 25 / 32 / 38
West Africa	8 / 16 / 18 / 58

Share of respondents (%)

■ No longer needed ■ Need is less ■ Need is the same ■ Need is greater

b. Smugglers' fees[b]

North Africa	6 / 37 / 57
West Africa	1 / 16 / 83

Share of respondents (%)

■ Went down ■ Stayed the same ■ Went up

c. Use of more dangerous routes[c]

North Africa	35 / 39 / 19 / 7
West Africa	42 / 26 / 21 / 11

Share of respondents (%)

■ Strongly agree ■ Agree ■ Neither agree nor disagree ■ Disagree

Source: MMC 2020.
Note: Survey was taken July 2–31, 2020. Responses of "Don't know/Prefer not to respond" are excluded from the totals used to calculate the percentages shown.
a. To the question, "How has the need for smuggling changed during the COVID-19 crisis?" 27 percent of 341 respondents in North Africa and 24 percent of 561 respondents in West Africa answered, "Don't know/Prefer not to respond." Their responses are excluded from the total shown.
b. To the question, "Have smugglers' fees changed since the start of the COVID-19 crisis?" 34 percent of 329 respondents in North Africa and 32 percent of 530 respondents in West Africa answered, "Don't know/Prefer not to respond." Their responses are excluded from the total shown.
c. To the question, "Are smugglers using more dangerous routes since the start of the COVID-19 crisis?" 4 percent of 329 respondents in North Africa and 9 percent of 530 respondents in West Africa answered, "Don't know/Prefer not to respond." Their responses are excluded from the total shown.

Figure O.4   **Share of European countries with labor shortages, by occupation, and share of foreign workers in those occupations, 2018–19**

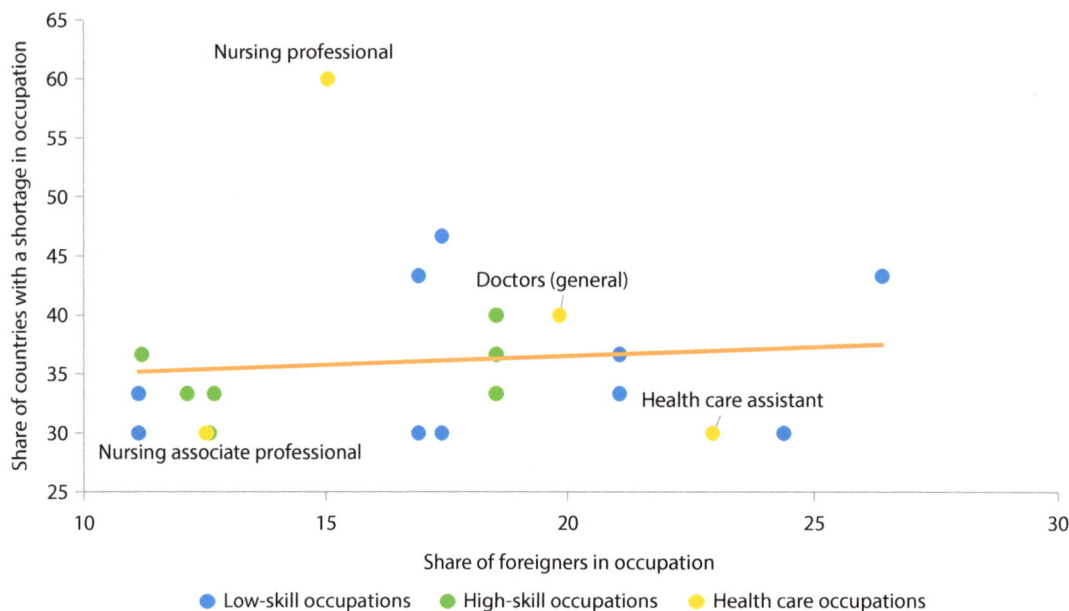

Sources: European Union Labour Force Survey (EU-LFS) 2018 data, Eurostat (https://ec.europa.eu/eurostat); EC 2020a.
Note: The x-axis is the 2018 share of foreigners in each occupation in the EU-28 (pre-Brexit) countries plus Iceland, Norway, and Switzerland, according to the EU-LFS. Shares are calculated using survey weights. The y-axis is the share of EU-28 countries (plus Norway and Switzerland but excluding Austria and France, which did not submit data) that reported a shortage in each occupation in the second half of 2019 (EC 2020a). Outliers across all occupations in the EU-LFS with a share of foreigners more than three standard deviations from the mean are excluded.

already experiencing food insecurity, including refugees in Turkey (figure O.7). Migrants were more likely than natives to be in poverty even before the pandemic. Then during the pandemic, they were less equipped to address the economic impacts because unemployment benefits, guaranteed minimum income schemes, and other safety nets are mostly reserved for nationals or long-term residents in most of the region's receiving countries (GFMD 2020; Lafleur and Vintila 2020).

The combination of budget constraints, reduced economic options, and mobility restrictions has stranded many migrants in the region. The International Organization for Migration (IOM) estimated that 2.75 million migrants whose movements were affected by COVID-19 were stranded worldwide as of September 2020 (IOM 2020). Of these, approximately 1.3 million people were in the Middle East and North Africa. This was particularly the case in the GCC countries.

Migrants' employment losses could also negatively influence the welfare of households in sending countries through the loss of remittance income. Some countries outside the Mediterranean region experienced these negative impacts in the first months

Figure O.5   Share of people with unmet health needs in selected Mediterranean countries, by place of birth, 2016

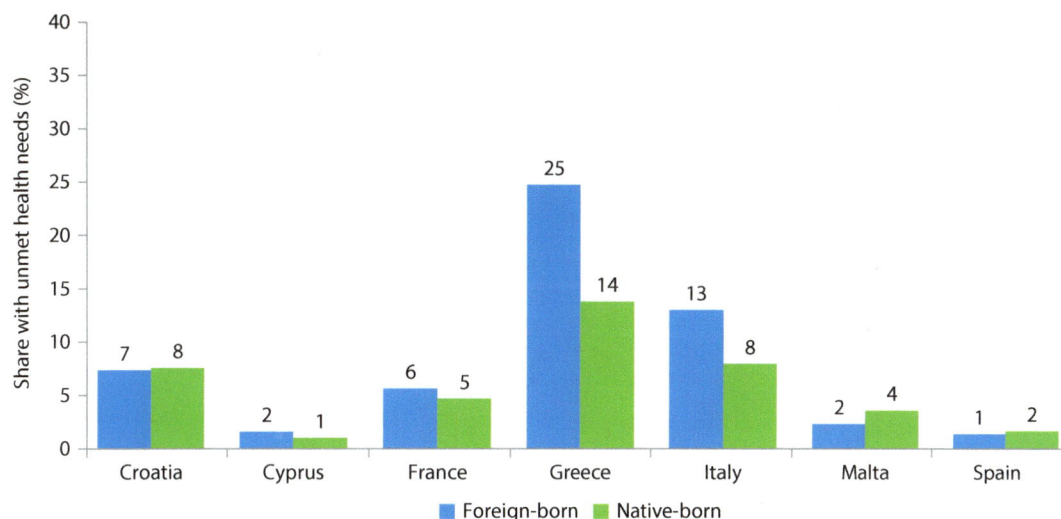

Source: OECD and EU 2018.

Note: Populations measured are those age 16 years and over. The shares are adjusted to account for the difference in age distribution between the foreign-born and native-born populations.

of the pandemic (Barker et al. 2020). In 2020, the World Food Programme projected that in 79 countries where it operates, at least 32.9 million people could be at risk of acute food insecurity from the loss of remittances (IOM and WFP 2020). However, despite these large overarching projected decreases, remittances dropped in some countries and rose in others in 2020 while steadily resurging in 2021.

Coupled with negative employment shocks, the interruptions in learning during the pandemic may have long-term implications for migrants' integration into their host communities. In addition to severe disruptions of economic activity worldwide, the crisis has led to prolonged closures of schools and training centers, with most countries trying to continue their activities using online platforms. Likewise, integration courses for adult migrants and refugees have also been suspended or delivered online. However, some subgroups of migrants faced considerable setbacks in the transition to distance learning owing to factors that preexisted the pandemic, such as language barriers and limited access to technology (figure O.8). These setbacks may lead many to drop out, as was the case in Germany, where only 38 percent of eligible adult migrants moved into the online integration courses in the first months of the pandemic (OECD 2020). These trends may have significant impacts on long-term integration. As several studies show, not only work experience but also language acquisition, skills development, and interactions with members of the host community play important roles in the economic and sociocultural integration of migrants and refugees (Chiswick and Miller 2014; Özden and Wagner 2020; Schuettler and Caron 2020; Zorlu and Hartog 2018).

Figure O.6   Change in employment rate between 2019 and 2020 in selected Mediterranean countries, by quarter and place of birth

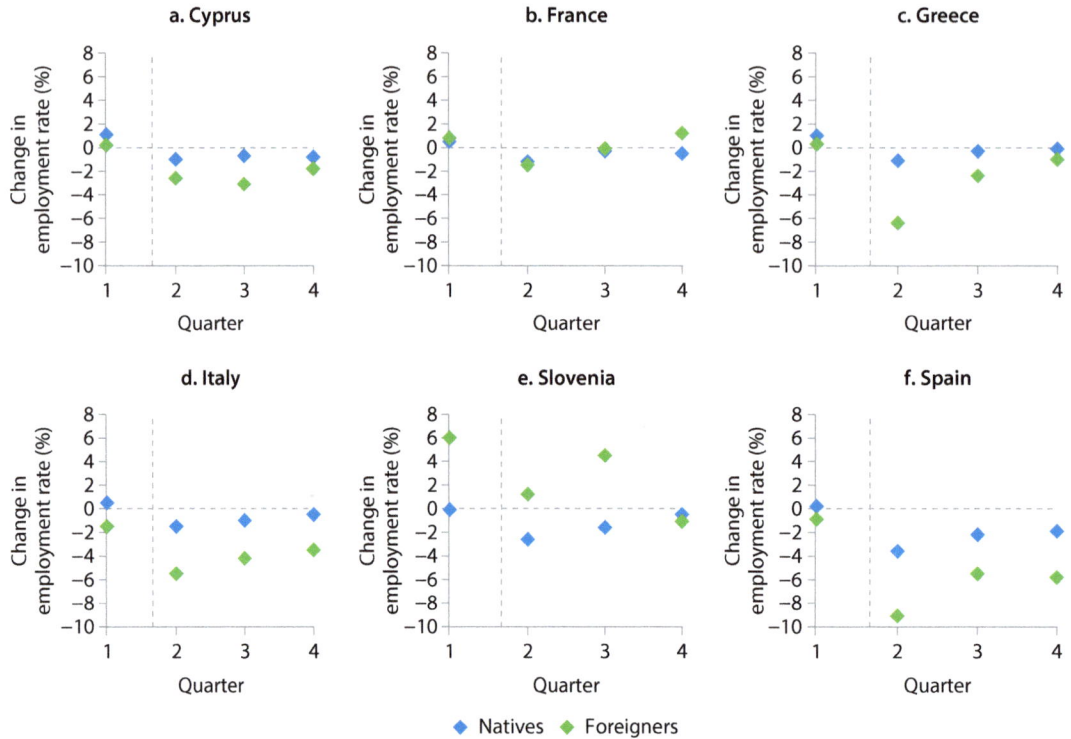

Source: Statistical Office of the European Union (Eurostat) database (https://ec.europa.eu/eurostat).
Note: The vertical line designates the onset of the COVID-19 pandemic in March 2020.

Figure O.7   Food insecurity among refugee households in Turkey, before the pandemic

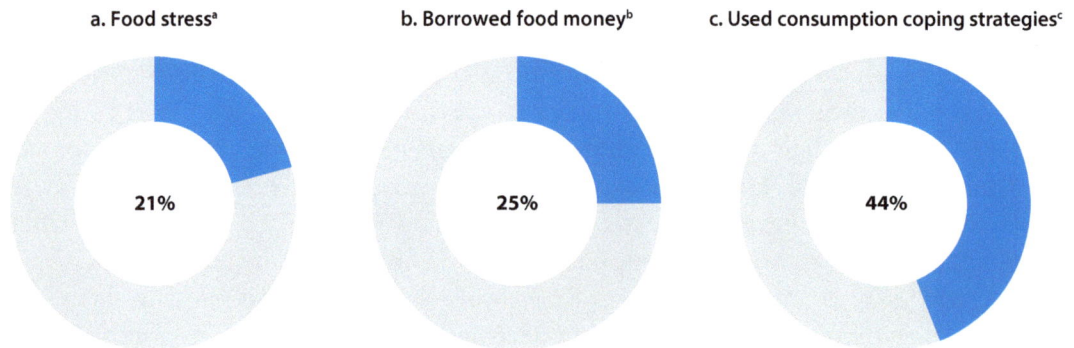

Source: WFP 2020.
a. Food stress was indicated by allocation of more than 65 percent of total household expenditure on food.
b. Percentage is the share of refugees who bought food with money they had borrowed in the three months preceding the World Food Programme (WFP) Comprehensive Vulnerability Monitoring Exercise (CVME).
c. Food-related consumption coping strategies included eating less-preferred, less-expensive foods; reducing meal portion sizes or the number of meals eaten per day; limiting adult intake so children can eat; and borrowing food or relying on help from friends or relatives.

Figure O.8   ICT availability at home for 15-year-old students in selected Mediterranean countries, 2018

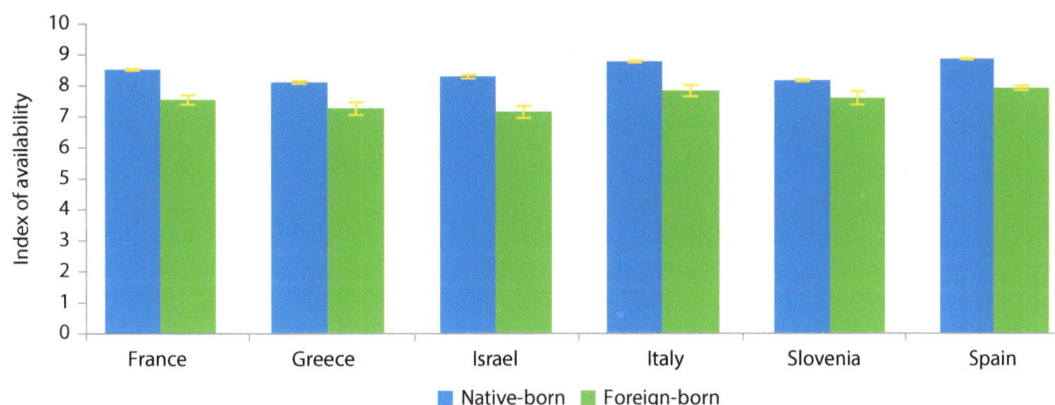

Source: Organisation for Economic Co-operation and Development (OECD) Programme for International Student Assessment (PISA) 2018 database (https://www.oecd.org/pisa/data/2018database/).
Note: The "native-born" group does not include second-generation immigrants. The results do not differ significantly when second-generation immigrants are included in the "native-born" group. The gold error bars indicate the standard error. The "index of availability" is a sum of how many of 10 specified information and communication technology (ICT) devices or connections the student has available at home. Foreign-born students with at least one native-born parent are also excluded from the analysis.

Openness to migration, and ultimately integration, also could be limited by the rising adverse sentiments toward migrants. An emerging number of studies point to the link between COVID-19 and antiforeign sentiments. Several studies find that public opinion toward immigrants turned more negative and that exclusionary attitudes increased (Lu and Sheng 2020; Ratha et al. 2021; Yamagata, Teraguchi, and Miura 2021). However, the important role played by migrants in responding to the crisis may also positively affect attitudes toward migration, since crises do not inevitably mean that natives' views will worsen (Dennison and Geddes 2020). Nonetheless, if misinformation is not addressed and if migration is perceived as an even more salient issue after the pandemic, negative attitudes could pose major challenges to migrants' integration in the long term.

Countries' policy responses

Countries and economies in the extended Mediterranean region adapted their migration systems to better manage migration as new challenges emerged during the global public health crisis. Mobility restrictions increased risks for people on the move. Worker shortages threatened economic recovery. Concentrated COVID-19 outbreaks among migrant workers increased the risk of transmission to local populations. As these different challenges emerged, Mediterranean and GCC countries and economies responded with varying degrees of success.

Recognizing the important role played by migrant workers, the region's countries and economies have introduced exemptions to allow entry. During the pandemic, several countries have simplified administrative procedures and loosened requirements to make sure that migrants were available to help countries address the health and economic impacts of the crisis. For instance, Spain sped up the processes of recognizing foreign doctors' and nurses' professional qualifications and of granting visas for immigrants—including asylum seekers with pending cases—in these health care professions (Moroz, Shrestha, and Testaverde 2020). In most EU countries, occupations that justified continued admission during the COVID-19 crisis included (a) health care professionals, health researchers, and eldercare professionals; (b) transport personnel engaged in haulage of goods, plus other transport staff; and (c) seasonal workers employed in agriculture (EC 2020b).

Governments also increased health and social welfare protection for migrants, showing that systems can become more flexible in response to shocks. Some European and GCC countries expanded health care access for migrants during the pandemic (Moroz, Shrestha, and Testaverde 2020). Several EU countries also introduced communication campaigns to inform migrants and refugees about the risks associated with COVID-19 and about transmission prevention measures and support services available during the crisis. Countries within and outside the region have also taken measures to include migrants in social protection schemes during the pandemic. For example, migrant workers with permits could apply for the federal stimulus payment in Italy and for pandemic-specific unemployment benefits in Ireland (Moroz, Shrestha, and Testaverde 2020). A direct cash transfer scheme benefiting refugees that was already in place in Turkey—the Emergency Social Safety Net (ESSN), funded by the EU and implemented by the Turkish Red Crescent—was expanded between June and July 2021 to help refugees cope with the negative impacts of the pandemic (IFRC and TRC 2021). The Jordanian government, together with the United Nations Children's Fund (UNICEF), provided emergency cash transfers to refugee daily-wage workers who were vulnerable to income losses because of the pandemic and lockdown measures (Hagen-Zanker and Both 2021).

Lessons learned and policy recommendations

This report suggests that migration can and should continue safely in the context of pandemics, that additional actions are needed to promptly respond to future shocks, and that prepandemic challenges must be addressed to maximize the benefit of migration for the whole region. Faced with the health challenges posed by the COVID-19 pandemic, countries initially imposed strict mobility restrictions but have since shown the capacity to lift these restrictions, establish health protocols, fast-track migration procedures, and extend coverage of basic services to limit the economic and health impacts of the crisis. Although these actions were key to addressing the immediate migration-related impacts of the pandemic, more systematic reforms would be important to address the remaining challenges posed by the COVID-19 pandemic as well as to better prepare to respond to various other future shocks. Figure O.9 presents a set of policy actions with the associated implementation timeline to

- Restart migration safely in the aftermath of a public health crisis such as the COVID-19 pandemic.
- Be ready to respond to different types of future shocks.
- Ensure the future sustainability of migration flows.

The unfolding of the COVID-19 pandemic and the policy actions implemented worldwide have generated important lessons that could inform the response to future shocks. Whereas some of the lessons learned focus on challenges typically arising from public health shocks, other lessons apply to a broader set of shocks, including those related to economic, conflict, or climate-related factors. Four main lessons have

Figure O.9   Proposed policy objectives and actions

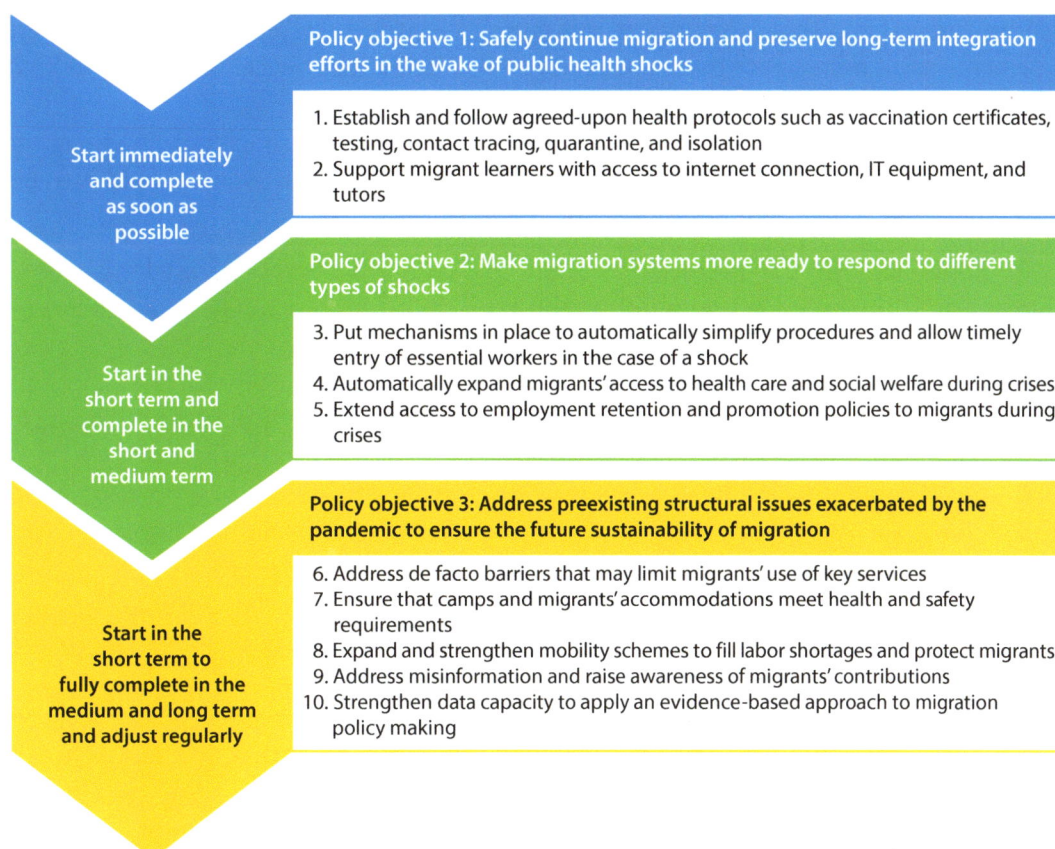

Start immediately and complete as soon as possible

Policy objective 1: Safely continue migration and preserve long-term integration efforts in the wake of public health shocks

1. Establish and follow agreed-upon health protocols such as vaccination certificates, testing, contact tracing, quarantine, and isolation
2. Support migrant learners with access to internet connection, IT equipment, and tutors

Start in the short term and complete in the short and medium term

Policy objective 2: Make migration systems more ready to respond to different types of shocks

3. Put mechanisms in place to automatically simplify procedures and allow timely entry of essential workers in the case of a shock
4. Automatically expand migrants' access to health care and social welfare during crises
5. Extend access to employment retention and promotion policies to migrants during crises

Start in the short term to fully complete in the medium and long term and adjust regularly

Policy objective 3: Address preexisting structural issues exacerbated by the pandemic to ensure the future sustainability of migration

6. Address de facto barriers that may limit migrants' use of key services
7. Ensure that camps and migrants' accommodations meet health and safety requirements
8. Expand and strengthen mobility schemes to fill labor shortages and protect migrants
9. Address misinformation and raise awareness of migrants' contributions
10. Strengthen data capacity to apply an evidence-based approach to migration policy making

Source: Original figure for this publication.
Note: IT = information technology.

emerged during the COVID-19 crisis that can inform countries' efforts to develop shock-responsive mobility systems:

1. Travel restrictions may have an impact in delaying contagion, but they are only a temporary solution that comes with non-negligible costs for employers, migrants, and sending countries. When the structural drivers of migration are strong, mobility restrictions do not necessarily halt migration flows, and they are likely to increase the vulnerabilities faced by people on the move.
2. Migrants play an important role in the workforce of many receiving countries and have been shown to be an essential resource in managing the health and economic impacts of the COVID-19 pandemic. Their contributions have been key in helping the receiving countries to address shocks associated with high risks and to promptly restart economic activity.
3. Applying human development policies equally to migrants and locals in the wake of large shocks keeps locals "safe," protects migrants, and keeps economies strong. In contrast, limiting migrants' access to health care, social welfare, active labor market programs, and adequate housing may cause them to adopt coping mechanisms that can slow down economic recovery, with severe short- and long-term implications. As such, expanding migrants' access to services even during crises, when overall fiscal space might be limited, is an investment with a strong economic rationale.
4. Sudden shocks can put long-term immigrant integration efforts at risk. Although it is important to address the immediate impacts of shocks, attention should also be paid to their potential scarring effects on migrants.

To conclude, the COVID-19 pandemic posed a severe test of migration systems both in the extended Mediterranean region and globally. The region's countries and economies responded to this public health shock but at great economic cost and with results that often revealed gaps in migration systems rather than resilience—the ability to adjust to shocks flexibly, recover quickly, and operate sustainably.

In resilient mobility systems, the underlying components—ranging from admission channels to provision of various services in the receiving and sending countries—are built with the flexibility to adapt to shocks. These systems require coordination between the sending and receiving countries to ensure that policy mechanisms are activated at different stages of the migration cycle to ensure continued and safe mobility when unexpected shocks occur.

This volume sets forth the policy objectives and actions that could rebuild and even strengthen migration systems in the wake of any large shock that disrupts people's movements, whether from a pandemic or from violent conflict, disaster, or climate change. As a whole, these proposed policy actions point toward a vision of migration resilience that, even during crises, can address key labor shortages, keep both migrant and native populations safer, sustain household incomes, and ameliorate blows to economic growth.

Despite the COVID-19 pandemic and the resulting travel restrictions, as the documented mobility trends show, the structural drivers of migration remained strong throughout the extended Mediterranean region. Whether this crisis can illuminate the way toward better adapting migration systems to future crises will depend on learning its lessons.

Notes

1. The "Mediterranean" countries and economies include Albania; Algeria; Bosnia and Herzegovina; Croatia; Cyprus; the Arab Republic of Egypt; France; Greece; Israel; Italy; Jordan; Lebanon; Libya; Malta; Montenegro; Morocco; Slovenia; Spain; the Syrian Arab Republic; Tunisia; Turkey; and West Bank and Gaza. Despite not bordering the Mediterranean Sea, Jordan is included given its importance as a receiver of Syrian refugees.
2. The GCC states include Bahrain, Kuwait, Oman, Qatar, Saudi Arabia, and the United Arab Emirates.
3. The asylum application data are from the Eurostat Asylum Database: https://ec.europa.eu/eurostat/web/migration-asylum/asylum/database.
4. Migrant route data are from the European Border and Coast Guard Agency (Frontex).

References

Aoun, R. 2020. "COVID-19 Impact of Female Migrant Domestic Workers in the Middle East." Gender-Based Violence Area of Responsibility (GBV AoR) HelpDesk Research Query, United Nations Population Fund, Geneva.

Barker, N., C. Davis, P. López-Peña, H. Mitchell, A. Mobarak, K. Naguib, M. Reimão, A. Shenoy, and C. Vernot. 2020. "Migration and the Labour Market Impacts of COVID-19." Working Paper No. 2020/139, United Nations University World Institute for Development Economics Research (UNU-WIDER), Helsinki.

Baruah, N., J. Chaloff, P. Hervé, H. Honsho, S. Nair, and P. Sirivunnabood. 2021. "Trends in Labor Migration in Asia." In *Labor Migration in Asia: Impacts of the COVID-19 Crisis and the Post-Pandemic Future*, 1–37. Tokyo: Asian Development Bank Institute; Paris: Organisation for Economic Co-operation and Development; Bangkok: International Labour Organization.

Chiswick, B., and P. Miller. 2014. "International Migration and the Economics of Language." Discussion Paper No. 7880, IZA Institute of Labor Economics, Bonn.

De Bel-Air, F. 2017. "Demography, Migration, and Labour Market in Qatar." Gulf Labour Markets and Migration (GLMM) Explanatory Note No. 3/2017, Migration Policy Centre, European University Institute, Florence.

De Bel-Air, F. 2018a. "Demography, Migration, and the Labour Market in Oman." Gulf Labour Markets and Migration (GLMM) Explanatory Note No. 7/2018, Migration Policy Centre, European University Institute, Florence.

De Bel-Air, F. 2018b. "Demography, Migration and Labour Market in Saudi Arabia." Gulf Labour Markets and Migration (GLMM) Explanatory Note No. 5/2018, Migration Policy Centre, European University Institute, Florence.

De Bel-Air, F. 2018c. "Demography, Migration, and the Labour Market in the UAE." Gulf Labour Markets and Migration (GLMM) Explanatory Note No. 1/2018, Migration Policy Centre, European University Institute, Florence.

De Bel-Air, F. 2019a. "Demography, Migration, and the Labour Market in Bahrain." Gulf Labour Markets and Migration (GLMM) Explanatory Note No. 1/2019, Migration Policy Centre, European University Institute, Florence.

De Bel-Air, F. 2019b. "Demography, Migration, and the Labour Market in Kuwait." Gulf Labour Markets and Migration (GLMM) Explanatory Note No. 3/2019, Migration Policy Centre, European University Institute, Florence.

EC (European Commission). 2020a. *Analysis of Shortage and Surplus Occupations 2020.* Luxembourg: Publications Office of the European Union.

EC (European Commission). 2020b. "Council Recommendation 2020/912 of 30 June 2020 on the Temporary Restriction on Non-Essential Travel into the EU and the Possible Lifting of Such Restriction." https://eur-lex.europa.eu/legal-content/EN/TXT/HTML/?uri=CELEX:32 020H0912&from=EN.

EPRS (European Parliamentary Research Service). 2021. "Migrant Seasonal Workers in the European Agricultural Sector." Briefing for the European Parliament, European Union, Luxembourg.

GFMD (Global Forum on Migration and Development). 2020. "Inventory of Social Protection Provisions for Temporary Migrant Workers in GCC Countries." Data tables, GFMD, https://www .gfmd.org/inventory-social-protection-provisions-temporary-migrant-workers-gcc-countries.

Giammarinaro, M. 2020. "The Impact and Consequences of the COVID-19 Pandemic on Trafficked and Exploited Persons." COVID-19 position paper, United Nations Office of the High Commissioner for Human Rights, Geneva.

Hagen-Zanker, J., and N. Both. 2021. "Social Protection Provisions to Refugees during the Covid-19 Pandemic: Lessons Learned from Government and Humanitarian Responses." Working Paper No. 612, Overseas Development Institute (ODI), London; and German Agency for International Cooperation (GIZ), Bonn.

Hale, T., N. Angrist, R. Goldszmidt, B. Kira, A. Petherick, T. Phillips, S. Webster, et al. 2021. "A Global Panel Database of Pandemic Policies (Oxford COVID-19 Government Response Tracker)." *Nature Human Behaviour* 5: 529–38.

IFRC and TRC (International Federation of Red Cross and Red Crescent Societies and Turkish Red Crescent Society). 2021. "Cash Assistance in Times of COVID-19: Impacts on Refugees Living in Turkey." Survey report, IFRC, Geneva; and TRC, Ankara.

IOM (International Organization for Migration). 2020. "COVID-19 Impact on Stranded Migrants." Brief, September 30, COVID-19 Return Task Force, IOM, Geneva.

IOM (International Organization for Migration). 2021. "Alarming Loss of Life on Way to Canaries Worsens in 2021." IOM News, September 24. https://www.iom.int/news /alarming-loss-life-way-canaries-worsens-2021.

IOM and WFP (International Organization for Migration and World Food Programme). 2020. "Populations at Risk: Implications of COVID-19 for Hunger, Migration and Displacement." Joint report, IOM, Geneva; and WFP, Rome.

Lafleur, J.-M., and D. Vintila, eds. 2020. *Migration and Social Protection in Europe and Beyond (Volume 1): Comparing Access to Welfare Entitlements.* International Migration, Integration and Social Cohesion in Europe (IMISCOE) Research Series. Cham, Switzerland: Springer.

Lu, R., and Y. Sheng. 2020. "From Fear to Hate: How the COVID-19 Pandemic Sparks Racial Animus in the United States." *COVID Economics* 39: 72–108.

MMC (Mixed Migration Centre). 2020. "Impact of COVID-19 on Migrant Smuggling." COVID-19 Global Thematic Update #1, MMC, Brussels.

Moroz, H., M. Shrestha, and M. Testaverde. 2020. "Potential Responses to the COVID-19 Outbreak in Support of Migrant Workers." Note, World Bank, Washington, DC.

OECD (Organisation for Economic Co-operation and Development). 2020. "What Is the Impact of the COVID-19 Pandemic on Immigrants and Their Children?" Policy brief, OECD, Paris.

OECD (Organisation for Economic Co-operation and Development). 2021. *International Migration Outlook 2021.* Paris: OECD Publishing.

OECD and EU (Organisation for Economic Co-operation and Development and European Union). 2018. *Settling In 2018: Indicators of Immigrant Integration.* Paris: OECD Publishing; Brussels: EU.

Özden, Ç., and M. Wagner. 2020. *Moving for Prosperity: Global Migration and Labor Markets.* Policy Research Report. Washington, DC: World Bank.

Ratha, D., E. J. Kim, S. Plaza, and G. Seshan. 2021. "Resilience: COVID-19 Crisis through a Migration Lens." Migration and Development Brief No. 34, Global Knowledge Partnership on Migration and Development (KNOMAD), World Bank, Washington, DC.

Schuettler, K., and L. Caron. 2020. "Jobs Interventions for Refugees and Internally Displaced Persons." Jobs Working Paper No. 47, World Bank, Washington, DC.

Sorkar, M. N. I. 2020. "COVID-19 Pandemic Profoundly Affects Bangladeshi Workers Abroad with Consequences for Origin Communities." Feature article, Migration Policy Institute, Washington, DC.

3RP (Regional Refugee and Resilience Plan in Response to the Syria Crisis). 2020. "3RP Turkey Consolidated: 2020 Appeal Overview." Financial appeal consolidation document, 3RP Turkey Chapter.

WFP (World Food Programme). 2020. "Comprehensive Vulnerability Monitoring Exercise (CVME), Round 4." Report, WFP Turkey Country Office, Ankara.

Yamagata, M., T. Teraguchi, and A. Miura. 2021. "The Relationship between Infection-Avoidance Tendencies and Exclusionary Attitudes toward Foreigners: A Panel Study of the COVID-19 Outbreak in Japan." Working paper. doi:10.31234/osf.io/x5emj.

Zorlu, A., and J. Hartog. 2018. "The Impact of Language on Socioeconomic Integration of Immigrants." Discussion Paper No. 11485, IZA Institute of Labor Economics, Bonn.

CHAPTER 1

COVID-19 and Migration in the Mediterranean Region

Introduction

The movement of people across countries surrounding the Mediterranean Sea has characterized this region for centuries. Given its unique position connecting Africa, Asia, and Europe, the Mediterranean Sea has been a bridge between different cultures throughout human history. Mobility flows across its shores date back to at least ancient Greek civilization and have continued in different forms since then. People have moved across the Mediterranean in all directions and with various reasons— whether to flee wars and famines, escape religious and political persecution, or to seek better lives and economic opportunities.

Migration is still a fact of life for many people living near the Mediterranean Sea. As of 2020, more than 40 million migrants were living in Mediterranean countries and economies and nearly 31 million in the Gulf Cooperation Council (GCC) states.[1] Given the important role of GCC states as hosts of many migrants throughout the Mediterranean, this report focuses on the extended Mediterranean region, defined as the region including both Mediterranean and GCC countries and economies (map 1.1).

Migrations flows to GCC countries are intertwined with those from Mediterranean countries. The GCC region is particularly important as a destination for emigrants from the southern Mediterranean region.[2] For example, as of 2020, nearly 2.5 million Egyptians—68 percent of all emigrants from the Arab Republic of Egypt—lived in Kuwait, Qatar, Saudi Arabia, and the United Arab Emirates. Similarly, 66 percent of all emigrants from Jordan, or more than half a million, lived in GCC states in 2020.

This report presents evidence on how the COVID-19 pandemic has affected mobility in the Mediterranean region, with the objective of informing policy

Map 1.1   The extended Mediterranean region

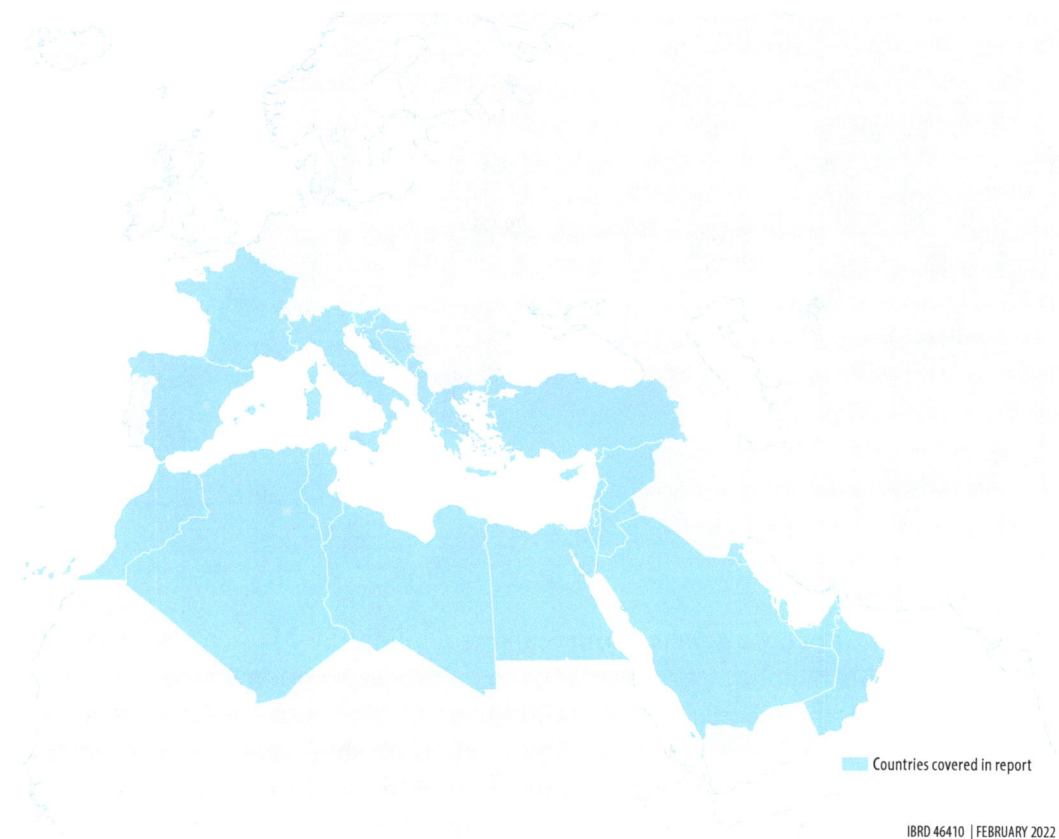

Countries covered in report

IBRD 46410 | FEBRUARY 2022

Source: World Bank.
Note: The extended Mediterranean region (shaded blue) includes Albania, Algeria, Bosnia and Herzegovina, Croatia, Cyprus, the Arab Republic of Egypt, France, Greece, Israel, Italy, Jordan, Lebanon, Libya, Malta, Morocco, Montenegro, Slovenia, Spain, the Syrian Arab Republic, Tunisia, Turkey, and West Bank and Gaza. It also includes the Gulf Cooperation Council states: Bahrain, Kuwait, Oman, Qatar, Saudi Arabia, and the United Arab Emirates.

responses that can help countries restart migration safely and better respond to future shocks. The COVID-19 crisis has posed severe challenges to lives and livelihoods across the globe. In the Mediterranean region specifically, migration has always been an important source of economic prosperity not only for migrants but also for the countries that send and receive them. Given the importance of migration to the economic and social well-being of the region's people, this report sheds light on the pandemic's short- and long-term impacts on these migrant and nonmigrant communities. In so doing, it also explores whether mobility can still be expected to play a central role in the Mediterranean region in the aftermath of the COVID-19 outbreak.

Distinguishing between new challenges posed by the COVID-19 crisis and pre-existing issues exacerbated by the pandemic, the report not only proposes policies for restarting migration safely amid the ongoing public health crisis but also recommends ways to better respond to future shocks and ensure the sustainability of migration flows. Whereas some of the proposed policy actions focus on challenges typically arising in the context of public health shocks, other actions represent suitable responses to a broader set of shocks, including those related to economic, conflict, or climate-related factors.

The report draws on emerging data and literature to provide a complete picture of how the pandemic has affected mobility in the region. The crisis hit the whole world rapidly—affecting data collection processes, among other things, and highlighting the shortcomings of traditional data, which are usually available only with some time lags (ILO 2020). Especially in the first months of the pandemic, the lack of comprehensive and timely data challenged policy makers' ability to make evidence-based decisions. This paucity of data has also limited researchers' ability to shed light on the complex dynamics triggered by the COVID-19 crisis, especially in areas such as migration, which suffered from the limited availability of granular data even before the crisis (UN 2019). For this reason, this report uses numerous data sources, which, while not perfect on their own, can still point to useful emerging trends when jointly explored. The evidence presented in this report focuses as much as possible on findings in the extended Mediterranean region. When such evidence is not available, the report presents evidence from other countries, emphasizing its potential applicability to the extended Mediterranean region.

The report is structured into four chapters:

- *Chapter 1* next discusses mobility trends in the extended Mediterranean region, how the pandemic has spread across these countries and economies, and how the crisis has affected mobility flows.
- *Chapter 2, "The Impacts of COVID-19 on Migrants and Their Families,"* focuses on the safety, health, and economic implications of the crisis for migrants and their families. It also documents the fluctuations in remittance flows—and their potential implications—to the sending communities during the pandemic.
- *Chapter 3, "Mobility-Related Implications of COVID-19 for Receiving Countries,"* focuses on the implications of restricted mobility for the receiving countries and for the longer-term trends that are yet to fully manifest but are important to acknowledge and understand. More specifically, the chapter also discusses (a) the implications of the crisis for factors such as education and skills acquisition that are crucial for migrants and refugees' long-term integration, and (b) the links between the health crisis and attitudes toward migration as well as their potential implications for future openness to migration.
- *Chapter 4, "Policy Directions,"* summarizes the findings of the report; presents lessons from various governments' COVID-19 responses to inform future efforts to address a broad set of shocks; and highlights the potential for new policy interventions to develop resilient mobility systems that can ensure the sustainability of migration in the years to come.

Mobility trends in the region

Over recent decades, the extended Mediterranean region has become increasingly important as a point of both departure and arrival for migrants seeking a better life. Although migration from, to, and across these countries and economies is not a new phenomenon, the migrant stock in the Mediterranean and GCC regions almost tripled in the past three decades, jumping from 24 million in 1990 to 71 million in 2020, with women accounting for almost 41 percent of the total.[3]

In relative terms, these figures equate to a jump from 15.8 percent of the world's total immigration being located in the Mediterranean and the GCC in 1990 to 25.5 percent in 2020 (a 61 percent increase), contrasting with the trends in other regions (figure 1.1). For example, during the same period, immigration to other states in the Middle East and North Africa decreased from 3 percent to 1.3 percent (a 57 percent decrease). The same was true for immigration to other states in Europe and Central Asia, dropping from 31.4 percent to 24.5 percent (a 22 percent decrease). Immigration to North America increased but by much less than in the extended Mediterranean region, from 18.1 percent to 21 percent (a 16 percent increase).[4]

Similarly, emigration from Mediterranean and Gulf economies has increased over the past 30 years, accounting for increasing shares of global emigration.[5] Opposite trends were evident in North America as well as the non-Mediterranean part of Europe and Central Asia: in both cases, emigration has decreased since 1990 as a share of the total world migration.[6]

Countries and economies in the extended Mediterranean region account for just 7.7 percent of the world's population (6.9 percent and 0.8 percent for the Mediterranean and GCC areas, respectively), but in 2020 they accounted for 14.7 percent of the world's emigrants (14.4 percent and 0.3 percent, respectively) and for 25.5 percent of all immigrants (14.5 percent and 11 percent, respectively), as shown in figure 1.1. In contrast, for example, East Asia and the Pacific in 2020 accounted for the largest regional share of global population (30.3 percent) but for just 14.4 percent and 10.3 percent of emigrants and immigrants, respectively. Meanwhile, South Asian countries made up 24 percent of the world's population but accounted for just 15 percent and 4 percent of the emigrants and immigrants, respectively. And Sub-Saharan African countries, with 14.4 percent of the world's population, had just 10.8 percent of the world's emigrants and 8.3 percent of immigrants.

Top receiving and sending countries and economies in the region

Migration patterns vary from country to country in both absolute and relative terms. Saudi Arabia, France, the United Arab Emirates, Spain, and Italy are the top five receiving countries, hosting approximately 44 million migrants, or 62 percent of the total, in the extended Mediterranean region (figure 1.2, panel c). In relative terms, the GCC states are the countries with the highest shares of migrants among

Figure 1.1   Share of world's population, emigrants, and immigrants, by region, 2020

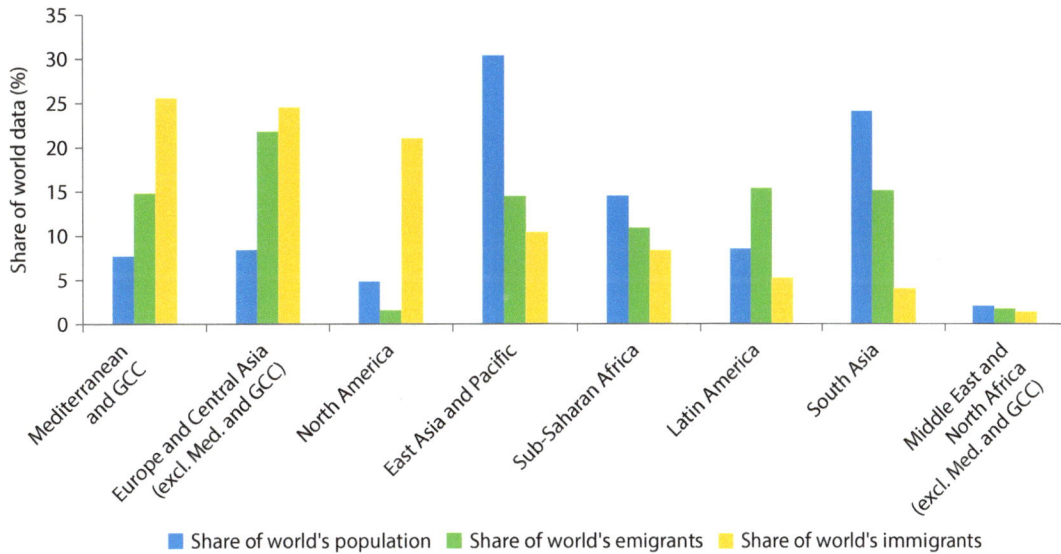

Source: International Migrant Stock 2020 dataset, Population Division, United Nations Department of Economic and Social Affairs: https://www.un.org/development/desa/pd/content/international-migrant-stock.
Note: "Mediterranean" includes Albania, Algeria, Bosnia and Herzegovina, Croatia, Cyprus, the Arab Republic of Egypt, France, Greece, Israel, Italy, Jordan, Lebanon, Libya, Malta, Montenegro, Morocco, Slovenia, Spain, the Syrian Arab Republic, Tunisia, Turkey, and West Bank and Gaza. GCC = Gulf Cooperation Council (Bahrain, Kuwait, Oman, Qatar, Saudi Arabia, and United Arab Emirates); Med. = Mediterranean.

the resident population, with the United Arab Emirates, Qatar, Kuwait, Bahrain and Oman at the top in the extended Mediterranean region (figure 1.2, panel a). By comparison, the countries in the northern Mediterranean with the highest shares of migrants among the resident population are Malta (23 percent), Cyprus (16 percent), and Spain (15 percent).[7]

The region's top five sending economies in absolute size of migration outflows are the Syrian Arab Republic, West Bank and Gaza, the Arab Republic of Egypt, Turkey, and Morocco (panel 1.2, panel d). Meanwhile, West Bank and Gaza, Bosnia and Herzegovina, the Syrian Arab Republic, Albania, and Croatia are the economies with the highest shares of nationals living abroad (figure 1.2, panel b).

Top migration corridors

Most of the migration in the extended Mediterranean region is intraregional. In 2020, of the region's 41 million migrants, 24 million settled elsewhere in the region—of whom 44 percent were women.[8] For example, more than three-quarters of all Moroccan emigrants and more than four-fifths of all Algerian emigrants settled in just a few other Mediterranean destinations.[9]

Figure 1.2   Top five migrant sending and receiving economies in the extended Mediterranean region, in relative and absolute terms, 2020

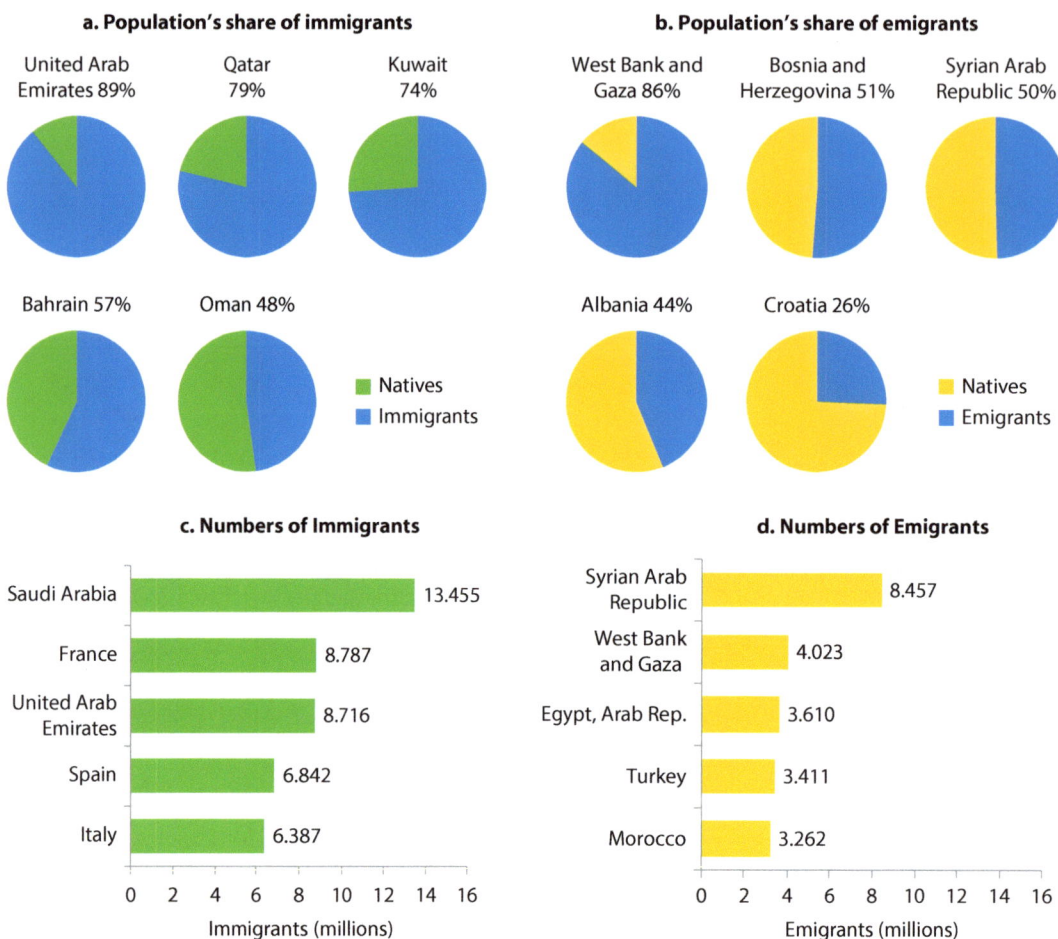

a. Population's share of immigrants

United Arab Emirates 89%   Qatar 79%   Kuwait 74%

Bahrain 57%   Oman 48%

- Natives
- Immigrants

b. Population's share of emigrants

West Bank and Gaza 86%   Bosnia and Herzegovina 51%   Syrian Arab Republic 50%

Albania 44%   Croatia 26%

- Natives
- Emigrants

c. Numbers of Immigrants

Saudi Arabia	13.455
France	8.787
United Arab Emirates	8.716
Spain	6.842
Italy	6.387

Immigrants (millions)

d. Numbers of Emigrants

Syrian Arab Republic	8.457
West Bank and Gaza	4.023
Egypt, Arab Rep.	3.610
Turkey	3.411
Morocco	3.262

Emigrants (millions)

Source: International Migrant Stock 2020 dataset, Population Division, United Nations Department of Economic and Social Affairs: https://www.un.org/development/desa/pd/content/international-migrant-stock.
Note: The "extended Mediterranean" region comprises 21 economies with Mediterranean coasts in addition to Jordan and the Gulf Cooperation Council (GCC) states: Bahrain, Kuwait, Oman, Qatar, Saudi Arabia, and United Arab Emirates.

Corridors between subregions. Figure 1.3 breaks down the intraregional migration corridors between the northern Mediterranean,[10] southern Mediterranean, and GCC. In 2020, the corridor used by the most migrants was from the southern Mediterranean to the northern Mediterranean (constituting over one-third of all intraregional migration), with the South–South corridor trailing just behind (at just over one-fourth of the total). There is hardly any North–South movement (only 0.7 percent), but North–North migration made up nearly 15 percent of the total intraregional migrant stock.

Despite little outmigration from the GCC countries to any of the other groupings, nor much North–GCC movement, a large flow of people moved from southern

Figure 1.3   Shares of intraregional Mediterranean and GCC migration, by corridor, 2020

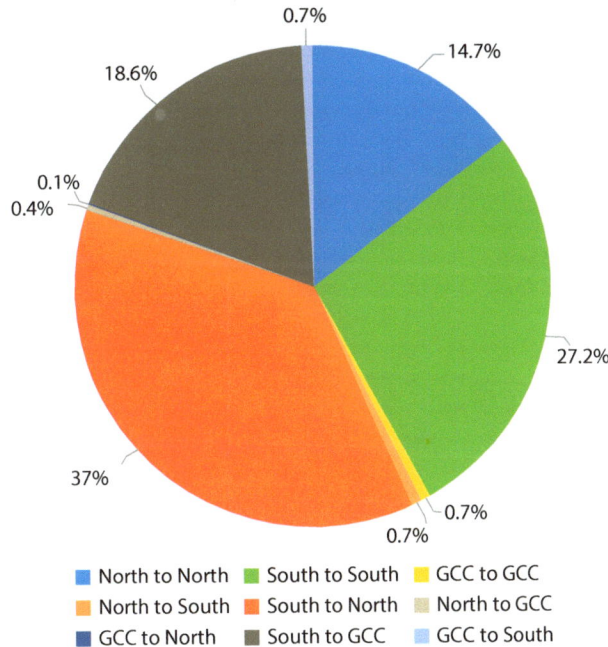

Source: International Migrant Stock 2020 dataset, Population Division, United Nations Department of Economic and Social Affairs: https://www.un.org/development/desa/pd/content/international-migrant-stock.
Note: "North" refers to Albania, Bosnia and Herzegovina, Croatia, Cyprus, France, Greece, Italy, Malta, Montenegro, Slovenia, Spain, and Turkey. "South" refers to Algeria, the Arab Republic of Egypt, Israel, Jordan, Lebanon, Libya, Morocco, the Syrian Arab Republic, Tunisia, and West Bank and Gaza. The Gulf Cooperation Council (GCC) includes Bahrain, Kuwait, Oman, Qatar, Saudi Arabia, and the United Arab Emirates.

Mediterranean to GCC economies, accounting for about 19 percent of the intraregional migrant stock.

Corridors between countries. By country, Algerian and Moroccan migration flows to France are the top two migration corridors, reflecting historical connection as a strong predictor of migration flows. Egyptian migration flows to Saudi Arabia and the United Arab Emirates are also among the top five corridors, confirming the strong pull of work opportunities in those destinations for foreigners from abroad (figure 1.4). While most migrants in GCC states are men, flows to northern Mediterranean countries tend to be more gender balanced.[11]

Top corridors for low- and high-skilled migrants. The share of migrants across skill levels varies by corridor, with most low-skilled Mediterranean intraregional migrants coming from southern Mediterranean economies. Although comparable data covering the education levels of migrants throughout the extended Mediterranean region are limited, data on a subset of countries can still be useful to provide a general picture of the skills content of various migration corridors.[12]

Figure 1.4   Top 20 migrant corridors in the combined Mediterranean and GCC region, 2020

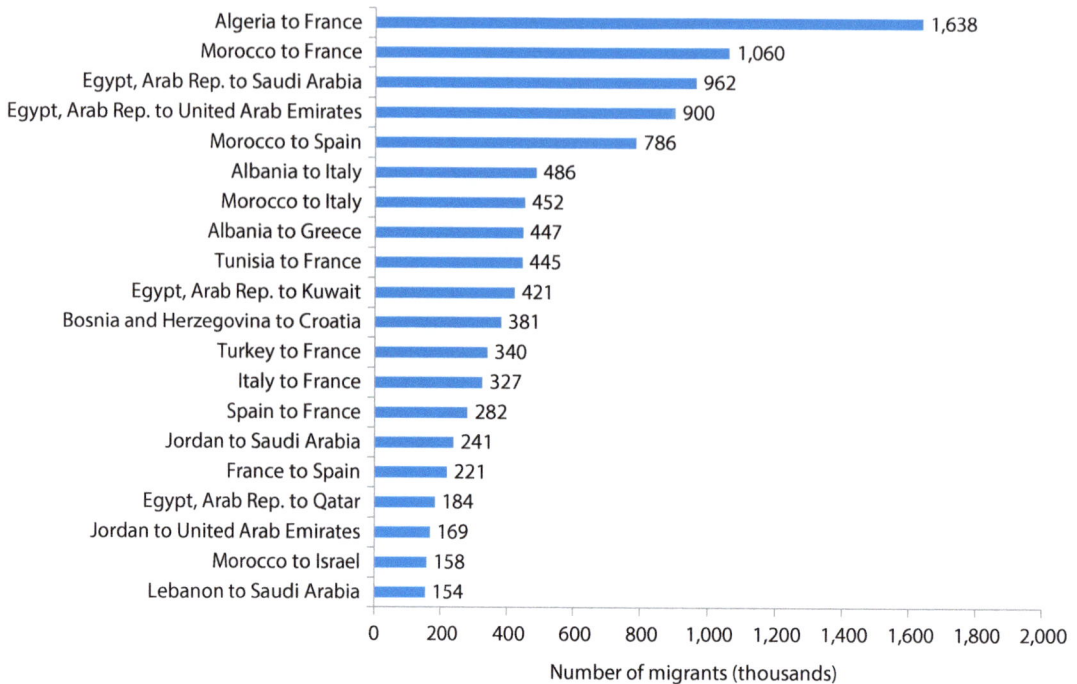

Corridor	Number of migrants (thousands)
Algeria to France	1,638
Morocco to France	1,060
Egypt, Arab Rep. to Saudi Arabia	962
Egypt, Arab Rep. to United Arab Emirates	900
Morocco to Spain	786
Albania to Italy	486
Morocco to Italy	452
Albania to Greece	447
Tunisia to France	445
Egypt, Arab Rep. to Kuwait	421
Bosnia and Herzegovina to Croatia	381
Turkey to France	340
Italy to France	327
Spain to France	282
Jordan to Saudi Arabia	241
France to Spain	221
Egypt, Arab Rep. to Qatar	184
Jordan to United Arab Emirates	169
Morocco to Israel	158
Lebanon to Saudi Arabia	154

Source: International Migrant Stock 2020 dataset, Population Division, United Nations Department of Economic and Social Affairs: https://www.un.org/development/desa/pd/content/international-migrant-stock.
Note: "Mediterranean" includes Albania, Algeria, Bosnia and Herzegovina, Croatia, Cyprus, the Arab Republic of Egypt, France, Greece, Israel, Italy, Jordan, Lebanon, Libya, Malta, Montenegro, Morocco, Slovenia, Spain, Tunisia, and Turkey. The figure excludes migrant-sending economies with active conflict (the Syrian Arab Republic and West Bank and Gaza). GCC = Gulf Cooperation Council (Bahrain, Kuwait, Oman, Qatar, Saudi Arabia, and United Arab Emirates).

The countries in the extended Mediterranean region for which data is available that account for the highest shares of the total intraregional low-skilled emigrants are Morocco (32 percent), Algeria (19 percent), and Albania (12 percent).[13] The countries with the largest shares of their intraregional emigrants being low-skilled are Turkey (68 percent), Morocco (63 percent), and Libya (61 percent), while the countries with the highest shares of their interregional emigrants being high-skilled are Morocco (20 percent), Bosnia and Herzegovina (19 percent), and Algeria (18 percent).[14]

As for the receiving countries, France, Italy, and Spain host the largest shares of the region's low-skilled immigrants, at 50 percent, 18 percent, and 16 percent, respectively. The countries that host the highest shares of the region's high-skilled immigrants are France, Croatia, and Spain, at 46 percent, 19 percent, and 13 percent, respectively.

Figure 1.5 and figure 1.6 show the specific corridors (for which data are available) where the largest shares of migrants are low-skilled and high-skilled, respectively. Although comparable data are not available for GCC countries, national data suggest

Figure 1.5   **Mediterranean corridors with the highest shares of low-skilled migrants, 2010**

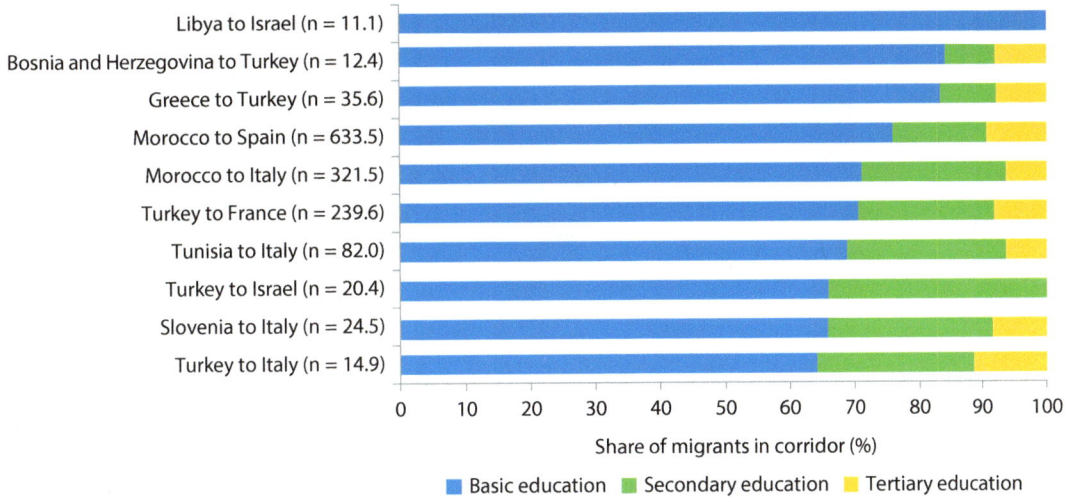

Share of migrants in corridor (%)

■ Basic education   ■ Secondary education   ■ Tertiary education

Source: Database on Immigrants in OECD and Non-OECD Countries (DIOC-E), 2010 data (https://www.oecd.org/els/mig/dioc.htm).

Note: "Low-skilled" is defined as having less than a secondary education. The numbers presented on the y-axis represent the number of total migrants expressed in thousands. Corridors with fewer than 10,000 total migrants are excluded. The examined Mediterranean destination countries include only those with adequate comparable data on migrants' education levels: Albania, Croatia, Cyprus, the Arab Republic of Egypt, France, Greece, Israel, Italy, Malta, Slovenia, Spain, and Turkey. OECD = Organisation for Economic Co-operation and Development.

Figure 1.6   **Mediterranean corridors with the highest shares of high-skilled migrants, 2010**

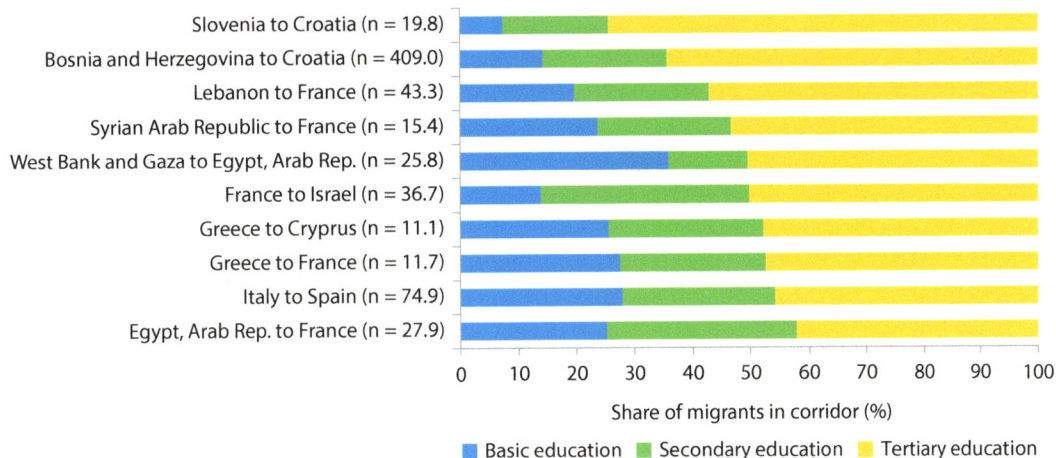

Share of migrants in corridor (%)

■ Basic education   ■ Secondary education   ■ Tertiary education

Source: Database on Immigrants in OECD and Non-OECD Countries (DIOC-E), 2010 data (https://www.oecd.org/els/mig/dioc.htm).

Note: High-skilled is defined as having a tertiary education or higher. The numbers presented on the y-axis represent the number total migrants expressed in thousands. Corridors with fewer than 10,000 total migrants are excluded. The examined Mediterranean destination countries include only those with adequate comparable data on migrants' education levels: Albania, Croatia, Cyprus, the Arab Republic of Egypt, France, Greece, Israel, Italy, Malta, Slovenia, Spain, and Turkey. OECD = Organisation for Economic Co-operation and Development.

that the bulk of the foreign workforce in these countries is low-skilled. In 2019, for instance, almost two-thirds of migrants in Saudi Arabia, many of whom come from Egypt and Syria, were low-skilled (World Bank 2020).

Refugee corridors. The Mediterranean is also a region where large flows of people are fleeing their homes. Approximately one in every three refugees in the world comes from or is hosted in the extended Mediterranean region, with the vast majority (nearly four-fifths) of refugees from the region remaining within the region.[15] Of these intraregional movements, Syrian flows to Turkey, Lebanon, Jordan, and Egypt as well as flows from West Bank and Gaza to Egypt are among the top five refugee corridors (figure 1.7).[16] Whereas these corridors were mainly dominated by men (96 percent)

Figure 1.7   Top 20 refugee corridors in the Mediterranean and GCC region, 2020

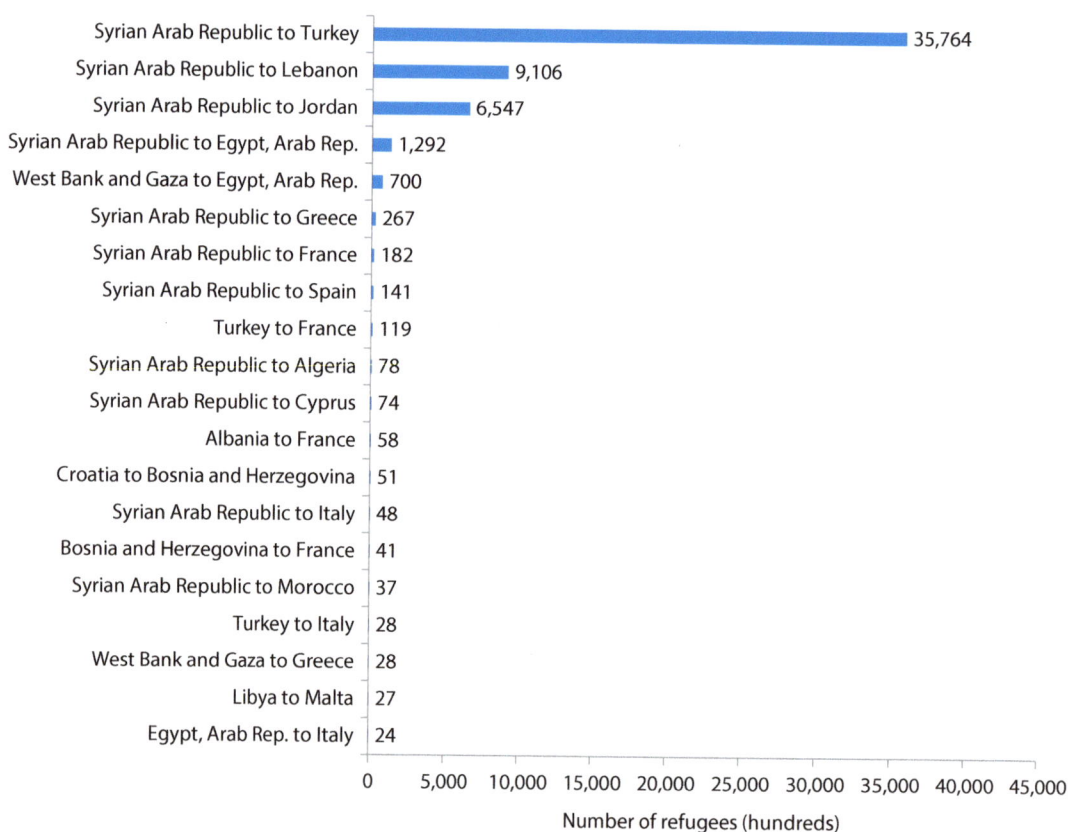

Corridor	Number of refugees (hundreds)
Syrian Arab Republic to Turkey	35,764
Syrian Arab Republic to Lebanon	9,106
Syrian Arab Republic to Jordan	6,547
Syrian Arab Republic to Egypt, Arab Rep.	1,292
West Bank and Gaza to Egypt, Arab Rep.	700
Syrian Arab Republic to Greece	267
Syrian Arab Republic to France	182
Syrian Arab Republic to Spain	141
Turkey to France	119
Syrian Arab Republic to Algeria	78
Syrian Arab Republic to Cyprus	74
Albania to France	58
Croatia to Bosnia and Herzegovina	51
Syrian Arab Republic to Italy	48
Bosnia and Herzegovina to France	41
Syrian Arab Republic to Morocco	37
Turkey to Italy	28
West Bank and Gaza to Greece	28
Libya to Malta	27
Egypt, Arab Rep. to Italy	24

Source: Refugee Data Finder database, United Nations High Commissioner for Refugees, https://www.unhcr.org /refugee-statistics/download/?url=5IkIF3.

Note: "Mediterranean" includes Albania, Algeria, Bosnia and Herzegovina, Croatia, Cyprus, the Arab Republic of Egypt, France, Greece, Israel, Italy, Jordan, Lebanon, Libya, Malta, Montenegro, Morocco, Slovenia, Spain, the Syrian Arab Republic, Tunisia, Turkey, and West Bank and Gaza. GCC = Gulf Cooperation Council (Bahrain, Kuwait, Oman, Qatar, Saudi Arabia, and United Arab Emirates).

up to 2005, the gender balance has significantly changed in recent years: in 2019, almost half of intraregional refugees (47 percent) were women.

Information on beneficiaries of a large refugee support program in Turkey, the Emergency Social Safety Net (ESSN) scheme, shows that a large share of the refugee beneficiaries (ranging from 55 percent to 80 percent across the 13 provinces included in the study) have at most a primary education (TRC 2020). Surveys of asylum seekers in reception centers in Italy and Greece show that 38 percent of respondents lack a primary school education, 33 percent have primary education, and 29 percent have secondary or higher education (World Bank 2018). A 2013 sample of Syrian refugees in Lebanon indicates that 30 percent have education levels below primary school, 41 percent have at least finished primary school, and 28 percent have secondary or higher education (ILO 2014).

Transit countries. Some destination countries in the extended Mediterranean region have at times become points of transit. Poor economic prospects in destination countries such as Italy and Greece have been shown to encourage migrants to move on to third countries in some cases (Düvell, Molodikova, and Collyer 2014; Jordan and Düvell 2002; Kuschminder, de Bresser, and Siegel 2015; Roman 2006). The same is true for some North African destinations. For example, Tunisia—a destination country for many Sub-Saharan African migrants—has been hit economically by the pandemic, inducing many of the migrants who settled there to cross the Mediterranean Sea (UNODC 2021). Migrants may also gain access to information and social networks in transit, which influences their decisions on when and where to move (Brekke and Brochmann 2014; Koser and Pinkerton 2002; Lutterbeck 2013). Wittenberg (2017) also finds that people may leave their first countries of asylum because of lack of legal protection and migrate on to third countries, pulled by factors such as better living conditions, work prospects, or social protection.

On the other hand, some transit countries have become final destinations. For instance, migrants and refugees intending to reach Europe often interrupt their journeys in transit countries such as Morocco or Turkey because they lack resources (Collyer 2006; Schapendonk 2012). Other factors that influence migration patterns include the political situations and the availability of humanitarian assistance in sending countries as well as social networks and the border control policies of host countries (Brewer and Yükseker 2009).

Some migrants headed for Scandinavian countries remained in Italy once realizing that they would not be allowed to leave their first country of arrival before having their asylum applications approved (Brekke and Brochmann 2014). Similarly, although Greece was an intended transit point for more than 1 million migrants and asylum seekers who entered the European Union (EU) in 2015 and 2016, many of them remained stranded in the country after the EU-Turkey Statement entered into force at the end of March 2016. As a result, the number of asylum applications to Greece jumped from 13,000 in 2015 to 51,000 in 2016, reaching 77,000 in 2019.[17]

Drivers of migration

Migration in the extended Mediterranean region is driven by disparities between and within countries and economies in demographic patterns, economic opportunities, and stability of political institutions. Economic migration in the region has long been driven by long-standing and structural factors such as age and wage gaps. Migrants benefit from higher wages in the destination countries while simultaneously providing labor to reduce shortages. Migration flows and differences in gross domestic product (GDP) per capita (in purchasing power parity terms) between destination and origin countries are more strongly correlated in Mediterranean-to-Mediterranean corridors than in other corridors globally. The correlation is even stronger for South–North Mediterranean corridors specifically (Wahba 2021).

The age gap between countries in many cases is also significant. For example, the median age in France (41.7) is 12.8 years older than in Algeria (28.9), which sent most of its emigrants to France in 2020.[18] Similarly, the median age in Italy (46.5) is 12.2 years older than in Albania (34.3). An aging population in receiving countries may result in labor shortages, while a young population in sending countries with limited economic opportunities can lead to labor surpluses. Migration may then occur as a result of these demographic imbalances as labor moves to places where available jobs are unfilled.

In other cases, migrants are forced out of their homes, seeking refuge in a more stable country. Approximately 32 percent of the world's forcibly displaced persons come from countries in the Middle East and North Africa, such as Iraq, Syria, the Republic of Yemen, and others. Most of these displaced persons settle elsewhere in the Middle East, while many others seek refuge in Europe by crossing the Mediterranean Basin (Rozo 2021).

The distinction between voluntary and forced migration is not always clear-cut. Individual migrants' reasons for migrating may be mixed. People fleeing conflict or persecution may at the same time be leaving because of chronic poverty or poor living conditions, occupying a "grey area" on the spectrum of motives for migrating (Triandafyllidou, Bartolini, and Guidi 2019). For example, Touzenis (2017) explains that migrants from Bangladesh, India, and Pakistan are often primarily economic migrants who are simultaneously fleeing for political motives such as to escape the caste system or discrimination based on affiliation with a particular political party.

Furthermore, the routes and channels along which people move may have mixed groups of migrants. For instance, forced migrants and economic migrants often occupy the same transit routes and even means of transportation. Afghan, Bangladeshi, and Pakistani migrants are often mixed along the same irregular routes to the West, often via Turkey to Greece, though some are considered forced migrants and others economic migrants (Dimitriadi 2013; Koser 2010). The same is true for many migrants and asylum seekers of different nationalities crossing the Mediterranean Sea who have departed from Libya and other places in North Africa.

COVID-19 in the Mediterranean region

The northern Mediterranean region and some GCC countries were the epicenter of the COVID-19 crisis for most of the first half of 2020. In early spring 2020, Italy became the first European country to face large numbers of contagions, which had begun at the end of February 2020. Piecemeal closures were followed by total lockdowns to try to contain the virus that was overwhelming hospitals and health care workers, with only essential services remaining open. Reported cases jumped from virtually none to a few hundred cases a day at first and then to thousands of cases a day in March.

Countries hit hardest by cases and deaths. By the end of May 2020, Italy, France, and Spain were among the top 5 countries for the most casualties from the virus, with approximately 33,000 deaths in Italy, and 29,000 in both France and Spain. After a break during the summer, COVID-19 cases in the Mediterranean region peaked again in the fourth quarter of 2020. By April 2021, these figures reached 120,000, 104,000, and 80,000, respectively, with these countries remaining in the top 10 for number of deaths. GCC countries have also been hit particularly hard by the health impacts of the COVID-19 crisis. In the first wave of the pandemic, Qatar, Bahrain, and Kuwait were among the top 5 countries (with populations exceeding 1 million) for COVID-19 cases per capita.[19]

Although the subsequent COVID-19 waves hit other regions more severely, Mediterranean and GCC countries continued to struggle to limit the spread of the virus. During these waves of the pandemic, countries such as Brazil, India, Mexico, and others surpassed Mediterranean countries for the highest number of total deaths. Even so, by October 2021, Italy, France, and Spain still remained in the top 15 countries for highest absolute number of deaths due to COVID-19, with 132,000, 119,000, and 89,000 deaths, respectively. Bahrain remained on the top 15 list for COVID-19 cases per capita, joined by Slovenia, Israel, and Croatia.[20] By December 2021, many Mediterranean countries were still experiencing a large number of cases per capita (map 1.2), but only Bosnia and Herzegovina and Slovenia were among the top 15 countries in deaths per capita.[21]

Health system impacts. COVID-19 put the resilience of health systems everywhere to the test. By the end of 2020, the GCC was ranked second among regions in terms of administering the most COVID-19 tests per million (469,000 tests), following North America (604,000). The northern and southern Mediterranean regions had also administered relatively more tests than other regions—366,000 and 285,000 tests per million, respectively, by the end of December 2020. These figures contrasted starkly with those of other regions such as Sub-Saharan Africa, which had administered only 14,800 tests per million by the end of 2020. By October 2021, the GCC and northern Mediterranean regions had far surpassed North America for COVID-19 tests, having administered 905,000 and 762,000 tests per million, respectively, while in the same period Sub-Saharan Africa had only reached 17,500 tests per million.[22]

Map 1.2   Cumulative COVID-19 cases per capita, by country, January 2020 to December 2021

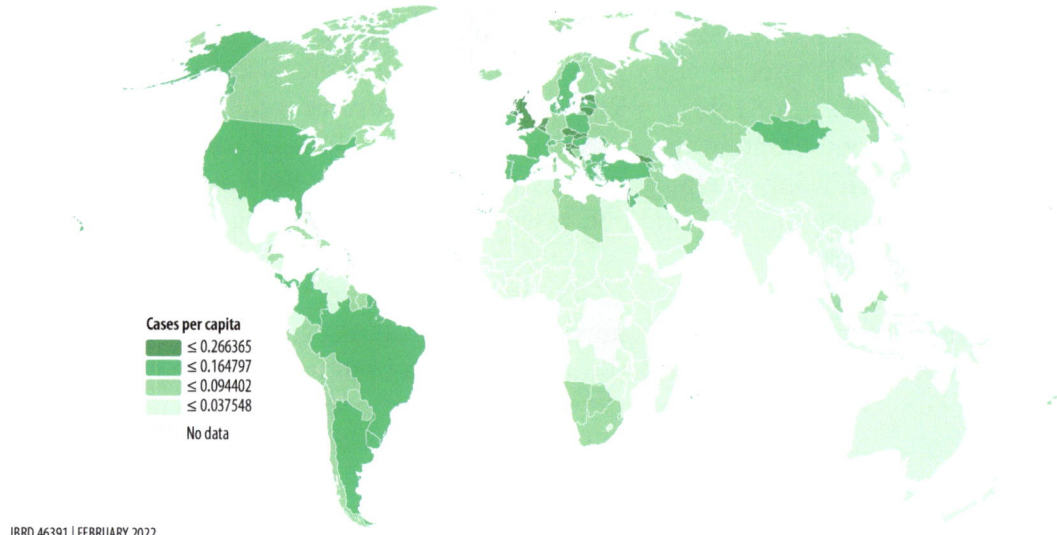

Cases per capita
- ≤ 0.266365
- ≤ 0.164797
- ≤ 0.094402
- ≤ 0.037548
- No data

IBRD 46391 | FEBRUARY 2022

Source: World Bank, using data from the COVID-19 Data Repository, Center for Systems Science and Engineering, Johns Hopkins University: https://github.com/CSSEGISandData/COVID-19.

Several countries in Sub-Saharan Africa have health care systems that are already overburdened by health needs such as reproductive health, mental health, immunization, care for chronic illness, and other endemic diseases that have broken out in large numbers in the past 10 years. Many Sub-Saharan countries already faced a shortage of health care workers before the pandemic, with only 0.2 physicians per 1,000 inhabitants across the subcontinent in 2020 (as opposed to 3.7 and 2.6 in Europe and North America, respectively) (Lau, Hooper, and Zard 2021). The COVID-19 pandemic only exacerbated these labor shortages in a health care system that was already fragile and lacking infrastructure.

Economic consequences. In addition to the health impacts and loss of lives, the extended Mediterranean region experienced severe economic disruptions. In 2020, the euro area experienced an overall GDP contraction of 6.5 percent—well above both the global average contraction of 3.4 percent and the impacts on the region after the 2008–09 Global Financial Crisis (OECD 2021a). Between 2020 and 2021, the euro area's economy grew by 5.2 percent, slightly less than the world average of 5.6 percent.

In the European countries facing significant challenges in containing the spread of the virus and in those that heavily rely on tourism, output declines were even more severe. For instance, GDP in 2020 dropped by 9 percent in both Greece and Italy, and by 9 percent and 10.8 percent in France and Spain, respectively (OECD 2021a). The pandemic's economic consequences also hit the southern Mediterranean area and the GCC states, with real GDP dropping by as much as 31 percent in Libya, by 20 percent in Lebanon, and by 9 percent in Tunisia (World Bank 2021b). That the COVID-19 crisis has more severely affected the most vulnerable groups, such as women and youth—causing an increasing number of people to fall into poverty—has been a reason of particular concern.

Recovery prospects. Recovery trajectories were also unequal across the extended Mediterranean region. Although the deployment of effective vaccines triggered a strong recovery in many European countries in 2021, growth trajectories were still below their pre-COVID expected paths (OECD 2021b). The euro area was expected to grow by 5.2 percent in 2021 and by 4.3 percent in 2022, while the Middle East and North Africa was expected to have a more modest recovery in 2021 (2.4 percent), especially in the GCC countries (2.2 percent), and with Lebanon's negative GDP growth expected to persist in 2021 (OECD 2021a; World Bank 2021a).

Apart from Spain, where GDP was projected to grow by only 4.5 percent between 2020 and 2021, GDP was projected to grow more quickly in 2021 in other Mediterranean countries such as France (6.8 percent), Greece (6.7 percent), and Italy (6.3 percent) as the tourism industry and domestic demand recover (OECD 2021a). However, because most of the populations in low-income countries have not been vaccinated and progress with vaccination campaigns has been slow in these countries, the emergence of new variants may pose additional future health and economic challenges for all countries (OECD 2021b).[23]

BOX 1.1   Issues with COVID-19–related data

The Johns Hopkins data on COVID-19 cases and deaths presented in this report have some limitations. First, different countries have administered different numbers of tests, which have also varied over time. Overall, northern Mediterranean countries have administered more tests per million people than have the southern Mediterranean and GCC countries and economies, especially during the second wave of the pandemic (figure B1.1.1).

Even within a region, testing capacity varies widely. For example, in Africa, by the end of December 2020, 10 countries accounted for over 70 percent of the COVID-19 tests administered in the whole continent (Petesch 2020).[a] Initial evidence suggests a positive correlation between the number of tests administered and the number of cases confirmed (figure B1.1.2).

Second, the capacity to report COVID-19 deaths and the ways of reporting them differ across countries, making it difficult to report the official death toll. For example, many countries do not count people who did not test positive for the virus before dying, which undercounts COVID-19 deaths

(continued on next page)

BOX 1.1 *continued*

Figure B1.1.1   COVID-19 tests per million people per day, by extended Mediterranean subregion, February 2020 to October 2021

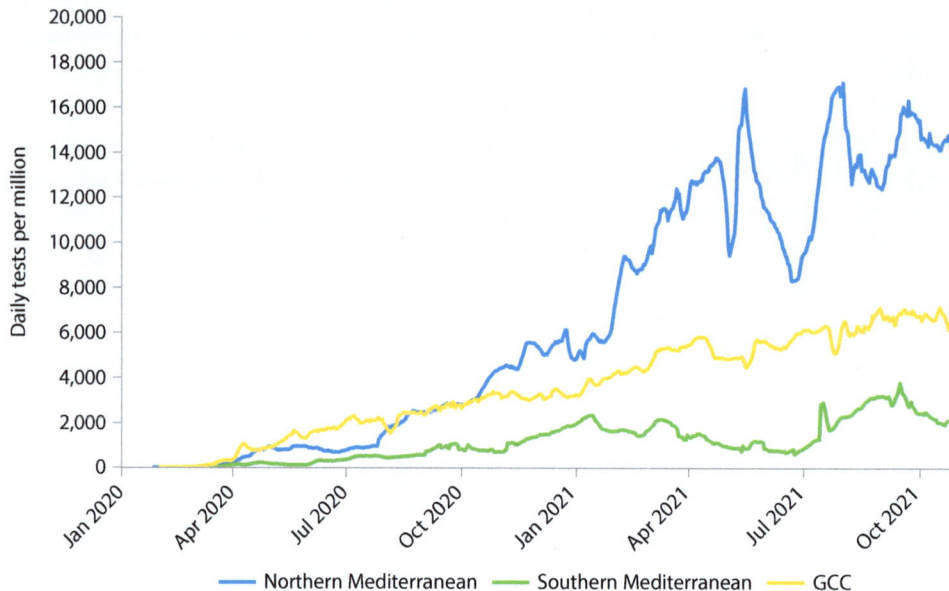

Sources: Coronavirus Pandemic (COVID-19) database of Our World in Data (https://ourworldindata.org /coronavirus); Coronavirus Resource Center, Center for Systems Science and Engineering, Johns Hopkins University (https://coronavirus.jhu.edu/).

Note: "Northern Mediterranean" includes Albania, Bosnia and Herzegovina, Croatia, Cyprus, France, Greece, Italy, Malta, Montenegro, Slovenia, Spain, and Turkey. "Southern Mediterranean" includes Algeria, the Arab Republic of Egypt, Israel, Jordan, Lebanon, Libya, Morocco, the Syrian Arab Republic, Tunisia, and West Bank and Gaza. GCC = Gulf Cooperation Council (Bahrain, Kuwait, Oman, Qatar, Saudi Arabia, and the United Arab Emirates).

especially in places with low testing capacity. In some areas, limited hospital resources have also created backlogs in the death counts, since they often lack the capacity to register death certificates for several days or weeks (*Economist* 2021a).

Counting "excess deaths" relative to prior years has been used as an alternate method of measuring deaths during the pandemic. An estimated 7–13 million excess deaths had occurred worldwide as of May 2021 (*Economist* 2021b). However, many people may have also died indirectly from the pandemic, as people were in many cases less likely to seek care for other illnesses, which also blurs the number of excess deaths reported.

(continued on next page)

BOX 1.1 *continued*

Figure B1.1.2 **Daily new confirmed COVID-19 cases in relation to daily tests, extended Mediterranean versus non-extended Mediterranean regions, January 2020 to October 2021**

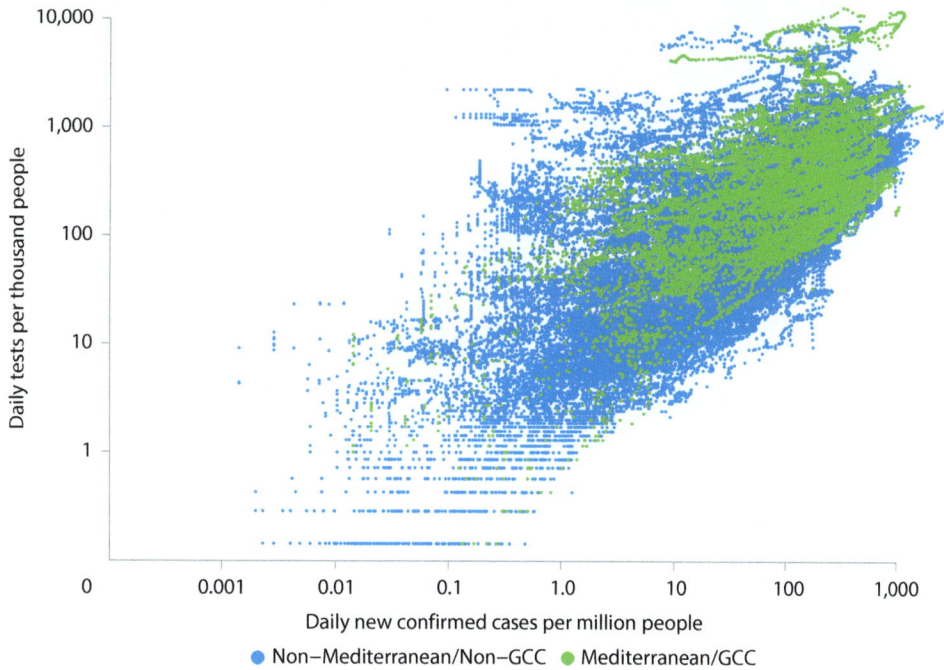

Sources: Coronavirus Pandemic (COVID-19) database of Our World in Data (https://ourworldindata.org /coronavirus); Coronavirus Resource Center, Center for Systems Science and Engineering, Johns Hopkins University (https://coronavirus.jhu.edu/).

Note: "Mediterranean" includes Albania, Algeria, Bosnia and Herzegovina, Croatia, Cyprus, the Arab Republic of Egypt, France, Greece, Israel, Italy, Jordan, Lebanon, Libya, Malta, Montenegro, Morocco, Slovenia, Spain, the Syrian Arab Republic, Tunisia, Turkey, and West Bank and Gaza. GCC = Gulf Cooperation Council (Bahrain, Kuwait, Oman, Qatar, Saudi Arabia, and the United Arab Emirates).

a. These 10 African countries were Cameroon, the Arab Republic of Egypt, Ethiopia, Ghana, Kenya, Morocco, Nigeria, Rwanda, South Africa, and Uganda.

Management and adjustment of mobility in response to the pandemic

During the initial months of the pandemic, most countries around the world introduced strong measures to limit the risk of transmission, especially at a time when other precautionary measures such as testing and vaccines were not in place. Lockdowns that limited mobility within national borders were imposed in most countries to contain the spread of the virus. Starting in March 2020, all extended Mediterranean countries and economies also imposed international mobility restrictions.

Travel restrictions

By the end of March 2020, federal and subnational governments had issued 43,300 travel measures across every country worldwide and 70 travel bans (Benton et al. 2021). From March 19 until the end of May 2020, every country or economy in the Mediterranean and GCC region had a full or partial ban on the entry of foreigners (figure 1.8).

With only one or two exceptions for brief stints of time, every economy in the region maintained some form of travel restriction until November 2021. Restrictions eased a bit in the last few months of 2020, with around half of the region's economies allowing foreigners to enter with only a screening or quarantine period upon arrival in November 2020. However, restrictions were strictly reinforced in the early months of 2021, with approximately three-quarters of the region's economies again having a full or partial entry ban for foreigners in February 2021.

On the African continent, 90 percent of African Union (AU) countries introduced at least some travel restrictions by the beginning of April 2020 (AUDA-NEPAD 2020). Many of these closures started as targeted measures such as bans on travelers

Figure 1.8   Share of Mediterranean and GCC countries and economies with mobility restrictions, by type, 2020–21

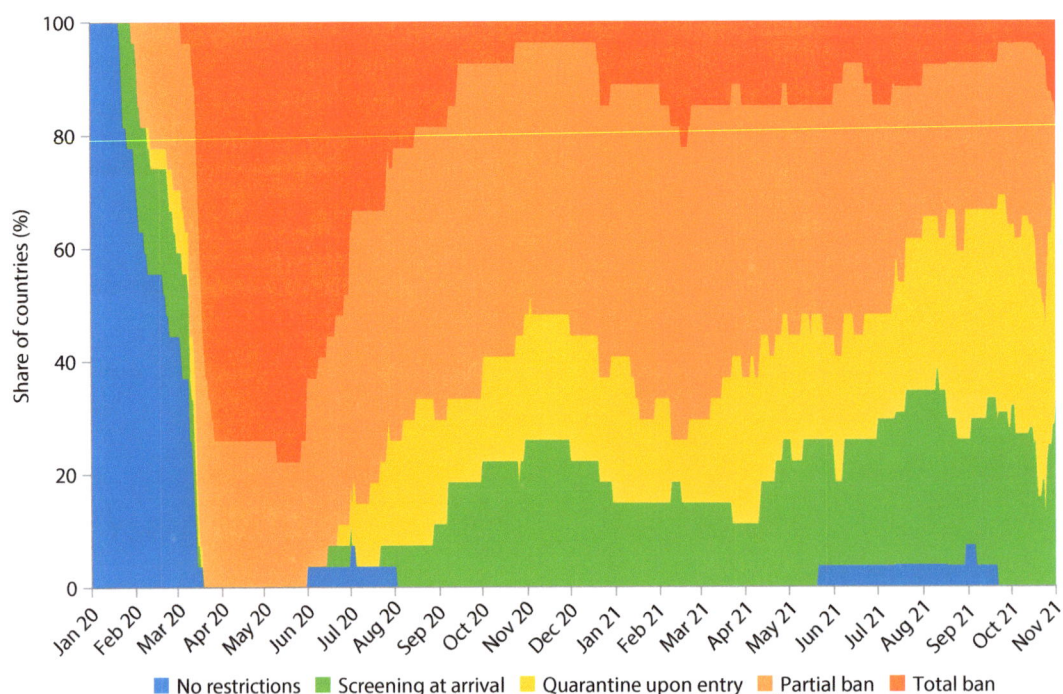

Source: Hale et al. 2021.

Note: The data cover 21 Mediterranean countries and economies as well as the Gulf Cooperation Council (GCC) countries: Bahrain, Kuwait, Oman, Qatar, Saudi Arabia, and the United Arab Emirates. Data for Montenegro were unavailable.

from high-risk areas, and some quickly turned toward complete halting of international flights. Similar to countries in the Mediterranean region, by June 2020, many AU countries moved toward lesser restrictions such as requiring a negative PCR test before one's flight to enter the country or other screenings or even quarantine upon arrival.[24] By April 2021, nearly all AU countries had implemented these measures. Backlogs at land border crossings have slowed mobility as well, and some have argued that the discrepancy in the strictness of mobility between land and air arrivals has led to some wealth inequalities between those who can afford flights and those who cannot (Lau, Hooper, and Zard 2021).

Point-of-entry closures

Seaports, airports, and land border crossing points of entry had all decreased their operations, with many closing entirely for long periods. As of the second week of June 2020, such restrictions included the following (IOM 2020a):

- *Seaports, rivers, and lakes:* Of the seaport, river, and lake points of entry assessed worldwide by the International Organization for Migration (IOM), 22 percent were fully closed, and 57 percent were partially closed. The Middle East and North Africa was the region with the highest share of ports fully closed (19 percent). These mobility restrictions affected the journeys of migrant workers in 40 percent of the locations and those of refugees, irregular migrants, and returnees in 34 percent, 35 percent, and 27 percent of the locations, respectively.
- *Land border crossing points:* Of the land border crossings assessed worldwide, 48 percent were fully closed and 35 percent were partially closed during the same period. The regions with the most land border closures were Southeastern Europe, Eastern Europe, and Central Asia, with 287 of the combined 405 assessed points of entry fully closed. West and Central Africa and the Middle East and North Africa were also facing tight land border crossing closures during this period. Apart from regular travelers and nationals, irregular migrants were the most affected, with 45 percent of land border closures affecting irregular migrants.
- *Airports:* Airports were not excluded from these closures. Of the 763 airports assessed worldwide, 31 percent were fully closed and 43 percent were partially operational, with the Mediterranean region particularly affected. The two regions with the highest percentage of full airport closures were the Middle East and North Africa (19 percent) and the combined Southeastern Europe, Eastern Europe, and Central Asia region (18 percent).

A later round of assessment by the IOM showed that, as of mid-October 2021, 10 percent of the assessed seaports, rivers, lakes, and airports used as points of entry were still closed, 29 percent were partially closed, and 53 percent were fully operational (IOM 2021). West and Central Africa had the highest share of its points of entry fully closed (17 percent), while the European Economic Area was the region with the highest share of points of entry fully operating (82 percent).[25] In the Middle

East and North Africa region, 59 percent of these points of entry were fully operational as of October 2021.

The disruptions in airport operations affected the number of passengers on flights connecting the region for several months. Flights within the Mediterranean region were reduced dramatically. Immediately following the airport closures, as described above, flights between the southern and northern Mediterranean areas were cut in half. The number of passengers on flights in April and May 2020 were down 92 percent compared with the previous year (Benton et al. 2021). Unlike North–North and South–South flights, which rebounded to near normal levels toward the third and fourth quarters of 2020 (figure 1.9, panels a and b), flights between the southern and northern Mediterranean countries only began rebounding in summer 2021 (figure 1.9, panel c).

Slowdowns in mobility inflows

Visa issuances as well as actual migration flows in Europe and the GCC were also affected in 2020 relative to 2019. Issuances of new visas or permits by European Organisation for Economic Co-operation and Development (OECD) countries dropped by 35 percent on average in January to June 2020 compared with the same period in 2019. In Greece and Israel, the 2020 numbers were less than half those in 2019. In France, after an initial drop, numbers returned to their 2019 levels by June 2020 (OECD 2020).

Permanent and temporary migrants. Overall, the number of permanent migrants to OECD countries decreased by more than 30 percent in 2020, to fewer than 4 million.

Figure 1.9 Flights in the Mediterranean region, by subregion, October 2019 to October 2021

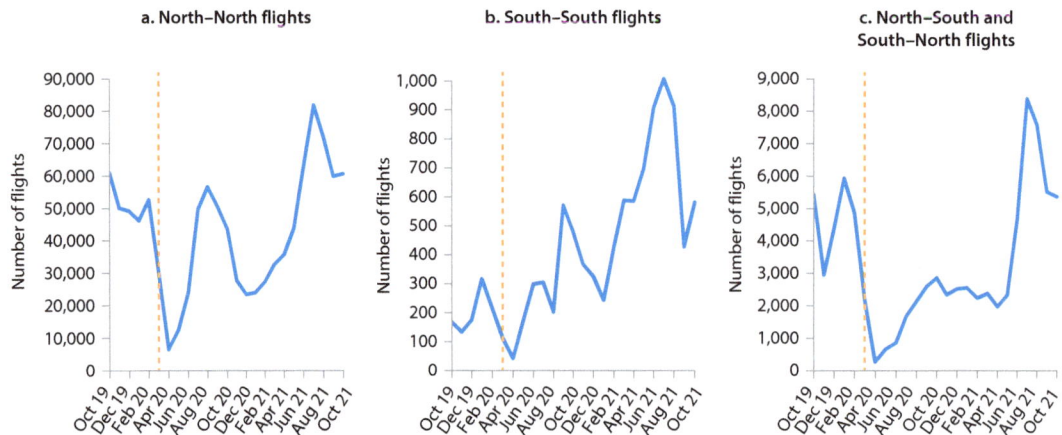

Source: Strohmeier et al. 2021.

Note: The flight data cover 871 airports in 20 Mediterranean countries. "North" includes Albania, Bosnia and Herzegovina, Croatia, Cyprus, France, Greece, Italy, Montenegro, Slovenia, Spain, and Turkey. "South" refers to Algeria, the Arab Republic of Egypt, Israel, Jordan, Lebanon, Libya, Morocco, the Syrian Arab Republic, and Tunisia. The vertical line designates the onset of the COVID-19 pandemic in March 2020.

In France and Spain—among the top five OECD destination countries for permanent migrants—permanent migration decreased to 229,700 (–21 percent) and 209,200 (–38 percent), respectively. Similarly, migration to Italy and Israel decreased to 124,300 (–35 percent) and 19,700 (–41 percent), respectively.

Declines in migration flows were even larger when taking the halt in temporary migration into account. The impact on seasonal migration varied widely among countries, for example, dropping by 57 percent in Italy and increasing by 2 percent in France between 2019 and 2020 (OECD 2021a).

Similar trends were seen in some GCC countries. The United Arab Emirates suspended the issuance of entry visas for nearly seven months after the start of the pandemic (Baruah et al. 2021a). In Saudi Arabia, the number of work visas in the first half of 2020 was down 31 percent from the year prior, and in the second half of 2020 it was down by 91 percent compared with the same period in 2019 (Baruah et al. 2021b).

Asylum seekers. Processing of asylum applications for forced migrants faced slowdowns as well. Between 2019 and 2020, the number of new asylum applications in EU Mediterranean countries[26] dropped by 37 percent overall (to approximately 242,000) (figure 1.10) and in the OECD overall by 31 percent (to just 830,000) (OECD 2021b). Just after the pandemic started spreading in the extended Mediterranean region, first-instance asylum applications in these countries and economies dropped by 99 percent—from 37,545 in February 2020 to just 455 in April 2020. Although the number of applications rebounded somewhat by July 2020, prepandemic levels were not reached in most of the region, and the number of applications tapered off again toward year-end when a second wave of the pandemic began. According to Eurostat data, only 15,730 applications were filed in December 2020, and these numbers remained low until late fall 2021.[27]

In Cyprus and Italy, the number of first-instance asylum applications returned to 2019 levels in 2021 (figure 1.10, panels a and d). But for other EU Mediterranean countries including Malta, France, Spain, and Greece—the latter three of which had, respectively, the EU's second, third, and fourth highest number (after Germany) of asylum applications in 2019—asylum applications remained stagnantly low in 2021 (figure 1.10, panels b, c, e, and f). The number of resettled refugees in OECD countries also hit record lows in 2020 (OECD 2021a).

Arrivals of migrants and asylum seekers were only partially halted by the pandemic. Overall, land and sea arrivals of migrants and asylum seekers to Europe dropped during March to July 2020 relative to the same period in 2019. However, by the end of 2020, this figure rebounded and increased even further, as 2.5 times more people arrived through irregular channels along the central Mediterranean route in 2020 than in 2019 (UNODC 2021).[28]

By 2021, land and sea arrivals to the EU had rebounded to 2019 levels (figure 1.11, panel a), but the trends of *where* migrants were arriving shifted, with fewer arriving in Greece and more arriving in Spain and especially Italy. The number of arrivals to Greece dipped at the beginning of the pandemic in March 2020 and never

Figure 1.10   First-instance asylum applications in selected European Mediterranean countries, 2019 to 2021

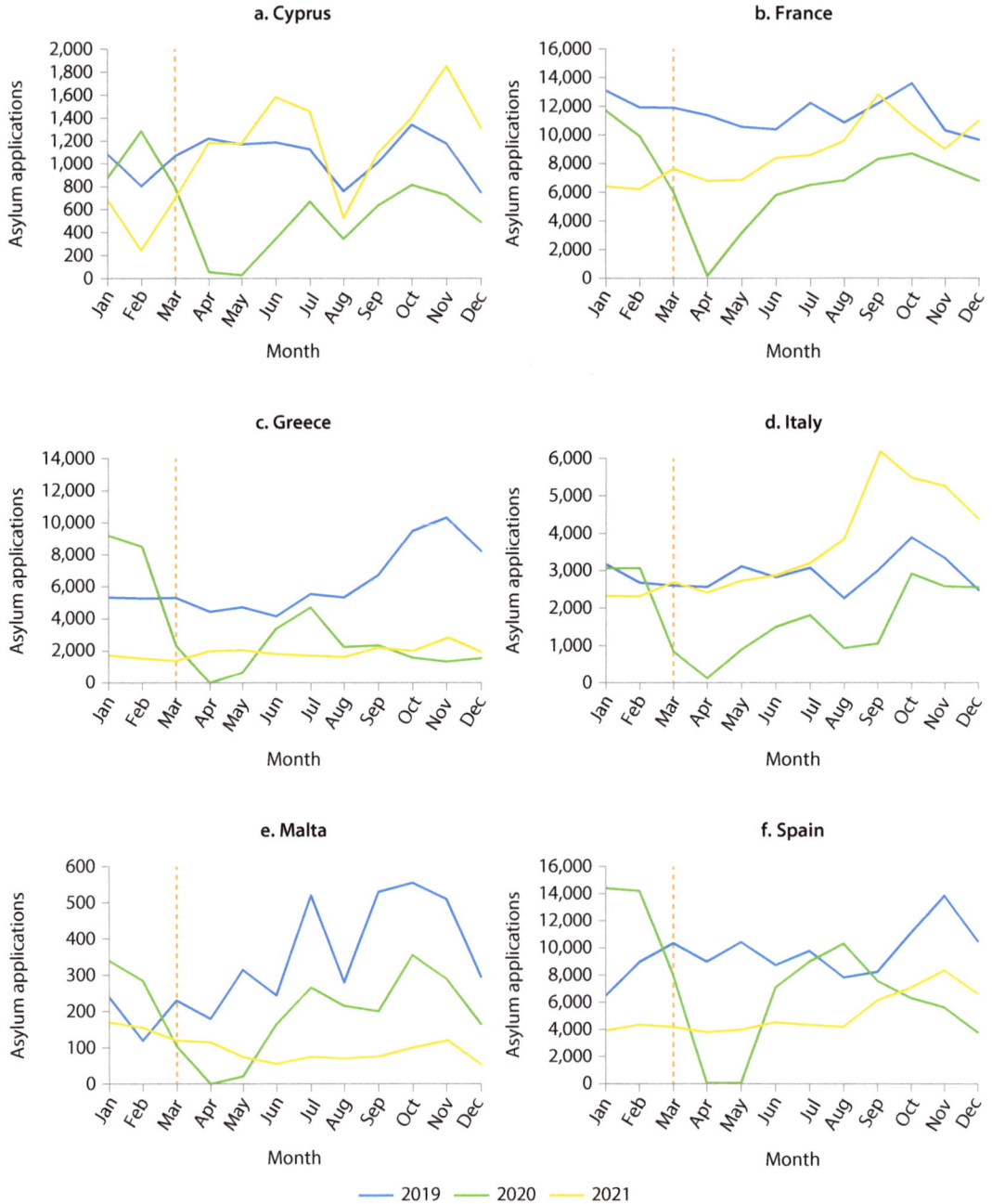

Source: Asylum Database, Eurostat: https://ec.europa.eu/eurostat/web/migration-asylum/asylum/database.
Note: The vertical line designates the onset of the COVID-19 pandemic in March 2020 and each subsequent one-year mark.

rebounded throughout all of 2020 and 2021 (figure 1.11, panel c). On the other hand, after a slight decline between March and August 2020, arrivals to Spain were higher in 2020 than in 2019 and even higher in 2021 than compared to both 2019 and 2020 levels (figure 1.11, panel d). Spain became, for the first time, one of the top OECD destination countries for asylum seekers (OECD 2021b). Similarly, although lower in March, arrivals to Italy were consistently higher during most of 2020 than in 2019—and substantially higher throughout 2021 than in the two years prior (figure 1.11, panel b).

While COVID-19 was a large direct factor in people's intention to migrate, measures to limit the spread of COVID-19 also amplified the economic stress in some sending countries, which further motivated people to move. A study shows that

Figure 1.11   **Land and sea arrivals at the EU's main points of entry and in selected Mediterranean countries, 2019 to 2021**

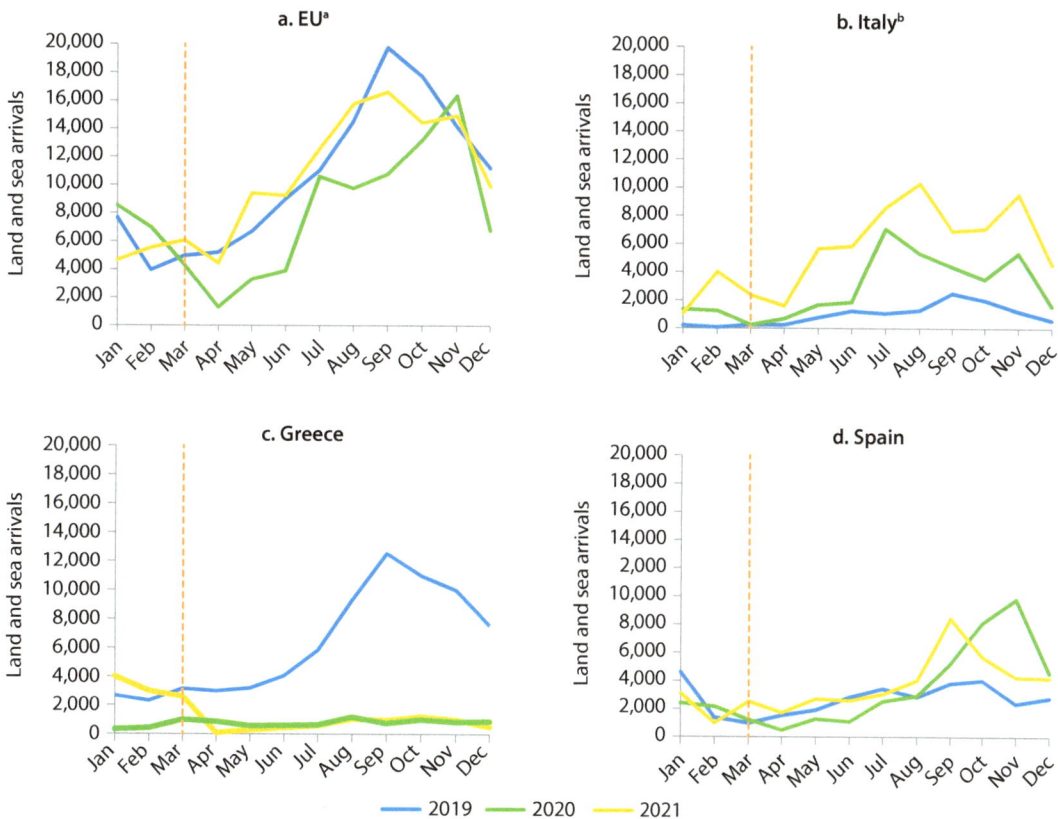

Source: United Nations High Commissioner for Refugees (UNHCR) Operational Data Portal on Refugee Situations, Mediterranean Situation monthly data (https://data2.unhcr.org/en/situations/mediterranean).

Note: The vertical line designates the onset of the COVID-19 pandemic in March 2020 and the subsequent one-year mark in March 2021.

a. Panel a encompasses the main points of entry to the European Union (EU), as defined by the UNHCR data: (1) sea arrivals to Cyprus, Greece, Italy, Malta, and Spain; and (2) land arrivals to Greece and Spain.

b. Only sea arrivals to Italy are documented.

25 percent of West and Central Africans cited COVID-19 as having an impact on other factors influencing their migration decisions—for example, exacerbating other economic stressors that drove them to leave (Horwood and Frouws 2021).

These findings are also confirmed by Facebook data on the number of foreign users in selected destinations. Facebook location data trends show that the number of foreigners from the global South located in the global North dropped significantly during the pandemic, partly because of border closures and backlogged visa processing.[29] (See box 1.2 for a description of limitations of the data used in this subsection.) In France, the number of Algerians dropped by 36 percent, the number of Nigerians by 12 percent, and the number of Moroccans by 12 percent (figure 1.12, panels a, b, and c). In Italy, however, the number of migrants did not seem to decrease as much as in other countries. This may be in part because the closure of borders and formal channels led to an increased reliance on informal channels, particularly along the central Mediterranean route, along which Italy is a primary point of arrival.

The number of Senegalese migrants in Europe, on the other hand, did not decrease as much as migrants of other nationalities (figure 1.12, panel d). In 2018, a crackdown on migration through Morocco to Europe led Senegalese migrants to increasingly use the Atlantic route through the Canary Islands to Europe. Transit via the Atlantic route has resurged because a severe depletion of fish off the Senegalese coast in 2020 led many people to lose their livelihoods. Many Senegalese migrants therefore continued their journeys to Europe along the Atlantic route despite the global pandemic (Shryock 2020).

Issues affecting returnees

The pandemic also pushed many migrant workers to return home. Although data on returnees are scarce, several disaggregated statistics show similar trends of rapid and widescale returns. Within the first 10 days after the pandemic struck Europe in mid-March 2020, of the 900,000 Bulgarians in other European countries (many of whom occupy seasonal agricultural and eldercare jobs) 100,000 returned home (Erizanu 2020). Many Bulgarians returned home out of necessity because they lacked health care coverage in their Western European host countries (Paul 2020).

The demand for return assistance increased worldwide. As of October 2020, the IOM had received 115,000 requests for return assistance globally (IOM 2020c). Between April and June 2020, Ethiopia assisted over 15,300 people in their return from nearby countries (Kuwait, Lebanon, Saudi Arabia, and others). Many of these returnees had lost their livelihoods in their destinations (IOM 2020d).

In some cases, the return of high-skilled migrants has been seen as a "reverse brain drain" phenomenon. According to the Italian foreign ministry, the number of young, working-age Italians who returned home in 2020 increased by 20 percent compared with 2019. Many of these young professionals returned because teleworking gave

BOX 1.2   Data limitations in measuring migration flows during the COVID-19 pandemic

Several of the data sources used in this chapter to explain migration flows come with some limitations. First, several bureaucratic agencies were fully or partially closed during early periods of the pandemic, slowing down the processing of visas, permits, and asylum applications. Second, some of the applications for asylum and visas may have been filed by migrants who were already in Europe when the pandemic struck. Thus, the drops in the processing and issuance of these legal documents may reflect the limited capacity of government agencies to supply migrants with legal documents at that time rather than an actual drop in migration flows or demand for such documents.

Second, the use of Facebook's advertising platform to collect data is a relatively new methodology. Pötzschke and Braun (2017) first used Facebook advertising as a more effective way to target survey participants, and they found this survey methodology could reach previously hard-to-reach populations. Zagheni, Weber, and Gummadi (2017) were among the first to use the Facebook advertising platform to estimate international migrant stocks. Comparing their statistics with the US Census Bureau's American Community Survey, they conclude that despite some sources of bias, this bias can be estimated and corrected.

Figure B1.2.1   Destinations of emigrants from Senegal, by data source

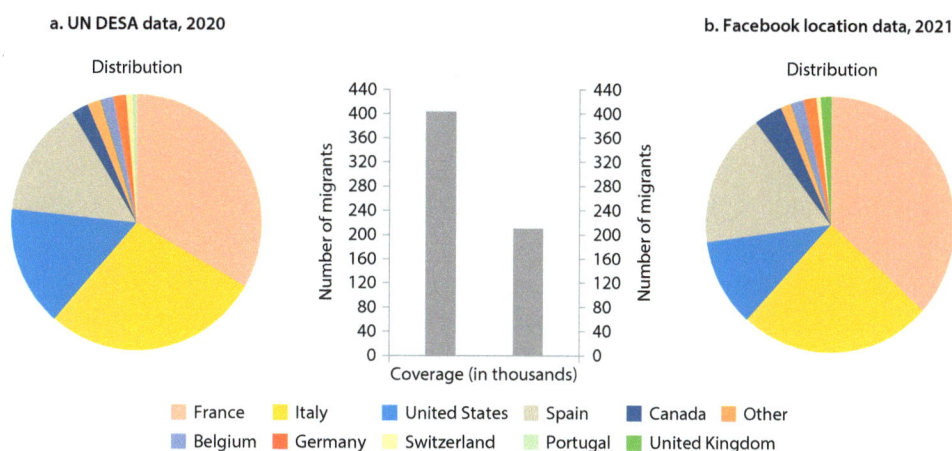

a. UN DESA data, 2020

b. Facebook location data, 2021

Distribution

Distribution

Coverage (in thousands)

Number of migrants

France   Italy   United States   Spain   Canada   Other
Belgium   Germany   Switzerland   Portugal   United Kingdom

Sources: International Migrant Stock 2020 dataset, Population Division, United Nations Department of Economic and Social Affairs (UN DESA): https://www.un.org/development/desa/pd/content/international-migrant-stock; World Bank internal data collection from Facebook's advertising platform.

(continued on next page)

BOX 1.2 *continued*

Figure B1.2.2 **Destinations of emigrants from Nigeria, by data source**

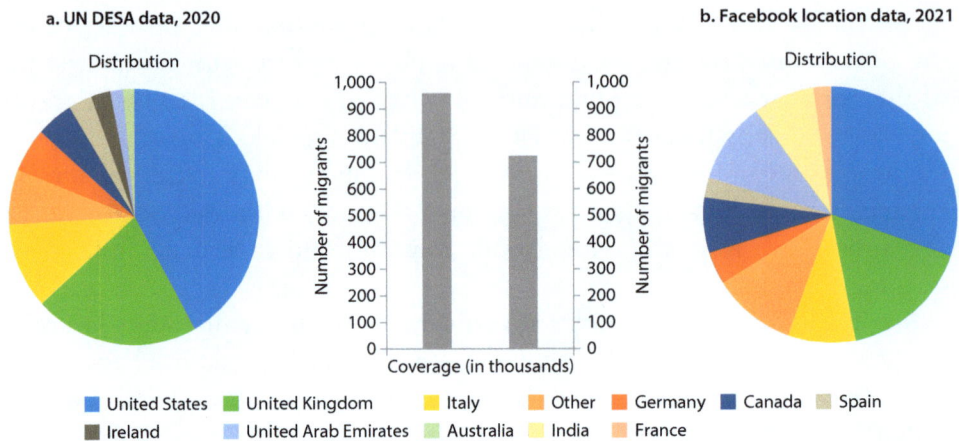

a. UN DESA data, 2020

b. Facebook location data, 2021

Distribution

Distribution

Coverage (in thousands)

■ United States ■ United Kingdom ■ Italy ■ Other ■ Germany ■ Canada ■ Spain
■ Ireland ■ United Arab Emirates ■ Australia ■ India ■ France

Sources: International Migrant Stock 2020 dataset, Population Division, United Nations Department of Economic and Social Affairs (UN DESA): https://www.un.org/development/desa/pd/content/international-migrant-stock; World Bank internal data collection from Facebook's advertising platform.

However, Facebook data also have several limitations. First, numbers of migrants are rounded to the nearest thousand, so there is some measurement error. Second, besides the fact that not everyone uses Facebook, these data could also capture the presence of foreigners in a country who are not necessarily migrants, such as tourists, travelers for business, and so on. Third, not every country supports Facebook's advertising platform. Rampazzo and Weber (2020) report that only 17 African countries support the platform and that United Nations Department of Economic and Social Affairs (UN DESA) estimates of African migrants abroad in other African countries are 64 percent higher than their estimates using Facebook data. When comparing the Facebook 2021 data with UN DESA 2020 data, for some nationalities such as Senegalese emigrants, the distribution of the data is relatively similar, though the coverage of the Facebook data is only about half that of the UN DESA data. On the other hand, the Facebook data have a wider coverage of Nigerians abroad, though the distribution across destinations is not entirely compatible with the UN DESA data.

Despite its nuances, the Facebook data has the benefit of being collected more frequently and at a smaller level of regional granularity. However, given the incomplete penetration of Facebook data in capturing all people on the move, the biases in the data should be corrected (Zagheni, Weber, and Gummadi 2017) and interpreted with caution.

Figure 1.12 Changes in migrant stocks from selected African countries to selected destination countries, April 2020 to January 2021

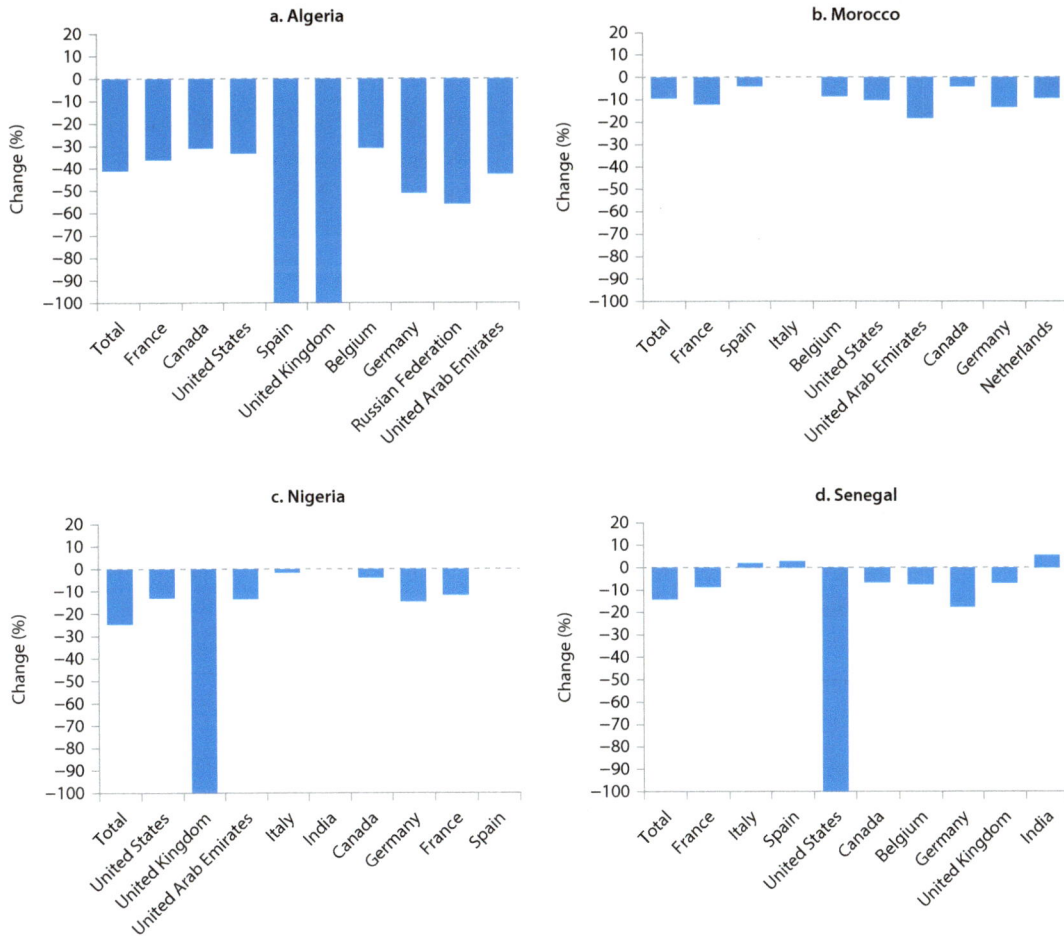

Source: World Bank internal data collection from Facebook's advertising platform.
Note: Destination countries were selected based on available data.

them the option to work remotely from their home country. The government is encouraging these return migrants to stay because it could promote innovation, competition, and tax revenue (Bubola 2021). Similarly, in spring 2020, more than 1.5 million Romanians and 54,000 Poles returned home from countries such as Italy, Spain, and other Western European countries (Paul 2020).

Although this phenomenon has been leading to a shortage of essential workers in host countries, this reverse migration is increasing the human capital of the sending countries. Bakalova et al. (2021) estimate that across the EU, 2.7–3.7 million migrants in white-collar occupations could potentially return home and work remotely, including 2–2.6 million to other EU member states and 321,000 to 446,000 to countries in the Middle East and North Africa.

On the other hand, border closures, strained budgets, and logistical difficulties led many migrants to become stranded. For example, from March to July 2020, Morocco closed its borders, preventing seasonal agricultural migrant workers abroad from returning home (Le Coz and Newland 2021). An estimated 2.75 million migrants whose movements were affected by COVID-19 were stranded worldwide in October 2020 (IOM 2020b). Of these 2.75 million, approximately 1.3 million people were in the Middle East and North Africa, 201,000 were in the European Economic Area and Switzerland, and 58,000 were in Eastern Europe and Central Asia. In June 2020, in West and Central Africa, the IOM counted approximately 50,000 migrants stranded at international borders, in transit centers, or in quarantine (Schöfberger and Rango 2020). For instance, when the Niger government closed its borders, 764 migrants were stranded at the Algerian border in quarantine, and 256 migrants were stranded at the Libyan border (MMC 2020).

Predeparture measures such as presenting negative PCR tests, among others, presented challenges for many people on the move. For example, difficulty in getting a test left more than 2,000 Nigerians stranded in transit in Libya in the early months of the pandemic (Lau, Hooper, and Zard 2021). In the United Arab Emirates, migrant workers were stranded for months after being laid off in the midst of the pandemic, trying to secure a way to return home (Horwood and Frouws 2021).

The effectiveness of travel restrictions: a call for research

Historical research has generally shown that border and travel restrictions do not stop virus transmission. Some historical research indicates that travel restrictions, especially if not implemented in a timely manner, have no effect on the spread of diseases. Brownstein, Wolfe, and Mandl (2006) look at the temporary reduction in air travel due to restrictions following the September 11, 2001, terrorist attacks on the spread of the flu virus, and they find that only immediate air travel closures would have an impact on containing the virus.

A recent study by Clemens and Ginn (2020) concludes that the case for permanent limits on international mobility to reduce the harm of future pandemics is weak. Using data on the influenza pandemics that began in 1889, 1918, 1957, and 2009, they find that a 50 percent reduction in prepandemic international mobility is associated with a one- to two-week delay in arrival of the virus to a destination and no detectable reduction in final mortality. They find no evidence that delayed arrival correlates systematically with lower morbidity or mortality in any of the pandemics. In a review of past research, Bier (2020) similarly shows that largely reducing air traffic can only slightly delay a pandemic—by one to six weeks at best—but not stop it (Bajardi et al. 2011; Cooper et al. 2006; Epstein et al. 2007; Ferguson et al. 2006;

Flahault et al. 2006; Germann et al. 2006; Hollingsworth, Ferguson, and Anderson 2006; Tomba and Wallinga 2008). Despite having only minimal effects on the spread of the virus, these closures have shown to be logistically difficult to implement and to cause economic disruptions (Colizza et al. 2007).

The effectiveness of recent border and travel restrictions in stopping the spread of COVID-19 is still unclear. Reviewing the literature, Islamaj, Kim, and Le (2021) highlight research with three different conclusions:

- Some papers find that the closure of borders or travel restrictions during the COVID-19 pandemic had little effect on transmission (Askitas, Tatsiramos, and Verheydan 2020; Bonardi et al. 2020; Weber 2020).
- Other papers find that restrictions to international air travel have sizable effects, particularly if measures were implemented early (Chinazzi et al. 2020; Keita 2020). For example, in a localized study, Costantino, Heslop, and MacIntyre (2020) find that the full travel bans reduced cases in Australia by 86 percent. On the other hand, Eckardt, Kappner, and Wolf (2020) find that border controls during the first wave of COVID-19 had limited effectiveness in 18 Western European countries.
- Finally, using a simulated model, assuming there were no reductions in travel, Russell et al. (2020) find that by May 2020, in 102 of the 136 countries studied, international travel would account for more than 10 percent of the total COVID-19 incidence. However, they also find that by September 2020, international travel would have accounted for less than 10 percent of the total incidence rate in 106 of the 162 countries studied if no travel restrictions had been implemented.

Russell et al. (2020) therefore conclude that (a) the effectiveness of border closures depends upon how near a country's incidence rate is to the tipping point for exponential spread of the virus, and (b) policy makers should take into account local incidence, epidemic growth, and travel volumes before implementing restrictions. More research is needed to better understand the effectiveness of border and travel restrictions on viral transmission during the COVID-19 pandemic.

Notes

1. Mediterranean migration data are from the International Migrant Stock 2020 dataset of the Population Division, United Nations Department of Economic and Social Affairs (UN DESA): https://www.un.org/development/desa/pd/content/international-migrant-stock. Throughout this volume, "Mediterranean" countries and economies include Albania, Algeria, Bosnia and Herzegovina, Croatia, Cyprus, the Arab Republic of Egypt, France, Greece, Israel, Italy, Jordan, Lebanon, Libya, Malta, Montenegro, Morocco, Slovenia, Spain, the Syrian Arab Republic, Tunisia, Turkey, and West Bank and Gaza. Jordan is also included, given its importance as a receiver of Syrian refugees. The Gulf Cooperation Council (GCC) states include Bahrain, Kuwait, Oman, Qatar, Saudi Arabia, and the United Arab Emirates.
2. Southern Mediterranean countries and economies include Algeria, the Arab Republic of Egypt, Israel, Jordan, Lebanon, Libya, Morocco, the Syrian Arab Republic, Tunisia, and West Bank and Gaza.

3. Mediterranean and GCC migration data throughout this section are from the International Migrant Stock 2020 dataset of the Population Division, United Nations Department of Economic and Social Affairs (UN DESA): https://www.un.org/development/desa/pd/content/international-migrant-stock.

4. "North America" is defined as Bermuda, Canada, and the United States (including Puerto Rico, and US Virgin Islands).

5. These countries accounted for 12.9 percent of the world's emigrants in 1990 and 14.7 percent in 2020 (International Migrant Stock 2020 dataset of the Population Division, UN DESA: https://www.un.org /development/desa/pd/content/international-migrant-stock).

6. From 1990 to 2020, the share of the world's emigrants from North America dropped from 1.8 percent to 1.5 percent, and the share of the world's emigrants from Europe and Central Asia excluding the Mediterranean countries dropped from 31.1 percent to 21.7 percent (International Migrant Stock 2020 dataset of the Population Division, UN DESA: https://www.un.org/development/desa/pd /content/international-migrant-stock).

7. Data on the top receiving and sending countries are from the International Migrant Stock 2020 dataset, Population Division, UN DESA: https://www.un.org/development/desa/pd/content /international-migrant-stock.

8. The top 10 sending countries to Mediterranean and GCC countries that are outside this extended Mediterranean region are (in this order) India, Pakistan, Bangladesh, Indonesia, Romania, the Philippines, Germany, the Republic of Yemen, Sri Lanka, and Bulgaria. The top 10 destinations of Mediterranean and GCC emigrants that are outside the region are Germany, the United States, Canada, the United Kingdom, Australia, Belgium, Switzerland, Serbia, the Netherlands, and Austria. Data on the top migration corridors are from the International Migrant Stock 2020 dataset of the Population Division, UN DESA: https://www.un.org/development/desa/pd/content/international-migrant-stock.

9. For Moroccan emigrants, the top extended Mediterranean destination countries include France, Spain, Italy, and Israel. For Algerian emigrants, the top extended Mediterranean destination countries include France, Spain, Israel, Italy, and Morocco. Rankings are based on the International Migrant Stock 2020 dataset of the Population Division, UN DESA: https://www.un.org/development/desa/pd /content/international-migrant-stock.

10. Northern Mediterranean states include Albania, Bosnia and Herzegovina, Croatia, Cyprus, France, Greece, Italy, Malta, Montenegro, Slovenia, Spain, and Turkey.

11. In 2020, 51.5 percent of migrants in Northern Mediterranean destinations were female as opposed to 27.8 in GCC destinations. Data for the male–female shares of migrants are also from the International Migrant Stock 2020 dataset of the Population Division, UN DESA: https://www.un.org/development /desa/pd/content/international-migrant-stock.

12. The region includes the following destination countries for which data are available: Albania, Croatia, Cyprus, Egypt, France, Greece, Israel, Italy, Malta, Slovenia, Spain, and Turkey. All data on emigrant and immigrant skill levels are from the Database on Immigrants in OECD and Non-OECD Countries (DIOC-E), 2010 data (https://www.oecd.org/els/mig/dioc.htm).

13. Low-skilled is defined as having less than a secondary education.

14. High-skilled is defined as having a tertiary education or higher.

15. The top 10 refugee destinations that are outside of the extended Mediterranean region are (in this order) Germany, Iraq, Sweden, Sudan, Austria, the Netherlands, the United States, Serbia, Switzerland, and the United Kingdom. All data on refugee migration corridors are from the Refugee Data Finder database, of the United Nations High Commissioner for Refugees (UNHCR), https://www.unhcr.org /refugee-statistics/download/?url=5IklF3.

16. The figure does not include refugees from West Bank and Gaza under the United Nations Relief and Works Agency for Palestine Refugees in the Near East (UNRWA) mandate.

17. Asylum Database, Eurostat: https://ec.europa.eu/eurostat/web/migration-asylum/asylum/database.

18. Median age data are from the International Migrant Stock 2020 dataset of the Population Division, UN DESA: https://www.un.org/development/desa/pd/content/international-migrant-stock.

19. Qatar was first, with 20,095 cases per million of population; Bahrain (second) had 6,945 cases per million; and Kuwait (fourth) had 6,428 cases per million. All data in this section on COVID-19 case counts and death counts per country are from the COVID-19 Data Repository, Center for Systems Science and Engineering, Johns Hopkins University: https://github.com/CSSEGISandData/COVID-19.

20. Bahrain was 2nd, with 168,679 cases per million of population; Slovenia (5th) had 160,818 cases per million; Israel (6th) had 146,625 cases per million; and Croatia (14th) had 115,700 cases per million. Countries with a population less than 1 million are excluded.
21. Bosnia and Herzegovina was 3rd, with 3,972 deaths per million of population, and Slovenia (13th) had 2,611 deaths per million.
22. Data from the Johns Hopkins Coronavirus Resource Center, Center of Systems Science and Engineering (https://coronavirus.jhu.edu/2021). See box 1.1 regarding data limitations.
23. For instance, the Omicron variant, discovered in late 2021, was classified by the World Health Organization as a variant of concern.
24. The polymerase chain reaction (PCR) test for COVID-19 is a molecular test to detect genetic material of the virus that causes COVID-19. It is considered the most accurate and reliable of the available COVID-19 tests.
25. The European Economic Area includes the EU countries as well as Iceland, Liechtenstein, and Norway.
26. The Mediterranean countries that are also EU member states include Croatia, Cyprus, France, Greece, Italy, Malta, Slovenia, and Spain.
27. Data on asylum applications are from Eurostat's Asylum Database, https://ec.europa.eu/eurostat/web/migration-asylum/asylum/database.
28. The central Mediterranean route connects specifically Libya, Tunisia, Algeria, and Egypt, with primarily Italy, as well as Greece and Malta.
29. Findings referring to Facebook data are based the World Bank's internal data collection from Facebook's advertising platform.

References

Askitas, N., K. Tatsiramos, and B. Verheyden. 2020. "Lockdown Strategies, Mobility Patterns and COVID-19." Discussion Paper No. 13293. IZA Institute of Labor Economics, Bonn.

AUDA-NEPAD (African Union Development Agency–New Partnership for Africa's Development). 2020. "AUPA-NEPAD COVID-19 Digest." Issue No. 001-2020, AUPA-NEPAD, Midrand, South Africa.

Bajardi, P., C. Poletto, J. J. Ramasco, M. Tizzoni, V. Colizza, and A. Vespignani. 2011. "Human Mobility Networks, Travel Restrictions, and the Global Spread of 2009 H1N1 Pandemic." *PLoS ONE* 6 (1): e16591.

Bakalova, I., R. Berlinschi, J. Fidrmuc, and Y. Dzjuba. 2021. "COVID-19, Working from Home and the Potential Reverse Brain Drain." Working Paper No. 9104, Center for Economic Studies and Ifo Institute for Economic Research (CESifo), Munich.

Baruah, N., J. Chaloff, J. C. Dumont, and R. Kawasaki. 2021a. "The Future of Labor Migration in Asia: Post-COVID-19 Pandemic." In *Labor Migration in Asia: Impacts of the COVID-19 Crisis and the Post-Pandemic Future*, 38–59. Tokyo: Asian Development Bank Institute; Paris: Organisation for Economic Co-operation and Development; and Bangkok: International Labour Organization.

Baruah, N., J. Chaloff, P. Hervé, H. Honsho, S. Nair, and P. Sirivunnabood. 2021b. "Trends in Labor Migration in Asia." In Labor Migration in Asia: Impacts of the COVID-19 Crisis and the Post-Pandemic Future, 1–37. Tokyo: Asian Development Bank Institute; Paris: Organisation for Economic Co-operation and Development; and Bangkok: International Labour Organization.

Benton, M., J. Batalova, S. Davidoff-Gore, and T. Schmidt. 2021. "COVID-19 and the State of Global Mobility in 2020." Report, International Organization for Migration, Geneva; and Migration Policy Institute, Washington, DC.

Bier, D. J. 2020. "Research Provides No Basis for Pandemic Travel Bans." Research review, Cato Institute, Washington, DC.

Bonardi, J. P., Q. Gallea, D. Kalanoski, and R. Lalive. 2020. "Fast and Local: How Did Lockdown Policies Affect the Spread and Severity of the Covid-19?" *Covid Economics* 23: 325–51.

Brekke, J.-P., and G. Brochmann. 2014. "Stuck in Transit: Secondary Migration of Asylum Seekers in Europe, National Differences, and the Dublin Regulation." *Journal of Refugee Studies* 28 (2): 145–62.

Brewer, K. T., and D. Yükseker. 2009. "A Survey on African Migrants and Asylum Seekers in Istanbul." In *Land of Diverse Migrations: Challenges of Emigration and Immigration in Turkey*, edited by A. İçduygu and K. Kirişci. Istanbul: Istanbul Bilgi University Press.

Brownstein, J. S., C. J. Wolfe, and K. D. Mandl. 2006. "Empirical Evidence for the Effect of Airline Travel on Inter-Regional Influenza Spread in the United States." *PLoS Medicine* 3 (10): e401.

Bubola, E. 2021. "The Pandemic Helped Reverse Italy's Brain Drain. But Can It Last?" *New York Times*, January 8.

Chinazzi, M., J. T. Davis, M. Ajelli, C. Gioannini, M. Litvinova, S. Merler, A. Piontti, et al. 2020. "The Effect of Travel Restrictions on the Spread of the 2019 Novel Coronavirus (COVID-19) Outbreak." *Science* 368 (6489): 395–400.

Clemens, M. A., and T. Ginn. 2020. "Global Mobility and the Threat of Pandemics: Evidence from Three Centuries." Discussion Paper No. 13947, IZA Institute of Labor Economics, Bonn.

Colizza, V., A. Barrat, M. Barthelemy, A.-J. Valleron, and A. Vespignani. 2007. "Modeling the Worldwide Spread of Pandemic Influenza: Baseline Case and Containment Interventions." *PLoS Medicine* 4 (1): e13.

Collyer, M. 2006. "Migrants, Migration and the Security Paradigm: Constraints and Opportunities." *Mediterranean Politics* 11 (2): 255–70.

Costantino, V., D. J. Heslop, and C. R. MacIntyre. 2020. "The Effectiveness of Full and Partial Travel Bans against COVID-19 Spread in Australia for Travellers from China." *Journal of Travel Medicine* 27 (5): taaa081.

Cooper, B. S., R. J. Pitman, W. J. Edmunds, and N. J. Gay. 2006. "Delaying the International Spread of Pandemic Influenza." *PLoS ONE* 3 (6): e212.

Dimitriadi, A. 2013. "Migration from Afghanistan to Third Countries and Greece." IRMA Background Report, Hellenic Foundation for European and Foreign Policy (ELIAMEP), Athens.

Düvell, F., I. Molodikova, and M. Collyer, eds. 2014. *Transit Migration in Europe*. International Migration, Integration and Social Cohesion in Europe (IMISCOE) Research Series. Amsterdam: Amsterdam University Press.

Eckardt, M., K. Kappner, and N. Wolf. 2020. "COVID-19 across European Regions: The Role of Border Controls." Online Working Paper No. 507, Competitive Advantage in the Global

Economy (CAGE) Research Centre, Department of Economics, University of Warwick, Coventry, UK.

Economist. 2021a. "COVID-19 Data: Tracking COVID-19 Excess Deaths Across Countries." Online COVID-19 data compilation with graphic detail, *Economist*, July 15 (last updated March 18, 2022): https://www.economist.com/graphic-detail /coronavirus-excess-deaths-tracker.

Economist. 2021b. "Modelling COVID-19's Death Toll: There Have Been 7m–13m Excess Deaths Worldwide during the Pandemic." Briefing, *Economist*, May 15. https://www.economist.com/briefing/2021/05/15/there-have-been-7m-13m -excess-deaths-worldwide-during-the-pandemic.

Epstein, J. M., D. M. Goedecke, F. Yu, R. J. Morris, D. K. Wagener, and G. V. Bobashev. 2007. "Controlling Pandemic Flu: The Value of International Air Travel Restrictions." *PloS ONE* 2 (5): e401.

Erizanu, P. 2020. "Stranded or Shunned: Europe's Migrant Workers Caught in No-Man's Land." *The Guardian*, April 16.

Ferguson, N. M., D. A. T. Cummings, C. Fraser, J. C. Cajka, P. C. Cooley, and D. S. Burke. 2006. "Strategies for Mitigating an Influenza Pandemic." *Nature* 442 (7101): 448–52.

Flahault, A., E. Vergu, L. Coudeville, and R. F. Grais. 2006. "Strategies for Containing a Global Influenza Pandemic." *Vaccine* 24 (44–46): 6751–55.

Germann, T. C., K. Kadau, I. M. Longini Jr., and C. A. Macken. 2006. "Mitigation Strategies for Pandemic Influenza in the United States." *PNAS* 103 (15): 5935–40.

Hale, T., N. Angrist, R. Goldszmidt, B. Kira, A. Petherick, T. Phillips, S. Webster, et al. 2021. "A Global Panel Database of Pandemic Policies (Oxford COVID-19 Government Response Tracker)." *Nature Human Behaviour* 5: 529–38.

Hollingsworth, T. D., N. M. Ferguson, and R. M. Anderson. 2006. "Will Travel Restrictions Control the International Spread of Pandemic Influenza?" *Nature Medicine* 12 (5): 497–99.

Horwood, C., and B. Frouws, eds. 2021. "Mixed Migration Review 2021: Reframing Human Mobility in a Changing World." Annual publication, Mixed Migration Centre, Geneva.

ILO (International Labour Organization). 2014. *Assessment of the Impact of Syrian Refugees in Lebanon and Their Employment Profile 2013*. Beirut: ILO Regional Office for the Arab States.

ILO (International Labour Organization). 2020. "COVID-19 Impact on the Collection of Labour Market Statistics." Note, ILO Department of Statistics (ILOSTAT), Geneva.

IOM (International Organization for Migration). 2020a. "IOM COVID-19 Impact on Ports of Entry: Weekly Analysis, 10 June 2020." Report, IOM, Geneva.

IOM (International Organization for Migration). 2020b. "COVID-19 Impact on Stranded Migrants." Brief, September 30, COVID-19 Return Task Force, IOM, Geneva.

IOM (International Organization for Migration). 2020c. "Immediate Action Required to Address Needs, Vulnerabilities of 2.75m Stranded Migrants." October 9, IOM, Geneva.

IOM (International Organization for Migration). 2020d. "IOM Ethiopia Assists Hundreds of Returning COVID-19 Affected Migrants." IOM News, June 9. https://www.iom.int/news /iom-ethiopia-assists-hundreds-returning-covid-19-affected-migrants.

IOM (International Organization for Migration). 2021. "IOM COVID-19 Impact on Points of Entry: Weekly Analysis, 13 October 2021." Report, IOM, Geneva.

Islamaj, E., Y. E. Kim, and D. T. Le. 2021. "The Spread of COVID-19 and Policy Responses." Research & Policy Brief No. 40, World Bank Malaysia Hub, Kuala Lumpur.

Jordan, B., and F. Düvell. 2002. *Irregular Migration: The Dilemmas of Transnational Mobility.* Cheltenham, UK: Edward Elgar.

Keita, S. 2020. "Air Passenger Mobility, Travel Restrictions, and the Transmission of the COVID-19 Pandemic between Countries." *Covid Economics* 9: 77–96.

Koser, K. 2010. "Dimensions and Dynamics of Irregular Migration." *Population, Space and Place* 16 (3): 181–93.

Koser, K., and C. Pinkerton. 2002. *The Social Networks of Asylum Seekers and the Dissemination of Information about Countries of Asylum.* London: Home Office Research, Development and Statistics Directorate.

Kuschminder, K., J. de Bresser, and M. Siegel. 2015. "Irregular Migration Routes to Europe and Factors Influencing Migrants' Destination Choices." Report, Maastricht Graduate School of Governance, Maastrict University, Netherlands.

Lau, L. S., K. Hooper, and M. Zard. 2021. "From Unilateral Response to Coordinated Action: How Can Mobility Systems in Sub-Saharan Africa Adapt to the Public-Health Challenges of COVID-19?" Policy brief, Migration Policy Institute, Washington, DC.

Le Coz, C., and K. Newland. 2021. "Rewiring Migrant Returns and Reintegration after the COVID-19 Shock." Policy brief, Migration Policy Institute, Washington, DC.

Lutterbeck, D. 2013. "Across the Desert, Across the Sea: Migrant Smuggling into and from Libya." In *Migration, Security, and Citizenship in the Middle East: New Perspectives*, edited by P. Seeberg and Z. Eyadat, 137–66. The Modern Muslim World Series. New York: Palgrave Macmillan.

MMC (Mixed Migration Centre). 2020. "Quarterly Mixed Migration Update: West Africa, Quarter 1 2020." Quarterly report, MMC, Geneva.

OECD (Organisation for Economic Co-operation and Development). 2020. "The Impact of Coronavirus (COVID-19) on Forcibly Displaced Persons in Developing Countries." Brief, OECD, Paris.

OECD (Organisation for Economic Co-operation and Development). 2021a. *OECD Economic Outlook, Volume 2021 Issue 2: Preliminary Version.* No. 110. Paris: OECD Publishing.

OECD (Organisation for Economic Co-operation and Development). 2021b. "The State of Global Education: 18 Months into the Pandemic." Report, OECD, Paris.

OECD, ILO, UNHCR, and IOM (Organisation for Economic Co-operation and Development, International Labour Organization, United Nations High Commissioner for Refugees, and International Organization for Migration). 2020. "2020 Annual International Migration and Forced Displacement Trends and Policies Report to the G20." Joint annual report, OECD, Paris; and ILO, UNHCR, and IOM, Geneva.

Paul, R. 2020. "Europe's Essential Workers: Migration and Pandemic Politics in Central and Eastern Europe during COVID-19." *European Policy Analysis* 6 (2): 238–63.

Petesch, C. 2020. "Increased Testing Needed as Africa Sees Rise in Virus Cases." Associated Press, December 31.

Pötzschke, S., and M. Braun. 2017. "Migrant Sampling Using Facebook Advertisements: A Case Study of Polish Migrants in Four European Countries." *Social Science Computer Review* 35 (5): 633–53.

Rampazzo, F., and I. Weber. 2020. "Facebook Advertising Data in Africa." In *Migration in West and North Africa and across the Mediterranean: Trends, Risks, Development and Governance*, 32–40. Geneva: International Organization for Migration.

Roman, H. 2006. "Transit Migration in Egypt." Euro-Mediterranean Consortium for Applied Research on International Migration (CARIM) Research Report No. 2006/01, Robert Schuman Centre for Advanced Studies (RSCAS) of the European University Institute, Florence.

Rozo, S. 2021. "Forced Displacement." Internal report, World Bank, Washington, DC.

Russell, T. W., J. T. Wu, S. Clifford, W. J. Edmunds, A. J. Kucharski, M. Jit, et al. 2020. "Effect of Internationally Imported Cases on Internal Spread of COVID-19: A Mathematical Modelling Study." *The Lancet Public Health* 6 (1): E12–E20.

Schapendonk, J. 2012. "Migrants' Im/Mobilities on Their Way to the EU: Lost in Transit?" *Tijdschrift voor Economische en Sociale Geografie* 103 (5): 577–83.

Schöfberger, I., and M. Rango. 2020. "COVID-19 and Migration in West and North Africa and across the Mediterranean." In *Migration in West and North Africa and across the Mediterranean: Trends, Risks, Development and Governance*, xx–xxxii. Geneva: International Organization for Migration

Shryock, R. 2020. "What's Driving the Deadly Migrant Surge from Senegal to the Canary Islands?" *The New Humanitarian*, December 7. https://www.thenewhumanitarian.org/news-feature/2020/12/7/senegal-canary-islands-migration-overfishing-coronavirus-restrictions#.

Strohmeier, M., X. Olive, J. Lübbe, M. Schäfer, and V. Lenders. 2021. "Crowdsourced Air Traffic Data from the OpenSky Network 2019–2020." *Earth System Science Data* 13 (2): 357–66. doi:10.5194/essd-13-357-2021.

Tomba, G. S., and J. Wallinga. 2008. "A Simple Explanation for the Low Impact of Border Control as a Countermeasure to the Spread of an Infectious Disease." *Mathematical Biosciences* 214 (1–2): 70–72.

Touzenis, K. 2017. *Free Movement of Persons in the European Union and Economic Community of West African States: A Comparison of Law and Practice*. Paris: United Nations Educational, Scientific and Cultural Organization.

TRC (Turkish Red Crescent Society). 2020. "Livelihood Transition of the ESSN – Capacity Mapping and Understanding Potential." Study of the Emergency Social Safety Net (ESSN) program, TRC, Ankara.

Triandafyllidou, A., L. Bartolini, and C. Guidi. 2019. *Exploring the Links Between Enhancing Regular Pathways and Discouraging Irregular Migration: A Discussion Paper to Inform Future Policy Deliberations*. Geneva: International Organization for Migration.

UN (United Nations). 2019. "Global Compact for Safe, Orderly and Regular Migration." UN General Assembly Resolution A/RES/73/195 (December 19, 2018).

UNODC (United Nations Office on Drugs and Crime). 2021. "West Africa, North Africa and the Central Mediterranean: Key Findings on the Characteristics of Migrant Smuggling in West Africa, North Africa and the Central Mediterranean." Research report, UNODC Observatory on Smuggling of Migrants, Vienna.

Wahba, J. 2021. "Economic Impact." Internal report, World Bank, Washington, DC.

Weber, E. 2020. "Which Measures Flattened the Curve in Germany?" *Covid Economics* 24: 205–17.

Wittenberg, L. 2017. "Managing Mixed Migration: The Central Mediterranean Route to Europe." Desperate Migration Series No. 3, International Peace Institute, New York.

World Bank. 2018. "Asylum Seekers in the European Union: Building Evidence to Inform Policy Makers." Report, World Bank, Washington, DC.

World Bank. 2020. "MoMRA's Low Income Labor Housing Strategy." Internal report, World Bank, Washington, DC.

World Bank. 2021a. *Global Economic Prospects, June 2021.* Washington, DC: World Bank.

World Bank. 2021b. "Middle East and North Africa Macro Poverty Outlook, Spring Meetings 2021." Biannual report, World Bank, Washington, DC.

Zagheni, E., I. Weber, and K. Gummadi. 2017. "Leveraging Facebook's Advertising Platform to Monitor Stocks of Migrants." *Population and Development Review* 43 (4): 721–34.

CHAPTER 2

The Impacts of COVID-19 on Migrants and Their Families

Introduction

This chapter describes the vulnerabilities faced by people on the move following the COVID-19 outbreak. The strong drivers behind mobility flows did not disappear during the pandemic, thus still pushing people to move but at higher risk, particularly for women. Migrants and refugees appear to be more vulnerable than nonmigrants to the health and economic impacts of the pandemic given the social and economic conditions they face. Furthermore, often because of their occupations and limited access to social welfare programs, migrants have experienced more severe economic impacts.

This chapter also shows that the health and economic risks to migrants during the pandemic may also have repercussions on migrants' families in sending countries. The negative impacts on migrant workers may trickle down to sending countries because of reduced remittances, which in turn reduce household income and increase food insecurity.

The sections of this chapter present detailed evidence on the (a) mobility-related vulnerabilities, (b) health risks, and (c) economic impacts on people on the move and their families during the COVID-19 crisis.

Mobility-related vulnerabilities of migrants and refugees during the pandemic

Initial data suggest that migrants have taken more dangerous routes to reach their destinations. In recent years, the central Mediterranean route has proven to be the deadliest passage for migrants and refugees in terms of both the death rate and the overall number of deaths.[1] Data on illegal border crossings show that since the start of the pandemic, the most commonly used migration routes have changed, possibly owing to border closures and other mobility restrictions. More migrants are using the central Mediterranean route and fewer are using the less dangerous eastern Mediterranean route (figure 2.1).[2]

Migration continues despite a greater risk

The number of people crossing from North Africa to Italy—along the deadliest route—was more than two and a half times higher in 2020 (approximately

Figure 2.1   Illegal border crossings to Europe, by route, January 2019 to August 2021

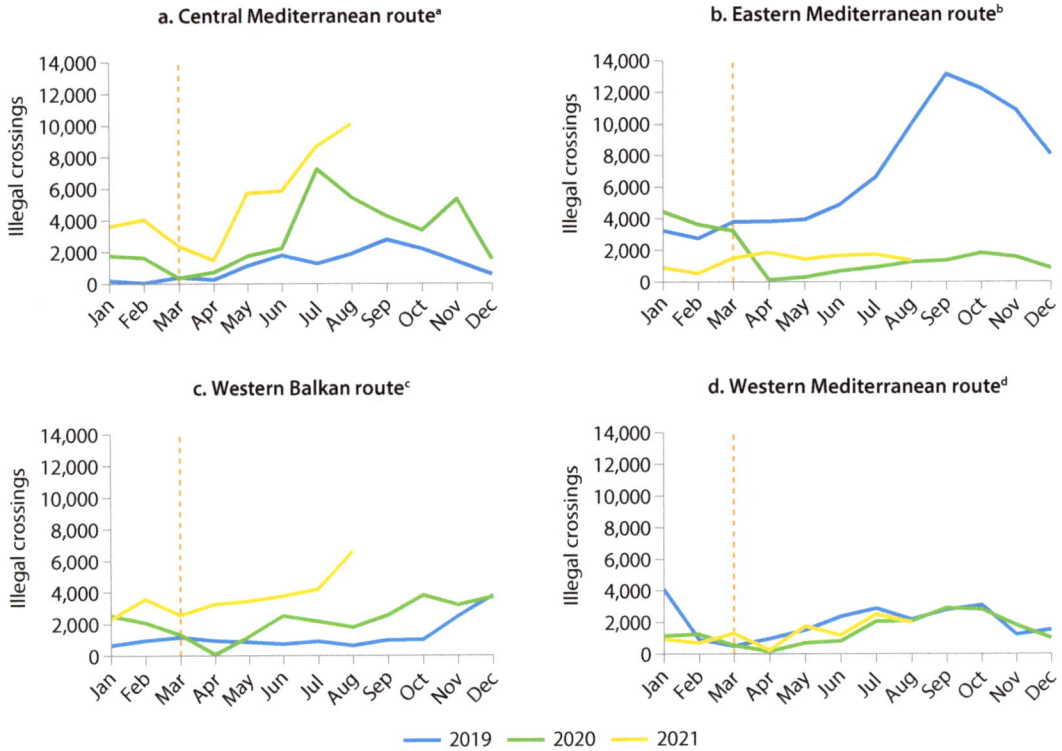

Source: European Border and Coast Guard Agency (Frontex), "Detections of illegal border-crossings" statistics (https://frontex.europa.eu/we-know/migratory-map/).

Note: The vertical line designates the onset of the COVID-19 pandemic in March 2020 and each subsequent one-year mark.

a. The central Mediterranean route connects the North African countries—primarily Libya but also Tunisia, Algeria, and the Arab Republic of Egypt—to primarily Italy and, in much smaller numbers, Malta and Greece.

b. The eastern Mediterranean route leads across the Mediterranean Sea from Turkey to Greece and Cyprus.

c. The western Balkan route leads across land from Turkey through Greece, North Macedonia, Serbia, Hungary, Croatia, Slovenia, and Austria.

d. The western Mediterranean route leads across the Mediterranean Sea from Morocco to Spain.

36,000 migrants) than in 2019. According to European Border and Coast Guard Agency (Frontex) data, the number of people along this route only increased further in 2021, to nearly 42,000 in the first eight months alone. The top nationalities of people who arrived via the central Mediterranean route in 2020 were Tunisians, Bangladeshis, and Ivorians. In Tunisia, COVID-19 exacerbated contemporary political shifts, poor economic conditions, and hyperinflation, inducing many people to leave. These trends also affected the Ivorians living in Tunisia (UNODC 2021).

The number of migrants arriving in Spain also increased in 2020, by 29 percent, but many people diverted their transit from the western Mediterranean route to the more dangerous western Atlantic route via the Canary Islands. While arrivals along the western Mediterranean route from Morocco and Algeria to Spain via Ceuta and Melilla (on the North African coast across from Gibraltar) dropped, arrivals through the western Atlantic route increased, mostly during the last quarter of 2020 (Bah et al. 2021) and throughout 2021. The increasing attempts to reach the Canary Islands also corresponded with a significant increase in the number of fatalities, which more than doubled in the first eight months of 2021 compared with the same period in 2020 (IOM 2021a). These figures suggest that the pandemic was not enough to dissuade people from migrating.

Increased exposure to smuggling and trafficking

Prolonged mobility restrictions may further limit regular migration and increase smuggling and trafficking. Mobility restrictions and backlogs in asylum processes (as discussed in chapter 1) have closed pathways for safe and regular migration. Even as legal pathways closed during the pandemic, conflict, violence, and persecution persisted, and poverty has been exacerbated. These systematic closures often lead migrants to take more dangerous routes, which leaves them (especially women) more exposed to exploitation and trafficking. For example, in the United States, human trafficking cases increased by an estimated 185 percent in 2020 relative to 2019. Similarly, in Colombia, the first four months of 2020 alone accounted for an estimated 20 percent increase in victims of trafficking when compared with all of 2019 (IOM 2021c).

As an additional problem, because of increased demand, smugglers may charge migrants exorbitant fees and further exploit the migrants as they try to pay these debts (Giammarinaro 2020; Sanchez and Achilli 2020; UNODC 2020).

Initial qualitative data confirm that an increasing number of people on the move turn to smugglers, pay higher smuggling fees, and face more risks to complete their journeys. According to a July 2020 survey of migrants by the Mixed Migration Centre (MMC), 38 percent of respondents in North Africa and 58 percent in West Africa reported an increase in the need to use smugglers (figure 2.2). And in a 2021 MMC survey of West and Central African migrants in 2021, 96 percent in Libya and

58 percent in Tunisia said they had used smugglers for at least part of their journey (Horwood and Frouws 2021).

Simultaneously, owing to increased demand, 57 percent of the North African respondents to the 2020 MMC survey and 83 percent of the West African respondents reported an increase in smugglers' fees since the start of the pandemic (figure 2.2). Some people pay their smugglers directly with their labor—an arrangement connected to greater risk of being trafficked into forced labor or sexual exploitation (UNODC 2021).

Furthermore, border closures and other mobility restrictions are leading smugglers to take more risks. Of the 2020 survey respondents, 74 percent in North Africa and 68 percent in West Africa said they "Agree" or "Strongly Agree" that smugglers have turned toward using more dangerous routes during this period (figure 2.2).

Heightened vulnerabilities of women migrants

Vulnerabilities are particularly severe for women, including domestic workers. During the pandemic, women have been differentially more at risk of harm to both their health and their livelihood (Giammarinaro 2020; UN Women 2020a). This vulnerability may be partly because of the types of occupations in which women are often employed. Domestic workers in cleaning or caregiving occupations are in direct contact with children, the elderly, and their families and therefore face high exposure to the virus. Conversely, pandemic-related lockdowns and other isolation measures simultaneously reduced households' demand for these workers. In Jordan, approximately 25,000 migrant domestic workers, or one-third of migrants in the occupation, lost their jobs in the initial months of the crisis (Aoun 2020).

Many domestic workers in the Middle East still work under kafala sponsorship programs for immigrants,[3] although some countries are now moving away from this system.[4] Under these programs, workers' health care coverage is employer-dependent and not guaranteed, potentially excluding those employed under this system from access to health care.

Migrant women and girls also have historically been more at risk of gender-based violence, domestic abuse, and sexual exploitation during epidemics (Wenham et al. 2020). Women, including but not limited to domestic workers, often have no other place to go during a pandemic and hence risk abuse and exploitation. For instance, cases of abuse against female domestic workers under the kafala system during lockdown have emerged in Lebanon (Aoun 2020). In a survey of Syrian refugees in Turkey during the pandemic's initial months, 13 percent of respondents reported experiencing conflict in their households, most likely a result of increased domestic violence (3RP 2020). In Istanbul, the city Security Directorate also reported a 38 percent increase in violence against women in the initial months of the pandemic (UN Women 2020b).

Figure 2.2   Changes in smuggling of migrants from West and North Africa since the beginning of the COVID-19 pandemic, as of July 2020

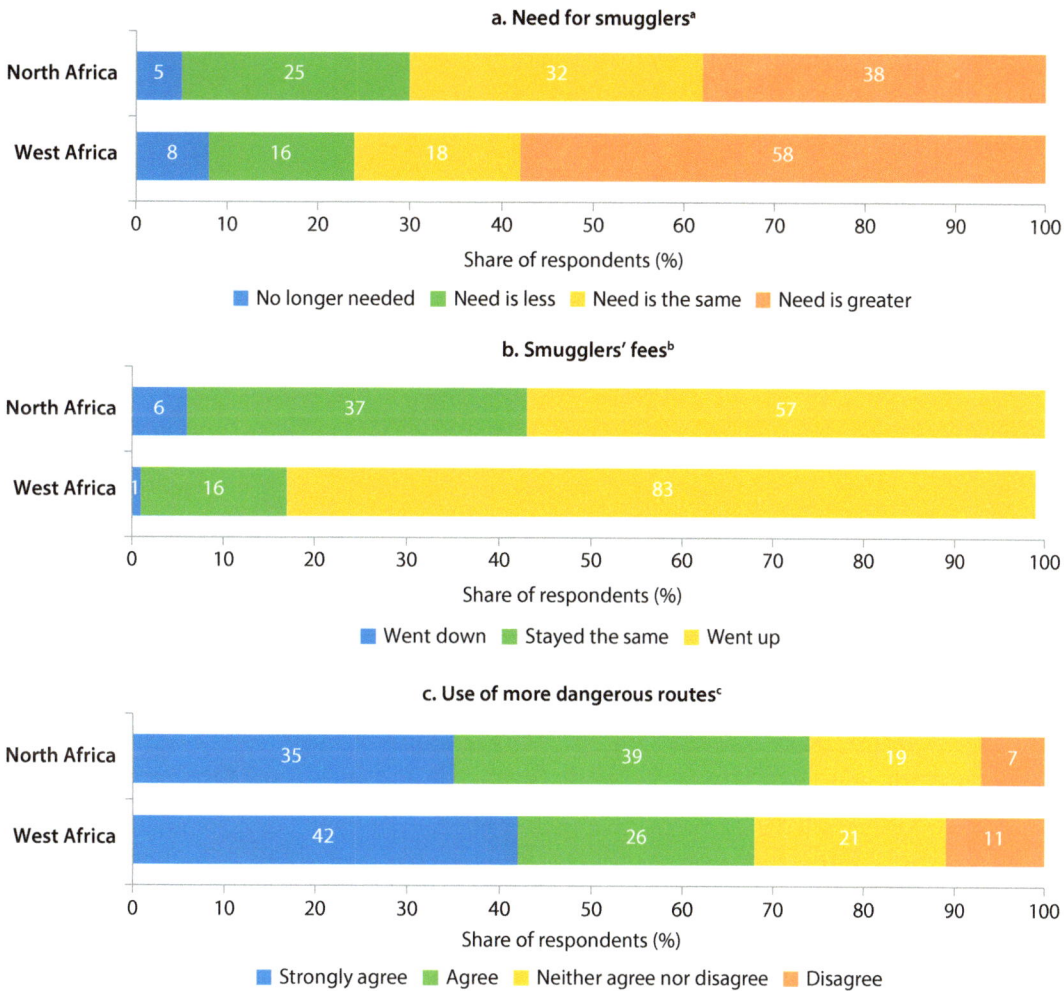

Source: MMC 2020.

Note: Survey was taken July 2–31, 2020. Responses of "Don't know/Prefer not to respond" are excluded from the totals used to calculate the percentages shown.

a. To the question, "How has the need for smuggling changed during the COVID-19 crisis?" 27 percent of 341 respondents in North Africa and 24 percent of 561 respondents in West Africa answered, "Don't know/Prefer not to respond."

b. To the question, "Have smugglers' fees changed since the start of the COVID-19 crisis?" 34 percent of 329 respondents in North Africa and 32 percent of 530 respondents in West Africa answered, "Don't know/Prefer not to respond."

c. To the question, "Are smugglers using more dangerous routes since the start of the COVID-19 crisis?" 4 percent of 329 respondents in North Africa and 11 percent of 530 respondents in West Africa answered, "Don't know/Prefer not to respond."

A mobile population at greater health risk

Direct COVID-19–related risks

Initial evidence suggests that migrants may face significantly higher health risks related to COVID-19 than nonmigrants. In some countries, migrants were about twice as likely to contract COVID-19 as natives. Although COVID-19 case and death data by immigration status are scarce, some studies have shed light on this correlation.

COVID-19 case trends. A report by the Organisation for Economic Co-operation and Development (OECD) shows that migrants are overrepresented among COVID-19 cases in several countries. For example, in Denmark, Norway, and Portugal, the share of foreign-born people who contract COVID-19 is more than twice that of the share of foreigners in the population (OECD 2020).[5] In Canada's Ontario Province, where only a quarter of the population are foreign-born permanent residents, this subpopulation accounted for 44 percent of COVID-19 cases. Similarly, in Sweden, immigrants make up 19 percent of the population but 32 percent of COVID-19 cases.

These initial trends are confirmed by studies across the globe:

- *In New York City,* people living in immigrant neighborhoods had a higher likelihood of testing positive for COVID-19 (Borjas 2020).
- *In Saudi Arabia,* the Saudi Ministry of Health reported in May 2020 that whereas migrants made up only 38 percent of the population, they accounted for 76 percent of new COVID-19 cases (Sorkar 2020).
- *In Bangladesh and Nepal* in April and May 2020, households with returned international migrants were twice as likely as households without returned migrants to have COVID-19 symptoms (Barker et al. 2020).
- *In Greece,* refugees and asylum seekers in reception and identification centers and reception sites were 2.5–3 times as likely to contract the virus as native Greeks between February and November 2020 (Kondilis et. al. 2021).

Serious COVID-19 illness. Migrants also appear to be more likely to end up in the hospital or even in the intensive care unit (ICU) after contracting the virus. A European study found that non-nationals in Italy were more likely than nationals to be admitted to the hospital too late, thus needing treatment in an ICU, with the biggest differences seen among patients from countries of origin with a lower human development index (ECDC 2021). Similarly, in Spain, non-Europeans were more likely to end up in the ICU. In Denmark, non-Western migrants made up only 9 percent of the population but accounted for 15 percent of COVID-19 hospital stays. In Sweden, Middle Eastern and African migrants were five times as likely as natives to end up in the ICU. And in Norway, the highest hospital rates were among (in this order) Pakistani, Iraqi, Turkish, and Somali migrants.

COVID-19 fatalities. Finally, migrants have exhibited higher COVID-19 fatality rates than natives in many cases. A study in Sweden of COVID-19 deaths up to May 2020 found that immigrants from low- and middle-income countries were almost twice as likely to die from the virus as those born in Sweden (Drefahl et al. 2020). This excess mortality was seen among people of all age groups but changed by country of origin. For instance, in Sweden, mortality risks were particularly high among (in this order) Somali, Lebanese, and Syrian migrants (ECDC 2021). The excess mortality in France—comparing deaths in March and April 2020 with those in 2019—was nearly twice as high for foreign-born as for native-born residents, and this excess mortality varied widely by region of origin (Papon and Robert-Bobée 2020). The percentage change in mortality ranged from a 22 percent increase among the native-born to a 114 percent increase for those of Sub-Saharan Africa origin (figure 2.3). And a study of all registered COVID-19 patients in Kuwait from February 24 to April 20, 2020, found that even after adjusting for age, gender, smoking habits, and selected comorbidities, foreigners had double the natives' risk of death or admission to the ICU as well as higher odds of contracting acute respiratory distress syndrome and pneumonia (Hamadah et al. 2020).

Heightened risk factors for COVID-19

Comorbidities and behavioral barriers. Preexisting comorbidities may make migrants and refugees more vulnerable to the virus. Groups with socioeconomic disadvantages are more likely to have serious health conditions and suffer more from chronic diseases, which can increase the risk of developing severe symptoms or dying from COVID-19.[6]

Figure 2.3   Excess mortality in France, by place of origin, March to April 2020

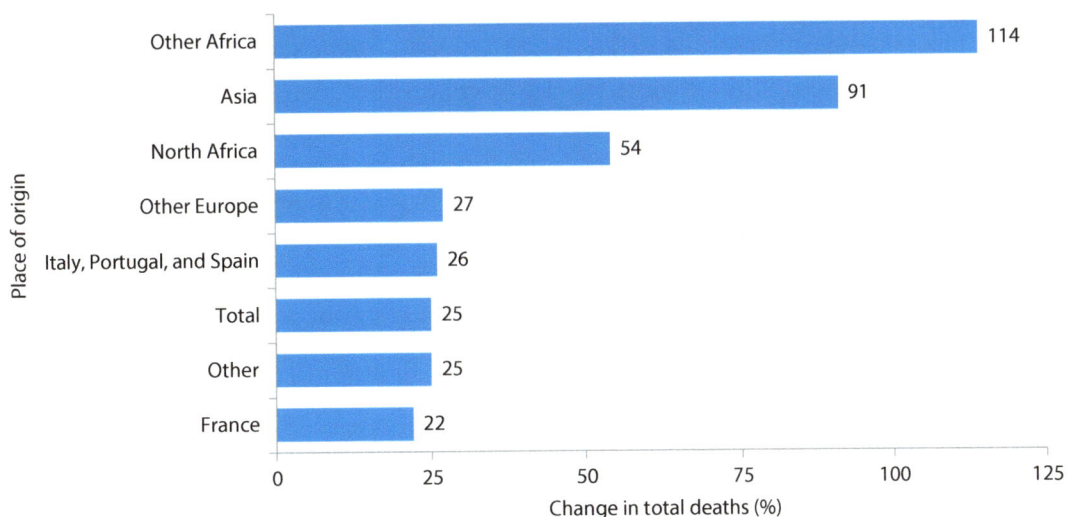

Source: Papon and Robert-Bobée 2020, using vital statistics data from France's National Institute of Statistics and Economic Studies (Insee).
Note: "Excess mortality" is measured as the increase in total deaths during March to April 2020 relative to total deaths in March to April 2019. "North Africa" includes Algeria, Morocco, and Tunisia.

Though migrants are often healthier on average than natives upon arrival to a host country (box 2.1), structural barriers in accessing health care and behavioral barriers such as procrastination in seeking health care because of time constraints or other cultural factors may put some immigrants at a health disadvantage (Garcés, Scarinci, and Harrison 2006). For instance, the migrant and refugee population in Europe faces a higher risk of ischemic heart disease and stroke as well as a higher incidence, prevalence, and mortality rate of diabetes than the host population (WHO 2018). According to a February 2020 study in China, whereas the COVID-19 death rate for those with no preexisting conditions was just over 1 percent, death rates from contracting COVID-19 were much higher for those with other illnesses—those with cardiovascular diseases (13.2 percent), diabetes (9.2 percent), chronic respiratory disease (8 percent), hypertension (8.4 percent), or cancer (7.6 percent) (WHO 2020).

BOX 2.1   The "healthy immigrant" paradox

Past research has shown that migrants are healthier overall than natives in their host communities. For instance, Aldridge et al. (2018) show that international migrants have a mortality advantage over natives across most disease categories. This might potentially be because of self-selection, since those who migrate may be the healthiest people from sending countries (Kennedy, McDonald, and Biddle 2006; Neuman 2014). Other studies have described a "salmon effect"—that people may return to their home countries when their health starts to deteriorate, so only the healthiest migrants remain abroad (Abraído-Lanza et al. 1999; Palloni and Arias 2004).

However, this effect seems to wear off gradually after arrival to new countries, and several studies have tried to explain this phenomenon. Though migrants who make the journey are often younger, healthier, and more fit to adapt to their new societies, over time, through acculturation to the habits of their host communities, their health outcomes converge with the mean of the destination (Jasso et al. 2004). Other studies have attributed this convergence of health status to an underutilization of health care services due to structural barriers such as language barriers or lack of transportation, legal documents, or health insurance (Garcés, Scarinci, and Harrison 2006); discrimination (Grove and Zwi 2006); and the poor working conditions or types of occupations in which immigrants are employed (Guintella and Mazzonna 2014; Orrenius and Zavodny 2009). Constant et al. (2018) find that the degree to which migrants assimilate healthwise depends on the migration policies in place and the degree to which host countries accommodate and assist migrants.

Living conditions. The living conditions of many migrants and refugees limit their ability to follow certain measures to prevent COVID-19. In New York City, neighborhoods where many people live together and occupy crowded spaces contribute to the spread of the virus (Almagro and Orane-Hutchinson 2022; Borjas 2020). The use of public transportation in the United States is also associated with higher probability of contracting COVID-19 (Benitez, Courtemanche, and Yelowitz 2020) and of death from it (McLaren 2020). Throughout the Mediterranean, migrants are by far overrepresented in the share of people occupying overcrowded housing (figure 2.4).

In the Gulf Cooperation Council (GCC) states as well, many migrants work in craft and manual labor occupations and live in tight living conditions or crowded compounds (Asi 2020). Such housing for migrant workers—with shared rooms, bathrooms, and cafeteria facilities—provides little means for social distancing, and hence migrant workers in these accommodations are the subpopulation most affected by the virus (Abu-Raddad et al. 2021).

It has also proven difficult to contain the spread of the virus in refugee settlements. Residents of the Cox's Bazar camps in Bangladesh—one of the world's largest refugee settlements, inhabited mostly by Rohingya refugees from Myanmar—report COVID-19 symptoms almost twice as frequently as members of the host community

Figure 2.4   Share of population in overcrowded housing, by origin status, in selected northern Mediterranean countries

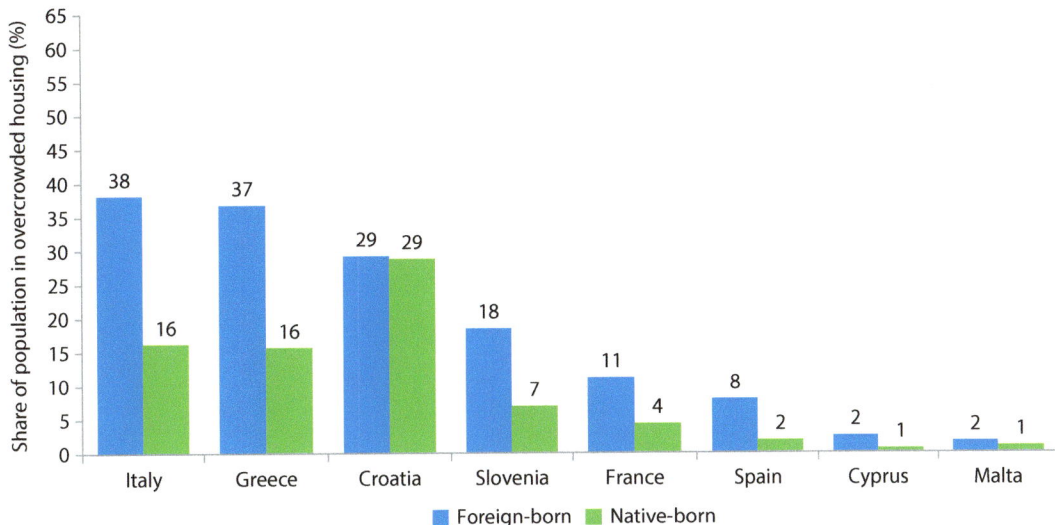

Source: World Bank, based on the European Union Statistics on Income and Living Conditions (EU-SILC) 2016 dataset.
Note: "Population" refers to all persons aged 16 and over living in ordinary housing. "Overcrowded housing" is defined as households that do not have at their disposal (a) at least one room per household, (b) one room per person or couple, (d) one room for each single person age 18 or older, (e) one room per two single people of the same gender aged 12–17, (f) one room for each single person aged 12–17 not included in the previous category, and (g) one room per two children under age 12.

(López-Peña et al. 2020). Another study, of refugee and asylum seeker reception facilities in Greece, identified 25 COVID-19 outbreaks between February and November 2020 and found that the likelihood of contracting the virus in these facilities was 2.5–3 times higher than in the Greek population (Kondilis et al. 2021). The situation was found to be particularly dire in the centers on the islands and along the Turkish border, where living conditions are worse (ECDC 2021).

In Turkey, the Izmir Bar Association found that despite finding 30 confirmed cases of COVID-19 in March 2020 in a refugee repatriation center, isolation rooms were still unavailable and cleaning procedures and access to doctors remained limited (Özvarış et al. 2020). Overall, among Syrian refugees in Turkey, 10 percent shared their housing with other families, 23 percent of which reported overcrowding being a problem in their homes. Furthermore, approximately half did not have enough soap to protect themselves during the COVID-19 pandemic (INDICATORS, IBC, and WATAN 2020).

"Health-risk" jobs. A significant share of migrants are employed in frontline jobs and therefore are more exposed to the health risks resulting from the pandemic. In the European Union-15 (EU-15), 42 percent of immigrants work in frontline jobs, which may put them at more risk of contracting the virus (Bossavie et al. 2020).

Figure 2.5 shows the share of the population in several northern Mediterranean countries who are employed in jobs that cannot be performed at home, as defined by Dingel and Neiman (2020).[7] In all northern Mediterranean countries presented

Figure 2.5   **Share of population in jobs that cannot be performed at home, by place of origin, in selected northern Mediterranean countries, 2018**

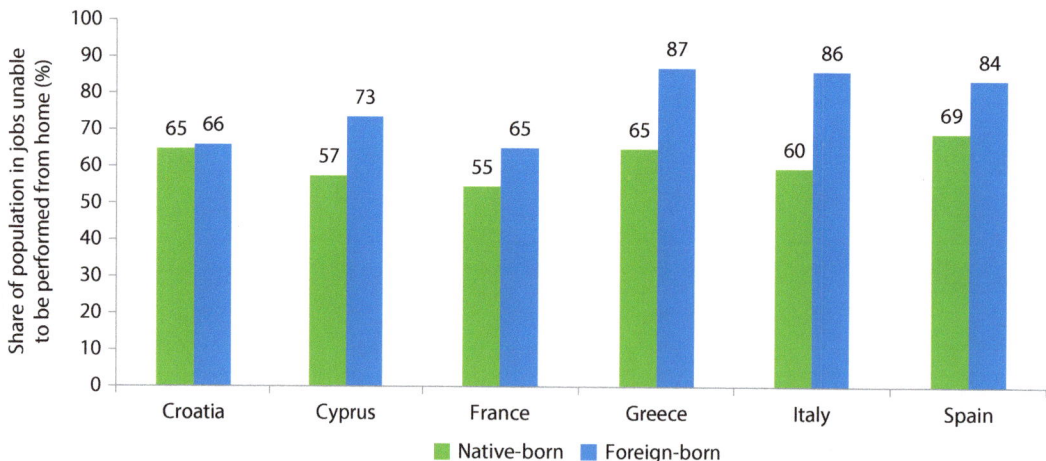

Source: World Bank, based on Dingel and Neiman 2020 and the European Union Labour Force Survey (EU-LFS) 2018 data.
Note: "Population" refers to the population age 15 and over. Jobs that cannot be performed from home are defined as in Dingel and Neiman (2020). For a more detailed description, see annex 2A.

in Figure 2.5, foreign-born residents are more likely than the host population to be employed in occupations that cannot be performed from home. Only a minority of foreign-born residents can work from home in Greece, Italy, and Spain. These findings are consistent with a study focused on New York City, where occupation appears to be a more important determinant than commuting patterns of whether a person contracts COVID-19 (Almagro and Orane-Hutchinson 2022).

Migrants' health care access in the northern Mediterranean

Access to benefits. In several EU countries, most migrants have legal access to health care benefits, albeit with certain limitations. Migrants' inclusion in the same health care scheme covering native residents depends on their documentation status, type of visa or duration of stay, and country of origin. For example, all the northern Mediterranean countries listed in table 2.1 provide health care to permanent residents, but Cyprus excludes extra-EU nationals from health care schemes entirely.[8] In Malta, extra-EU migrants must be working to obtain health care benefits.

Italy and Spain extend health care benefits to seasonal (temporary) workers as well. In Greece, this is also the case but only after migrants perform insured work

Table 2.1 Health care coverage of foreign workers in selected northern Mediterranean EU countries, 2020

Country	Permanent residents have access to health care	Temporary residents have access to health care	There are no differences between treatment of permanent residents and natives	There are no differences between treatment of temporary residents and natives	There are no differences between treatment of EU nationals and third-country nationals	Undocumented migrants have access to health care
Croatia	🟢	🟡	🟢	🟠	🟢	🟠
Cyprus	🟢	🟡	🟢	🟠	🟠	🟡
France	🟡	🟡	🟢	🟡	🟢	🟠
Greece	🟢	🟡	🟡	🟠	🟡	🟠
Italy	🟢	🟢	🟢	🟢	🟢	🟡
Malta	🟢	🟡	🟢	🟡	🟡	🟠
Slovenia	🟢	🟡	🟢	🟡	🟢	🟡
Spain	🟢	🟢	🟢	🟢	🟢	🟡

🟢 True   🟡 Partially true   🟠 False

Source: World Bank, based on information in Lafleur and Vintila 2020.

for a certain number of days. Meanwhile, Malta allows seasonal workers to receive health care with some fees if they are uninsured (meaning they have not paid contributions), and Slovenia allows uninsured seasonal workers to access emergency care only. Croatia includes seasonal workers unless they have not paid contributions, in which case they are covered only for emergency care, and Cyprus excludes seasonal workers from all health care except emergency services. Some countries, including Italy, Slovenia, and Spain, provide only emergency care to undocumented immigrants, while other countries exclude undocumented immigrants from their health care schemes entirely.

Other discrepancies regarding migrants' health care exist. For example, in Greece, although all foreign workers (both permanent and seasonal and from any country of origin) have health care benefits, extra-EU migrants are subject to a different definition of "family members" who can receive health care.

Unmet health care needs. In practice, even when migrants have access to health care, various factors or barriers may prevent them from using it, resulting in many unmet health needs (figure 2.6). Registration procedures are often complex or unfamiliar to migrants. Lack of knowledge about the health care system in addition to or combined with social isolation, low literacy levels, poverty, or a lack of financial resources (even for free services) may prevent migrants from seeking out health services. In some countries, a proof of residency is necessary to access the health care system, which excludes certain groups (including asylum seekers with pending cases) from accessing these benefits (see also box 2.2 for an example of barriers to refugees in accessing health care in Turkey).

Utilizing health care services may also have repercussions for some migrants. Even where undocumented migrants have some access to the health care system, they

Figure 2.6   Share of population with unmet health needs, by place of origin, in selected northern Mediterranean countries, 2016

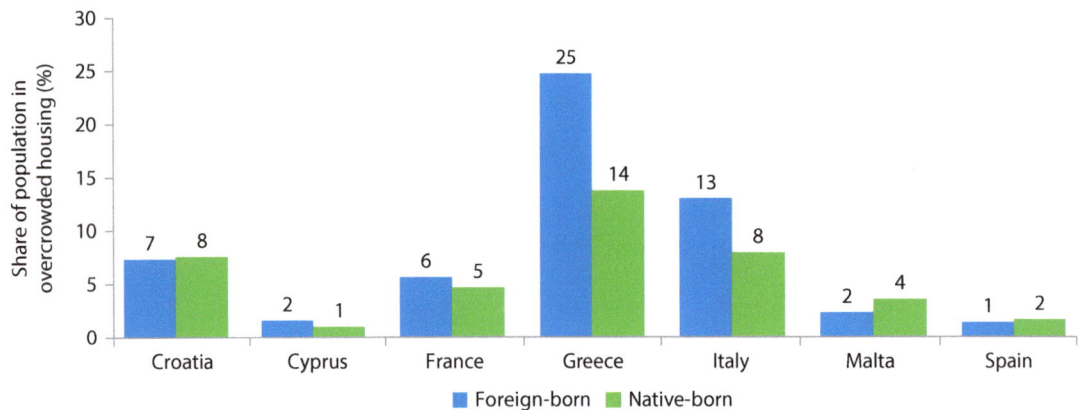

Source: OECD and EU 2018.
Note: "Population" refers to all residents aged 16 years and over. "Unmet health needs" refers to the share of people who reported needing but not receiving medical health care or dental care in the previous 12 months. The shares are adjusted to account for what outcomes would be if the foreign-born population had the same age distribution as the native-born population.

BOX 2.2   Refugees' access to health care in Turkey

Barriers to health care access have recently increased for refugees in Turkey. Until the end of 2019, migrants with temporary protection in Turkey had the same access to health care as Turkish citizens. Then in 2020, a new law required migrants with temporary protection or those seeking a residency permit to buy public or private health insurance, while undocumented immigrants were excluded entirely from this option. Though undocumented immigrants may receive emergency health care, they are required to pay for it in full before being released.

The COVID-19 pandemic has exacerbated these barriers to accessing health services. Requirements to pay out of pocket often discouraged migrants from seeking care during this period (Özvarış et al. 2020). Additionally, whereas 87 percent of Syrian refugees in Turkey reported having access to health services before the pandemic, only 25 percent reported having access after the COVID-19 outbreak (figure B2.2.1).

These findings are consistent with evidence from other parts of the world. A survey of forcibly displaced persons in several countries across Sub-Saharan Africa, South Asia, and the Middle East and North Africa found that the pandemic-induced economic shocks limited respondents' access to health care even further as it became more unaffordable (Tanner et al. 2021).[a]

Figure B2.2.1 Syrian refugees' access to health care in Turkey, before and after the onset of the COVID-19 pandemic

a. Prepandemic

b. Postpandemic

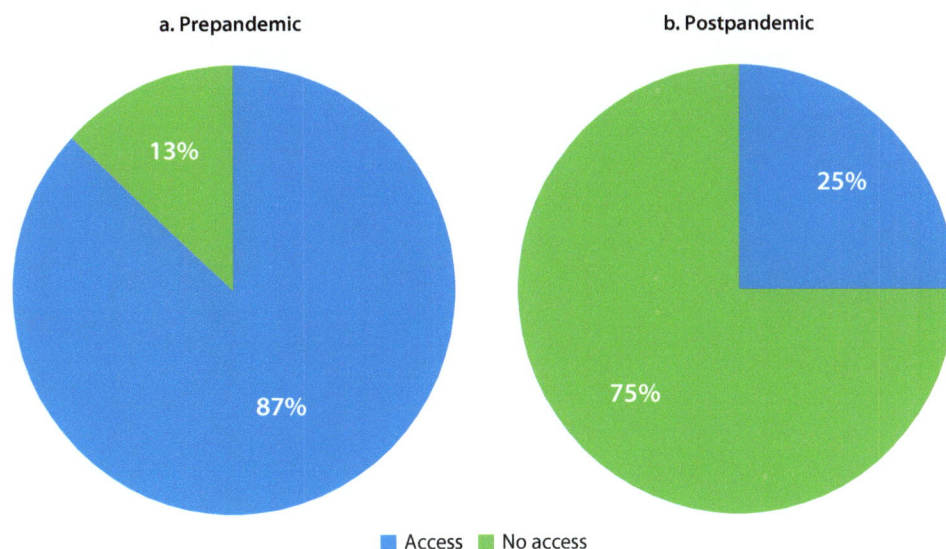

■ Access ■ No access

Source: RI 2020.
Note: Postpandemic figures were collected in May 2020. At that time, respondents (all from the Syrian Arab Republic) were also asked about their pre–COVID-19 situation.
a. The survey was conducted in Bangladesh, Chad, Djibouti, Iraq, Kenya, Uganda, and the Republic of Yemen.

might not use it for fear of legal consequences. The same fears may apply to regular migrants. For example, in France, using benefits may lower migrants' probability of renewing their residency permits via family reunification channels. Fear of discrimination in the provision of services may also discourage migrants from receiving needed care (Lebano et al. 2020; WHO 2018). Lack of training in routine data collection and health care professionals' limited experience in working with diverse populations may contribute to real or perceived implicit biases and hence to migrants' distrust of health care systems.

Health care access in the southern Mediterranean and GCC

Access to benefits. Countries and economies across the southern Mediterranean and the GCC also vary in how they include migrants in health care. In some of them, health care is covered by the state, and in others by employers, but still others exclude migrants from health care benefits entirely (table 2.2).[9]

In Morocco, for instance, the state provides access to government health care for all migrants who hold a work permit as well as for low-income migrants who are informally employed. Lebanon offers migrants and refugees access to free immunization

Table 2.2 **Health care coverage of foreign workers in selected southern Mediterranean and GCC countries, 2019**

Country	Laws explicitly detail how migrants are included in health care	Employers must cover migrant health care	Migrants must cover their own health care	State covers migrant health care	Undocumented migrants have access to health care
Bahrain	True	True	False	False	False
Kuwait	True	True	False	False	False
Lebanon	Partially true	Not available	Partially true	Partially true	Not available
Morocco	True	False	False	True	False
Oman	True	False	True	False	False
Qatar	True	True	False	False	False
Saudi Arabia	True	Partially true	Partially true	False	False
Syrian Arab Republic	True	False	False	True	Not available
United Arab Emirates	True	True	False	False	False

● True   ● Partially true   ● False   ● Not available

Source: World Bank, based on UN ESCWA 2020.
Note: GCC = Gulf Cooperation Council (Bahrain, Kuwait, Oman, Qatar, Saudi Arabia, and the United Arab Emirates).

and preventive treatment at public health centers and other outpatient services for a small fee regardless of nationality, but hospitalization services are not included.

Among the GCC countries, Bahrain, Kuwait, Qatar, Saudi Arabia, and the United Arab Emirates all require employers or sponsors to provide health insurance to their migrant workers. However, the conditions vary surrounding this form of health care. Bahrain provides an example of nondiscriminatory coverage for native and foreign workers, with some differences by gender. Oman excludes all migrants from health care except foreigners from Gulf states and non-GCC foreigners employed in government jobs (UN ESCWA 2020).

In a 2019 survey of migrants in Libya, only 26 percent of respondents reported having full access to medical services, with lack of documentation being one of the reported barriers. This figure was lower for newly arrived immigrants (22 percent) than for immigrants who had been in the country for more than a year (28 percent), suggesting that there is some advantage from better integration or ability to afford private health care over time (Teppert and Rossi 2020).

The copayment barrier. In some GCC and other Middle Eastern countries, migrants are required to pay fees for their health care, which are often unaffordable. In Saudi Arabia, for example, employer-sponsored health care programs have some limitations. Although employers must provide compulsory health insurance to migrants, patients must also contribute a fixed copayment for medical services, and whether a migrant can afford such a copayment is debatable. A 2014 study found that migrant workers in Saudi Arabia spent 10–30 percent of their income on medical copayments (Alkhamis, Hassan, and Cosgrove 2014).

Similarly, in Qatar, a decree passed in 2017 substantially increased the fees migrant workers must pay to stay in hospitals, receive outpatient care, or stay in public wards—a service that was previously free. Some other countries are moving in this same direction. In Jordan, until 2018, refugees could receive certain health care services free of charge and all others at a subsidized rate, which was generally affordable. Then in 2018, a policy change began requiring refugees to pay a higher rate (80 percent of the rate for noninsured foreigners), considerably raising the cost of health care for refugees, which may affect their use of health care services particularly in urban areas (Dajani Consulting 2018).

Limited access to vaccination programs

Only some countries in the extended Mediterranean region include de facto all migrants in national vaccination plans. The extent to which people on the move have been included in these health responses to the pandemic varies by country.

In 2018, the World Health Organization (WHO) noted that only 11 European WHO member countries had immunization programs considering migrants and refugees (WHO 2018). Focusing on COVID-19 vaccines, the International Organization for Migration (IOM) tracks the countries that include migrants in (a) their "de jure"

Figure 2.7   Inclusion of migrants in COVID-19 vaccination campaigns in countries in selected regions, as of May 2021

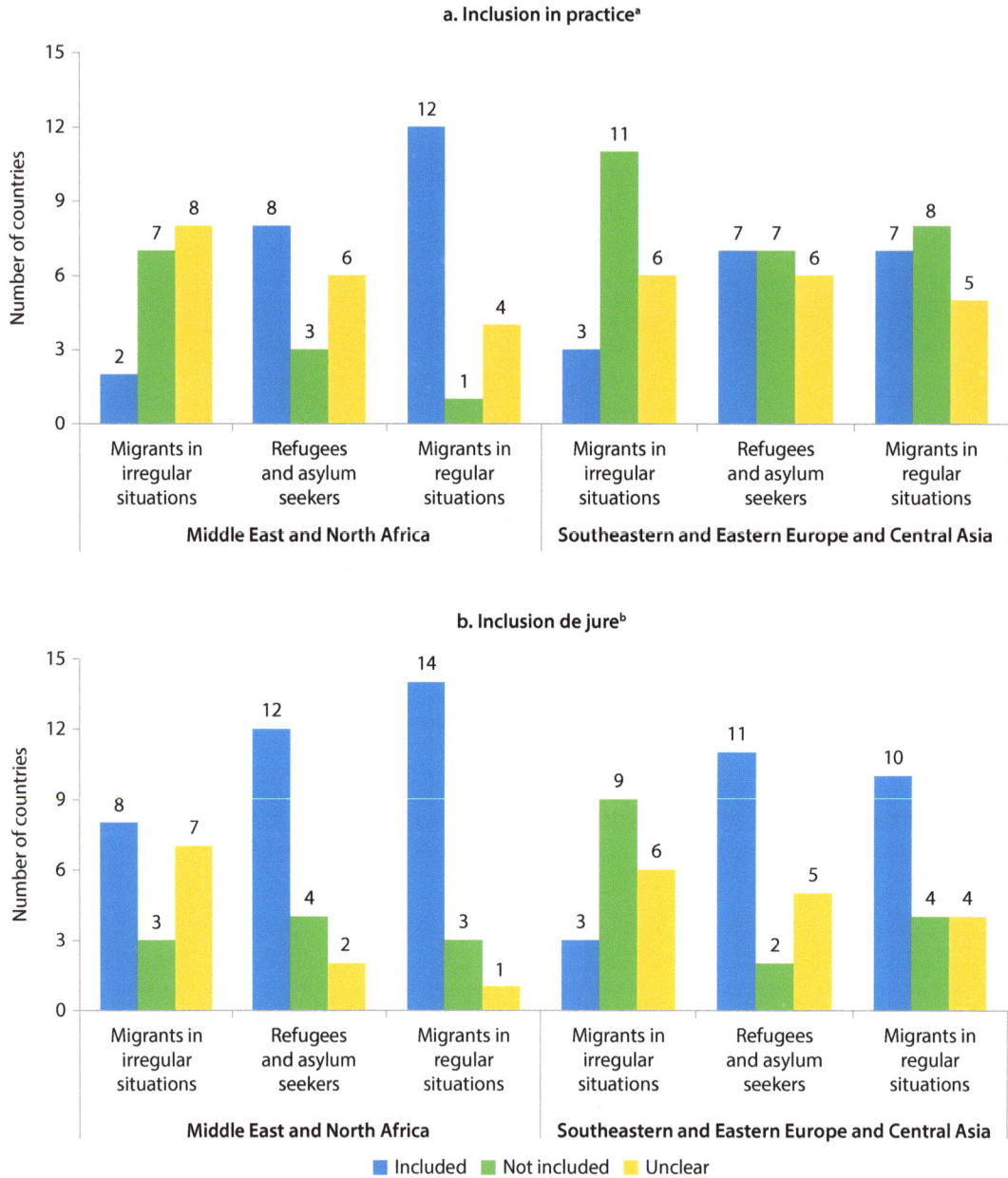

a. Inclusion in practice[a]

b. Inclusion de jure[b]

■ Included   ■ Not included   ■ Unclear

Source: IOM 2021b.

Note: The data cover 18 countries and economies in the Middle East and North Africa region and 20 countries in the combined regions of Southeastern and Eastern Europe and Central Asia. "Migrants in irregular situations," as defined by the International Organization for Migration (IOM), are persons who migrated "outside the laws, regulations, or international agreements governing the entry into or exit from the state of origin, transit, or destination." "Migrants in regular situations" are those who migrated according to such laws, regulations, or agreements, excluding refugees and asylum seekers.
a. "In practice" refers to inclusion in the actual administering of vaccines.
b. "De jure" refers to inclusion in National Deployment and Vaccination Plans.

National Deployment and Vaccination Plans, and (b) their vaccination schemes "in practice" (figure 2.7). The two sets of numbers show discrepancies for several reasons:

- Inclusion of migrants without mentioning them explicitly
- Differences in terminology between the country plan and the IOM/WHO
- Presence of unintended barriers to access for migrants, such as requiring documents for vaccination or migrant fear due to the lack of a firewall between health care providers and immigration authorities
- Avoidance of publicizing the inclusion of migrants to avoid backlashes.

IOM data show that several of the countries in the study do not include migrants in their vaccination campaigns, especially undocumented migrants.[10] While most of the 20 studied countries in Southeastern Europe, Eastern Europe, and Central Asia include refugees and asylum seekers in their plans, certain barriers in some of these countries seem to prevent them from accessing vaccines "in practice." Such barriers have also limited vaccination among refugees in Lebanon. Although the COVID-19 vaccination campaign launched in February 2021 does not exclude people on the basis of their nationality or residency status, low confidence in COVID-19 vaccination, distance from vaccination centers, low levels of literacy (including digital literacy), and refugees' fear of providing formal documentation are all factors that have resulted in unmet vaccination needs (Ahmed et al. 2021).

Language barriers and social exclusion make migrants more susceptible to lack of information or misinformation about the COVID-19 vaccine. Studies in Denmark, Norway, Sweden, and the United Kingdom find that different groups of migrants had lower vaccination rates than natives (ECDC 2021). In the United Kingdom, undocumented migrants, asylum seekers, and refugees are found to be hesitant about getting the vaccine owing to a lack of trust in health systems, low health literacy, and misinformation. On the other hand, in Qatar, a survey finds migrant workers to be more willing than natives to receive the vaccine, potentially because they are more eager to return to work or to travel to see family (Alabdulla et al. 2021). In Turkey, a June 2021 assessment shows that only 36 percent of refugee respondents were vaccinated against COVID-19. Lack of digital literacy, language barriers, lack of documentation, and lack of information were identified as the main causes for not getting vaccinated (UNHCR 2021).

The pandemic's economic impacts

The pandemic has had a severe impact on employment overall because of facility closures, inability to work from home, or voluntary resignations by many frontline workers to allay their safety concerns. The International Labour Organization (ILO) estimates that in 2020 the decline in global working hours relative to the last quarter of 2019 was equivalent to the loss of 255 million full-time jobs (ILO 2021a). In Southern and Western Europe, the equivalent of approximately 6 million and 5 million jobs were estimated to have been lost, respectively, while the corresponding figures were 6 million in North Africa and 5 million in the Arab states.[11]

These declines in working hours have had different implications for different parts of the world. The employment losses were the lowest in Europe because of the implementation of job retention schemes in many European countries (Apedo-Amah et al. 2020; Betcherman and Testaverde 2020). In Italy, for instance, employment and post-support labor income dropped by only 4 percent, whereas working hours declined by 23 percent. Women, youth, the self-employed, and low-skilled workers were the groups hit the most, while accommodation and food services, arts and culture, retail, and construction were the sectors with the highest number of job losses (ILO 2021a). Although labor markets in several Mediterranean and GCC countries have slowly recovered, non-negligible job losses relative to the fourth quarter of 2019 were still observed in 2021, especially in the Arab states (ILO 2021b).

Economic impacts on migrants

Employment impacts. Migrants tend to experience more severe economic impacts than native populations. Although the employment losses declined over time for

Figure 2.8 Difference in employment rate between 2019 and 2020, by quarter and place of origin, in selected northern Mediterranean countries

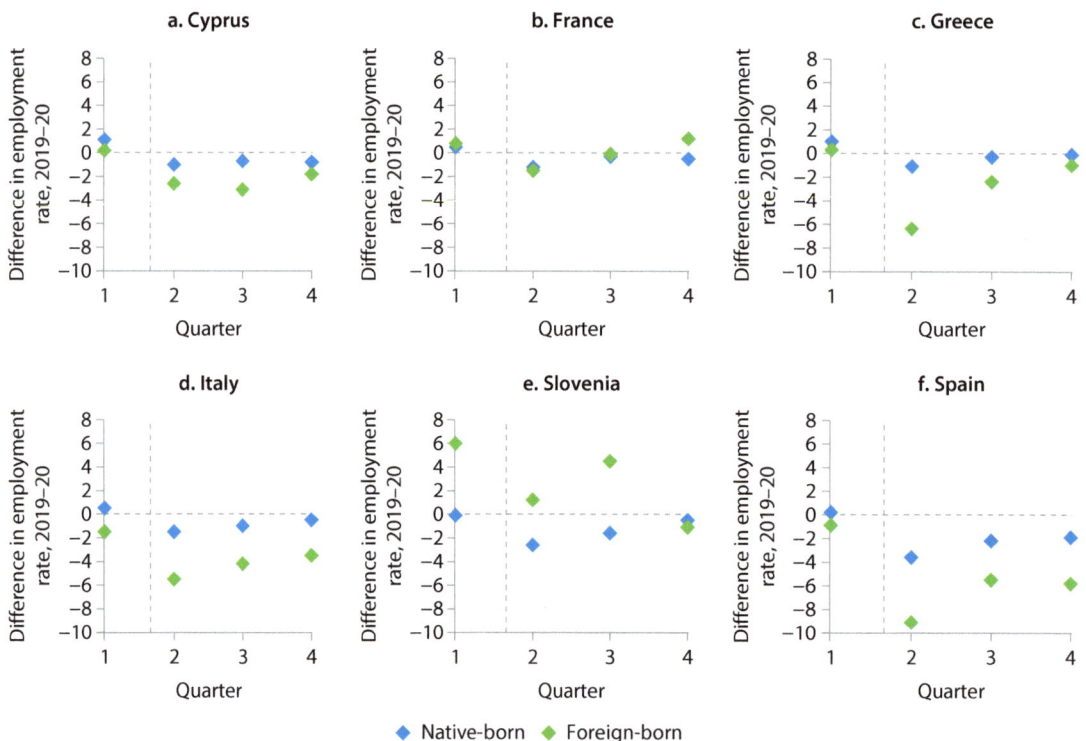

Source: Eurostat data (https://ec.europa.eu/eurostat).
Note: The vertical line represents the approximate point when the COVID-19 pandemic struck Europe in the first quarter of 2020.

both natives and foreigners, immigrants faced relatively higher drops in employment rates than natives in almost all Southern European countries as a result of the pandemic, especially in Cyprus, Greece, Italy, and Spain (figure 2.8). In Italy, 257,000 fewer migrants were employed in the second quarter of 2020 than in the same period of 2019. France and Spain saw similarly dire trends, with drops of 92,000 and 204,000 foreigners employed, respectively, in the same period.[12] Some countries, especially Italy, saw large drops in labor market participation as well (OECD 2021).

Though employment rates bounced back to 2019 levels in Croatia, France, and Malta by the first quarter of 2021 and in Greece by the second quarter, Eurostat data show that employment rates in other EU Mediterranean countries had not yet rebounded by the second quarter of 2021.[13] The same data show that the impact on foreigners' employment rates was still differentially worse than the impact on natives' employment rates into 2021.[14]

In GCC countries, some migrant workers also found themselves in precarious work situations. In addition to facing suspended contracts and reduced earnings, some migrant workers in the GCC states were repatriated. Some of the repatriated workers faced wage theft, because reclaiming unpaid earnings from their home countries presented a challenge. As such, many found themselves in debt bondage to those who had funded their travel to the GCC for work (Horwood and Frouws 2021).[15] These negative impacts on migrant workers in the GCC states were further exacerbated by the concurrent fall in oil prices, which resulted in dismissals and wage cuts (UNDP 2021).

Curtailed telework opportunities. Many migrants work in jobs that are not amenable to being performed at home, and therefore they might be at higher risk of being laid off. Borjas and Cassidy (2020) note that in the United States, immigrants experience higher rates of job loss for this very reason. Rahman (2020) shows that US regions where workers have low capacity to work from home tend to employ lower-skilled immigrant populations and have suffered higher unemployment due to COVID-19. Bossavie et al. (2020) find that, in the EU, 41 percent of natives as opposed to just 27 percent of immigrants are employed in jobs amenable to telework, and this gap is observed even when comparing workers of the same education level. Garrote Sanchez et al. (2021) confirm that migrants are more likely to be employed in face-to-face jobs or in jobs not amenable to telework, with migrants from outside the EU especially more vulnerable.

Among OECD countries, foreigners in Greece, Italy, and Spain are the least likely to be able to work remotely (Basso et al. 2020), as shown in figure 2.9. Furthermore, these three countries are among those exhibiting the biggest discrepancies between natives' and foreigners' ability to work from home. In line with these findings, Bossavie et al. (2020) show that 65 percent of natives as opposed to only 54 percent of immigrants are employed in "income-safe" jobs.

Figure 2.9   Share of the employed population who can work from home, by place of origin, in selected Mediterranean and non-Mediterranean countries, 2020

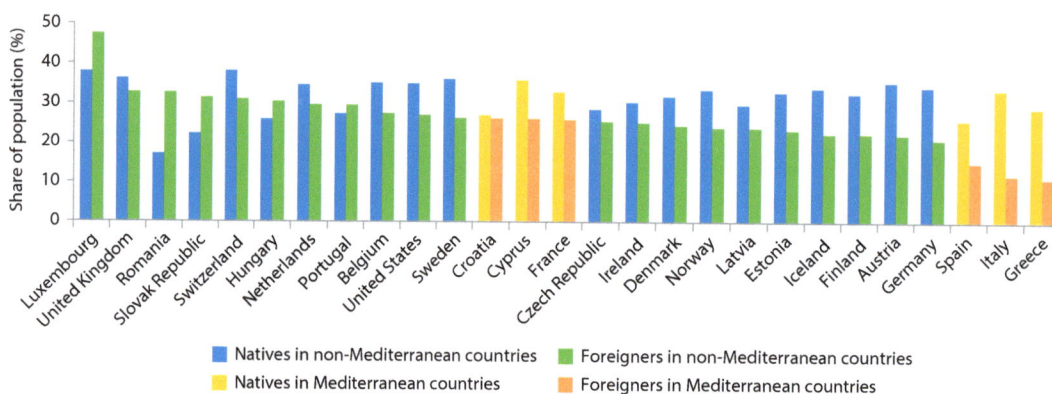

Source: World Bank calculations, based on Basso et al. 2020.
Note: "Population" refers to all working persons aged 15 and older. Ability to work from home is defined by Basso et al. (2020) as jobs that do not require workers to leave their home or to interact with coworkers or customers in person.

Refugee employment losses. Among migrants, refugees were particularly vulnerable. For instance, before the pandemic, 60 percent of employed refugees worked in sectors such as manufacturing, accommodation, and food services, which were particularly affected by the COVID-19 crisis. The corresponding share of natives working in these sectors was only 37 percent (IsDB 2021). For instance, in Turkey, more than 70 percent of refugees used to work in highly affected sectors, compared with about 45 percent of the host population (box 2.3).

Impacts on migrant poverty. Poverty rates have increased among people on the move, who were already more likely to be poor before the crisis. In Mediterranean EU countries, foreigners were more likely than natives to be in relative poverty before the pandemic. The relative poverty rates in these countries were even more dire for third-country nationals than for EU migrants, with third-country nationals having poverty rates more than double those of natives. For example, in France, whereas 12 percent of natives were living in relative poverty in 2016, 23 percent of EU foreigners and 41 percent of extra-EU foreigners were impoverished (figure 2.10).

Survey evidence also suggests the pandemic will lead to sharp increases in food insecurity across many countries in Sub-Saharan Africa, South Asia, and the Middle East (Tanner et al. 2021). In Jordan, poverty is estimated to have increased by 38 percentage points for Jordanians and by 18 percentage points among Syrian refugees, reflecting the fact that Syrians were already more likely to be living below the poverty line before the crisis (World Bank and UNHCR 2020).

In Lebanon, 1.7 million natives (an increase of 33 percentage points) and as many as 840,000 Syrian refugees (an increase of 56 percentage points) are expected to have fallen into poverty relative to before the pandemic. In Lebanon, many Syrians

BOX 2.3   Impact of COVID-19 on refugees in Turkey

Severe economic impacts during the pandemic were especially experienced by refugees in Turkey. In an April 2020 survey, 69 percent of refugees reported having lost their jobs as a result of COVID-19, and of those, 93 percent were their family's sole provider (IFRC and TRC 2020). In another survey conducted in the first few months of the pandemic, 83 percent of protection seekers (primarily Syrian nationals) who had been employed before the start of the pandemic saw a negative change to their employment status (3RP 2020).

Syrian-owned businesses in Turkey were also hit harder than native-owned businesses. While 70 percent of native-owned businesses reported the pandemic had a substantial impact on their operations, this share reached 81 percent for Syrian-owned businesses. Furthermore, 78 percent of Syrian businesses reported being unable to handle a second wave of COVID-19 as of August 2020, as opposed to 51 percent of native-owned businesses (figure B2.3.1).

According to TRC (2020), the share of protection needs before the pandemic (January to February 2020) were 33 percent for "financial situation," 20 percent for "legal documentation," and 17 percent for "child under risk." After the pandemic hit (April to May 2020), these shares shifted dramatically: "financial situation" more than doubled, to 67 percent, while the other two needs dropped to 12 percent and 8

Figure B2.3.1   Impact of the COVID-19 pandemic on Syrian-run and native-run businesses in Turkey, May 2020

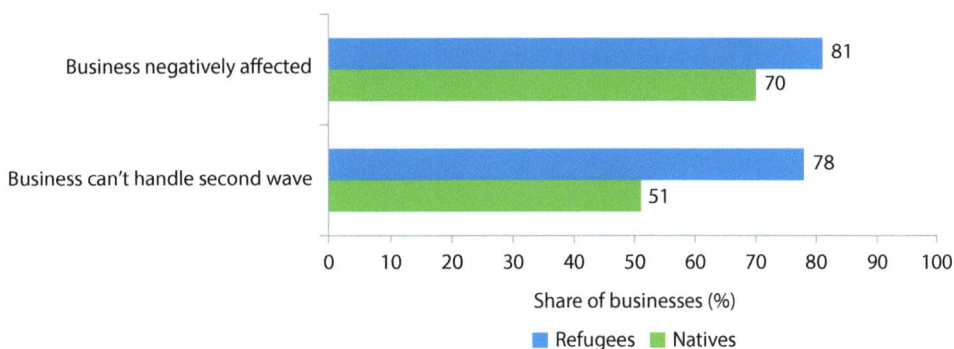

Source: UNDP 2020.
Note: Survey data were collected in August 2020.

(continued on next page)

BOX 2.3   *continued*

percent, respectively. Even after the COVID-19 crisis began, "health and psychosocial support" remained as the fourth priority, with 7 percent, showing that the number one focus for vulnerable refugees has not been COVID-19 but rather economic issues.

Even refugees who do not rely solely on work as primary income are facing difficulties in covering basic needs. According to a June 2021 inter-agency needs assessment in Turkey, only 47 percent of refugee respondents rely on work as the primary source of income (UNHCR 2021). Another 27 percent responded they rely on humanitarian assistance as the primary source of income, while 7 percent rely on community support, and another 7 percent rely on remittances. Of those who rely on any source as primary income *other* than humanitarian assistance, 31 percent rely on that as a secondary source of income. However, 56 percent claim to have *no* other source of income besides the primary source. Still, among those who received assistance, 88 percent responded that the amount received does not cover basic expenses and household needs. Food (69 percent), rent and housing (65 percent), and utilities (39 percent) were identified as the items for which the costs were harder to manage throughout the pandemic (UNHCR 2021).

Figure B2.3.2   **Food insecurity among refugee households in Turkey**

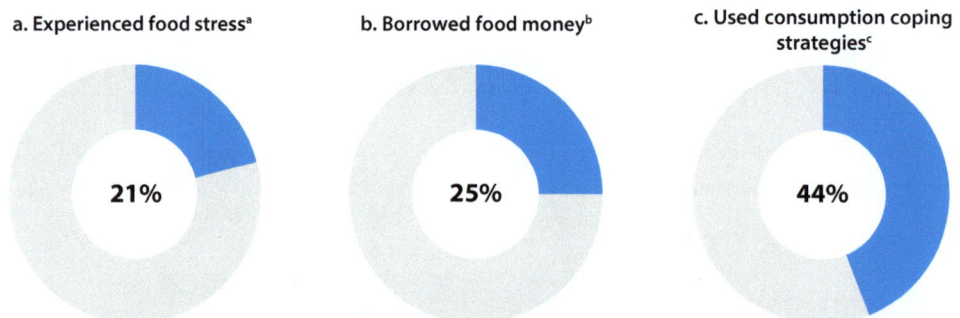

a. Experienced food stress[a]

21%

b. Borrowed food money[b]

25%

c. Used consumption coping strategies[c]

44%

Source: WFP 2020.
a. Food stress was indicated by allocation of more than 65 percent of total household expenditure for food.
b. Percentage is the share of refugees who bought food with money they had borrowed in the three months preceding the World Food Programme (WFP) Comprehensive Vulnerability Monitoring Exercise (CVME).
c. Food-related consumption coping strategies included eating less-preferred, less-expensive foods; reducing meal portion sizes or the number of meals eaten per day; limiting adult intake so children can eat; and borrowing food or relying on help from friends or relatives.

(continued on next page)

BOX 2.3   *continued*

Economic distress rapidly translated into food insecurity for refugees. The World Food Programme (WFP) found that among refugee households in Turkey, 21 percent of households (and 29 percent of female-headed households) were food stressed, 25 percent borrowed money for food, and 44 percent used consumption coping strategies such as reducing their number of meals or buying more inexpensive food (figure B2.3.2). The pandemic has only added to this stress, especially among refugees working informally who are not eligible for public benefits (3RP 2020).

Figure 2.10   Relative poverty rates of selected EU Mediterranean countries, by population origin category, 2016

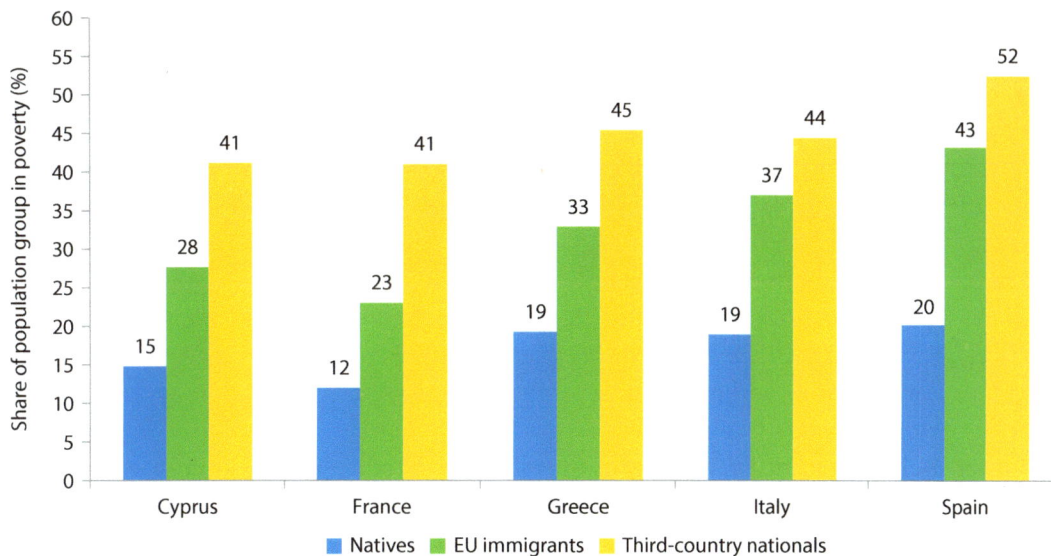

Source: OECD and EU 2018.
Note: "Population" refers to the population aged 16 and over living in ordinary housing. "EU immigrants" are those who migrated from one EU country to another. "Third-country nationals" are those who migrated from a non-EU country to the EU. The relative poverty rate is the share of people living below 60 percent of the median equivalized disposable income in each country. EU = European Union.

were living just above the poverty line before the pandemic, making them more vulnerable (3RP 2020). Modeling suggests that an additional 430,000 Syrians in Lebanon are projected to fall into poverty as a result of pandemic-induced job losses (Tanner et al. 2021).

Unemployment benefits in the northern Mediterranean. Some social welfare programs are available to migrants and refugees in the EU, but restrictions apply. For example, migrants' access to unemployment benefits depends not only on their legal status but also on the type and duration of visa they have (permanent versus seasonal) and their country of origin. In some cases, seasonal migrant workers and extra-EU workers have less access than permanent residents and other EU migrant workers (table 2.3).[16]

In Cyprus, France, Greece, Italy, Slovenia, and Spain, permanent residents may obtain the same contributory unemployment benefits as natives, and France extends full noncontributory unemployment benefits to permanent residents as well (Lafleur and Vintila 2020). However, in Croatia, third-country nationals are generally excluded from accessing this benefit, except for those originating from countries that have signed a bilateral social security agreement with Croatia covering unemployment benefits. And in Malta, third-country nationals must both have an employment license and be *long-term* residents to claim unemployment benefits.

As for seasonal workers, only in Cyprus and Slovenia can they receive full (contributory) unemployment assistance (Lafleur and Vintila 2020). Spain and Greece offer seasonal workers unemployment, but it is linked to the trajectory of previous contributions, so seasonal migrant workers are eligible for less. In France, resident requirements are very stringent, and seasonal workers are excluded entirely from unemployment assistance. In Italy, extra-EU seasonal workers are excluded. In Croatia and Malta, the same exclusions apply for seasonal third-country nationals as for permanent third-country nationals.

Every country excludes undocumented workers from claiming this benefit. Other barriers prevent migrants from claiming these benefits even where they have the right to them. For example, in France, accepting unemployment benefits may affect one's chance of naturalizing.

Other social assistance programs in the northern Mediterranean. In those EU countries with a guaranteed minimum income scheme, migrants tend to be partially or fully excluded from these benefits, as follows (Lafleur and Vintila 2020):

- *In Croatia and Slovenia,* only permanent residents or vulnerable groups such as asylum seekers, refugees, or unaccompanied minors may access this benefit.
- *In Cyprus,* foreigners from any country may claim this benefit after five years of residence, and non-EU foreigners must have been granted long-term residence status.
- *In France,* foreigners must hold a regular permit to access this benefit. For EU-foreigners, that includes permanent residents, those with residence through a family member, or those residing on work permits. For non-EU foreigners, this includes permanent residents, refugees, and those with authorization to work.
- *In Greece,* only permanent residents are included.

Table 2.3 Unemployment insurance coverage of foreign workers in selected northern Mediterranean EU countries, 2020

Country	Permanent residents can receive unemployment with contribution	Permanent residents can receive unemployment without contribution	Seasonal workers/ temporary residents can receive unemployment with contribution	Seasonal workers/ temporary residents can receive unemployment without contribution	There are no differences between treatment of permanent residents and natives	There are no differences between treatment of seasonal workers / temporary migrants and natives	There are no differences between treatment of EU nationals and third-country nationals
Croatia	Partially true	False	Partially true	False	Partially true	Partially true	False
Cyprus	True	False	True	False	True	True	True
France	True	True	False	False	True	False	True
Greece	True	False	Partially true	True	True	Partially true	True
Italy	Partially true	False	False	False	True	False	False
Malta	True	True	False	False	Partially true	Partially true	False
Slovenia	True	Not available	True	Not available	True	True	Partially true
Spain	True	False	Partially true	False	True	Partially true	True

● True   ● Partially true   ● False   ● Not available

Source: World Bank, based on information in Lafleur and Vintila 2020.

- *In Italy,* natives and EU foreigners and their families may access this benefit, but non-EU foreigners must have resided in Italy long term (10 years).
- *In Spain,* all foreigners with a residence permit may access this benefit, but the length of residency required to be eligible varies from six months in some regions to five years in others. Similarly, undocumented migrants' access of this benefit is dependent upon the decision of the regional governments.

Practical barriers, coupled with direct and indirect mechanisms of exclusion, often limit access to social welfare for migrants in northern Mediterranean countries. Practical barriers exist that are similar to those that limit migrants from accessing health care; they include complex program registration and benefits claims procedures, limited knowledge and awareness, and language barriers. On the administrative side, too, various direct and indirect mechanisms prevent migrants from accessing social welfare, such as strict requirements and limited administrative capacity (Lafleur and Vintila 2020). For example, in France and Greece, reliance on social assistance can negatively affect the renewal of migrants' residence permits, their applications for family reunification, or even their citizenship applications. Furthermore, in France, though unemployment benefits are accessible for third-country nationals, the strict definition of residence excludes foreigners who are students or temporary workers.

In Turkey, national governments and international actors have worked together to provide social protection in the form of direct cash transfers to refugees. Beginning in 2016, a direct cash transfer scheme in the form of monthly assistance through debit cards was made available to refugees in Turkey with funding from the EU. This program is intended to help vulnerable refugees with basic needs, encourage children's schooling, reduce household debt, and facilitate integration into national social protection schemes (WFP 2017). As of June 2020, more than 1.7 million refugees in Turkey had received this assistance through a partnership between the International Federation of Red Cross and Red Crescent Societies, the Turkish Red Crescent Society, and the Turkish Government (IFRC and TRC 2020).

Access to social benefits in the GCC. Migrant workers in the GCC region often have limited or no access to social protection programs. Given the temporary nature of migration in GCC states, few social safety net programs are in place targeting migrant workers (Nauk and Steinmayer 2014). Employers are mainly responsible for financing basic access to services for migrant workers, implying that, when laid off, migrant workers remain largely exposed to economic risks. For example, migrant workers in the GCC states have no access to unemployment benefits except for those in Bahrain. Likewise, pension benefits and family allowances are rare (GFMD 2020).

Figure 2.11 Remittances as a share of GDP in selected regions, by country or economy, 2020

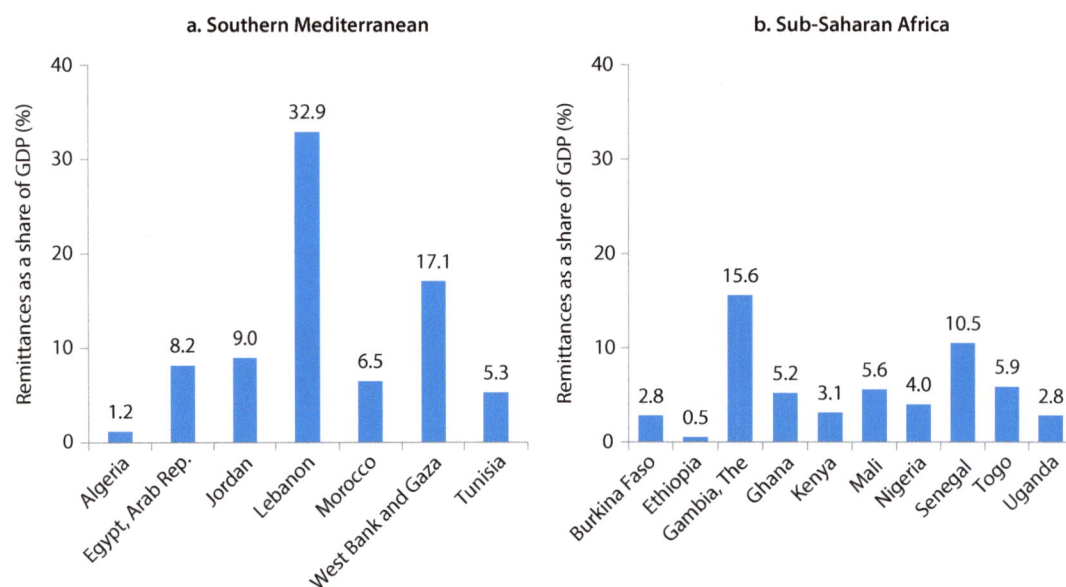

Source: World Bank, Annual Remittances Data (updated as of May 2021), https://www.worldbank.org/en/topic/migration remittancesdiasporaissues/brief/migration-remittances-data.

Economic impacts on families left behind: remittances

Remittances are a lifeline for many households in the extended Mediterranean region.[17] They account for a large portion of gross domestic product (GDP) in several southern Mediterranean countries (figure 2.11) and help to reduce poverty among recipient households.

In the Middle East and North Africa specifically, Adams and Page (2005) find that a 10 percentage point increase in remittances as a share of GDP decreases the number of people living in poverty by 5.7 percent. Adams (2011) reports that, among recipient households in low- and middle-income countries, 30–40 percent of household income comes from remittances, which helps to decrease both the level and severity of poverty. And in a 2019 survey of 523 migrants in Libya, 67 percent responded that the remittances they sent home were used for food, 51 percent responded they were used for other family expenses such as rent or utilities, and 47 percent responded they paid for health-related costs (Teppert and Rossi 2020).

The need for remittances was increasing as countries were hit economically by the COVID-19 pandemic.[18] In Morocco and Tunisia, most households reported a drop in income since the beginning of the pandemic, with 47 percent of Moroccans and 38 percent of Tunisians reporting a drop in income of more than 25 percent (ERF 2021).

Socioeconomically disadvantaged households are often employed in jobs that are not amenable to be performed from home and for this reason were hit the hardest during the crisis. For example, in the Arab Republic of Egypt and Morocco, people on the lower end of the income spectrum are less likely to be able to work from home and simultaneously faced larger drops in income in 2020. The data show that

Figure 2.12   Share of people able to work from home in Morocco and the Arab Republic of Egypt, by income quartile, 2020 to 2021

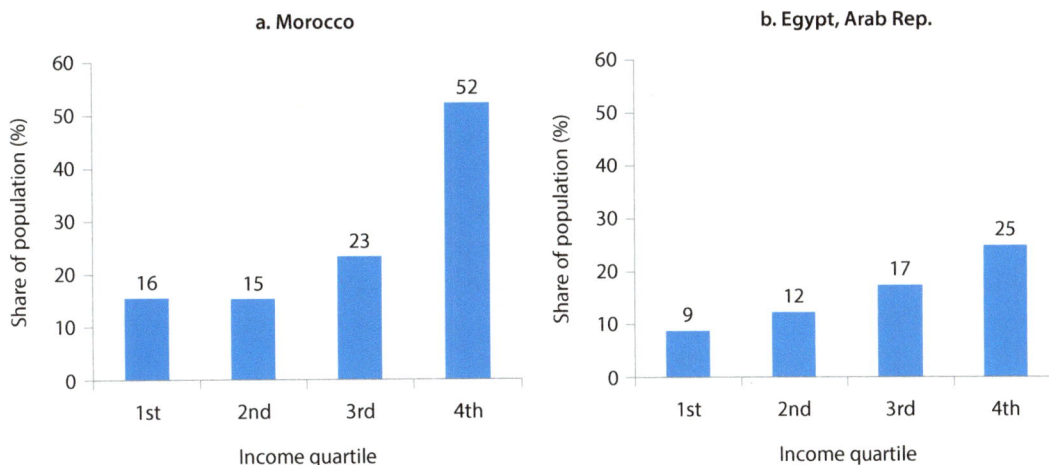

Source: ERF 2021.
Note: "Population" refers to a sample of mobile-phone users aged 18–64 years. Ability to work from home is self-reported.

whereas more than half of all Moroccans in the top income quartile had the ability to work from home during the pandemic, only 16 percent of those in the bottom quartile enjoyed the same freedom (ERF 2021), as shown in figure 2.12.

Remittances have therefore played an increasingly important role in helping households manage dire financial situations during the pandemic. By November 2020, 9 percent of Tunisians reported resorting to asking friends and relatives from abroad for money to cope with the financial stress caused by the pandemic (ERF 2021). And poverty in Tunisia is projected to increase by 7.3–11.9 percentage points as a result of the pandemic, with those in tourism and construction most affected (Kokas et al. 2021).

Drops in remittances may have significant effects on the migrant-sending communities. In 2020, the WFP projected that in 79 countries where it operates, at least 32.9 million people could be at risk of facing acute food insecurity because of the loss of remittances (IOM and WFP 2020). Drops in remittances had detrimental impacts on household welfare in Bangladesh and Nepal, where declines in earnings during the COVID-19 period were 25 percent greater among migrant households than among nonmigrant households (Barker et al. 2020). Such changes in migrant employment influence household welfare primarily through loss of remittance income. Declines in earnings translate into heightened food insecurity because remittances are necessary for meeting basic caloric needs for many households.

BOX 2.4   Costs of sending remittances in the extended Mediterranean region

The cost of sending remittances in the Mediterranean region varies widely by corridor. One of the objectives of the United Nations 2018 Global Compact for Safe, Orderly and Regular Migration is to "promote faster, safer and cheaper transfer of remittances and foster the financial inclusion of migrants" (UN 2019). As a benchmark, the Global Compact aims to (a) reduce the cost of sending remittances to less than 3 percent, and (b) eliminate any corridors with transaction costs greater than 5 percent by year 2030.

Figure B2.4.1 shows the 10 corridors with the highest and lowest costs of sending remittances in the extended Mediterranean region (including the GCC states). For example, in the third quarter of 2020, it cost roughly $25 to send $200 (12.5 percent) from Jordan to the Syrian Arab Republic but just $3 (1.5 percent) to send the same amount from Kuwait to Egypt. Among corridors within the Mediterranean and GCC states, just over half (52 percent) of the corridors had met the Global Compact's first object of transaction costs (below 3 percent), and 16 percent of the corridors still had transaction costs above the 5 percent mark.

(continued on next page)

BOX 2.4   *continued*

Figure B2.4.1   Corridors with the highest and lowest remittance transmission costs in the Mediterranean and GCC region, third quarter of 2020

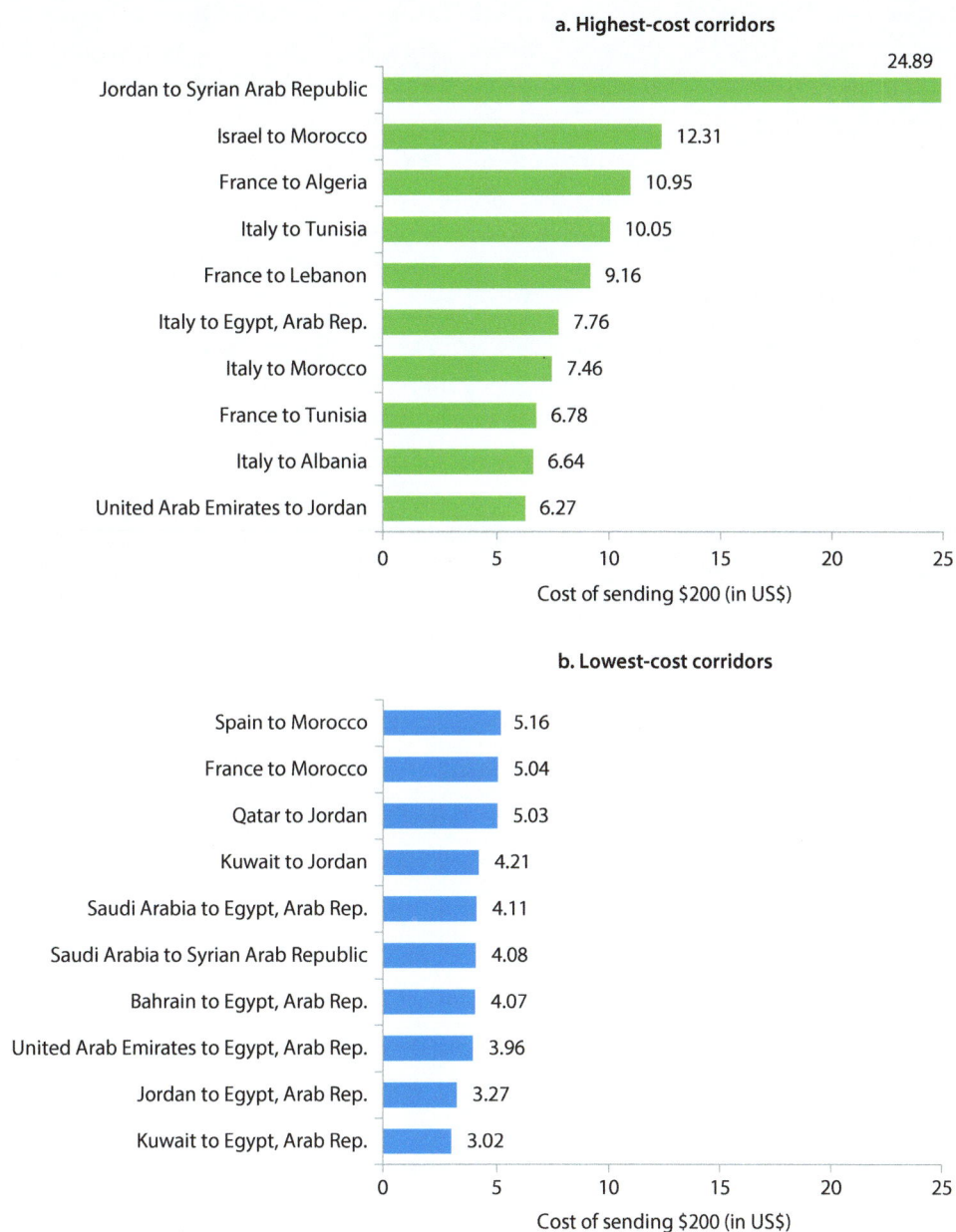

a. Highest-cost corridors

Corridor	Cost of sending $200 (in US$)
Jordan to Syrian Arab Republic	24.89
Israel to Morocco	12.31
France to Algeria	10.95
Italy to Tunisia	10.05
France to Lebanon	9.16
Italy to Egypt, Arab Rep.	7.76
Italy to Morocco	7.46
France to Tunisia	6.78
Italy to Albania	6.64
United Arab Emirates to Jordan	6.27

Cost of sending $200 (in US$)

b. Lowest-cost corridors

Corridor	Cost of sending $200 (in US$)
Spain to Morocco	5.16
France to Morocco	5.04
Qatar to Jordan	5.03
Kuwait to Jordan	4.21
Saudi Arabia to Egypt, Arab Rep.	4.11
Saudi Arabia to Syrian Arab Republic	4.08
Bahrain to Egypt, Arab Rep.	4.07
United Arab Emirates to Egypt, Arab Rep.	3.96
Jordan to Egypt, Arab Rep.	3.27
Kuwait to Egypt, Arab Rep.	3.02

Cost of sending $200 (in US$)

Source: World Bank Remittance Prices Worldwide database (https://remittanceprices.worldbank.org/).
Note: GCC = Gulf Cooperation Council (Bahrain, Kuwait, Oman, Qatar, Saudi Arabia, and the United Arab Emirates). Data reflect the remittance costs as of 2020q3.

Remittances fell in the months immediately after the start of the pandemic, leading to dire projections for the future of these financial flows. Economic shocks in migrant hosting countries affect the sending countries through drops in remittance inflows. Looking at the Great Recession in the United States, Caballero, Cadena, and Kovak (2021) show that in Mexican municipalities that had sent migrants to the areas of the United States with larger labor demand declines, remittances fell, emigration decreased, and return migration increased. Ratha et al. (2020) estimated that remittances would drop by 8 percent in 2020 and by 8 percent in 2021 in the Middle East and North Africa and by 9 percent in 2020 and 6 percent in 2021 in Sub-Saharan Africa.

Despite large overarching projected decreases, remittances dropped in some countries and rose in others in 2020 and completely resurged in 2021. Although they fell immediately after the start of the pandemic, by year end, the drops were not as dire as predicted, demonstrating the resilience of the remittance industry during the crisis.

Overall, remittances to the Middle East and North Africa region rose by 2.8 percent in 2020, but this increase was driven by remittances to a few North African countries, particularly Egypt and Morocco (Ratha et al. 2021b). Remittances to Egypt reached an all-time high, with an 11 percent increase in 2020 from the previous year. Similarly, remittances to Morocco and Tunisia rose by 6.5 percent and 2.5 percent, respectively. Remittances flowing out of Saudi Arabia increased by 11 percent, while those flowing out of the United Arab Emirates fell by 3.9 percent (Ratha et al. 2021a). Other countries in the region such as Jordan and Lebanon saw double-digit decreases in incoming remittances (figure 2.13).

Figure 2.13   Change in remittances to selected southern Mediterranean countries and economies, 2019–20

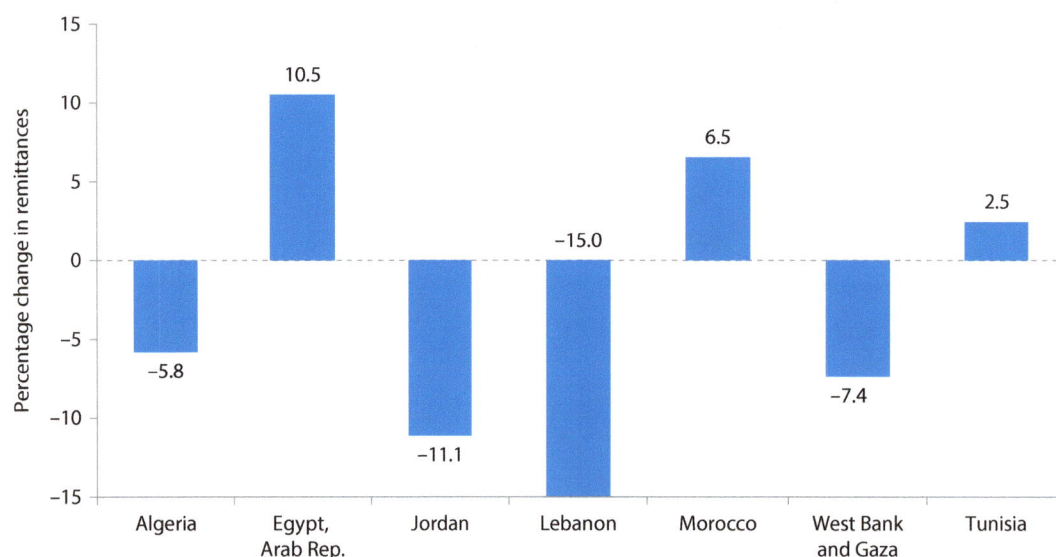

Source: World Bank, Annual Remittances Data (updated as of May 2021), https://www.worldbank.org/en/topic/migrationremittancesdiasporaissues/brief/migration-remittances-data.

In contrast to the Middle East and North Africa, remittances to the Sub-Saharan African region decreased by 14.1 percent during 2020 (Ratha et al. 2021b). This decrease was driven primarily by a significant drop in remittances to Nigeria, partially because of a policy that required money transfer agents to pay out in US dollars as opposed to the local currency. Excluding Nigeria, remittance flows to the region actually increased by 2.3 percent (Ratha et al. 2021a).[19] Remittances resurged in 2021, growing by 9.7 percent and 6.2 percent in the Middle East and North Africa and in Sub-Saharan Africa, respectively (Ratha et al. 2021b).

Annex 2A Methodology for defining jobs that cannot be performed from home

The definition of "jobs that cannot be performed at home" is derived from the methodology in Dingel and Nieman (2020). The authors use the Occupational Information Network (O*NET) work contexts and work activities survey datasets. First, jobs with the following work contexts are considered not amenable to being performed from home:

- The average worker uses email less that once per month;
- The average worker deals with physically aggressive people at least once per week;
- The majority of workers work outdoors every day;
- The average worker is exposed to diseases or infection at least once per week;
- The average worker is exposed to minor burns, cuts, bites, or stings at least once per week;
- The average worker spends the majority of time walking or running; or
- The average worker wears common or specialized safety equipment at least once per week.

Second, jobs in which the average worker said the following activities are very important are considered not amenable to being performed from home:

- general physical activities;
- handling and moving objects;
- controlling machines and processes (not computers or vehicles);
- performing for or working directly with the public;
- repairing and maintaining mechanical equipment;
- repairing and maintaining electrical equipment; or
- inspecting equipment, structures, or materials.

The O*NET 2010 codes are then matched to the International Standard Classification of Occupations (ISCO)-08 three-digit codes used in the European Union Labour Force Survey (2018) to construct the shares of jobs that cannot be performed from home, by place of origin.

Notes

1. The central Mediterranean route connects the North African countries—primarily Libya but also Tunisia, Algeria, and the Arab Republic of Egypt—to primarily Italy and, in much smaller numbers, to Malta and Greece. According to the Missing Migrants Project dataset of the International Organization for Migration (IOM), between 2018 and 2020, the central Mediterranean route was also the deadliest route per number of travelers. Of the migrants and refugees crossing this route, 1.3 percent die, as opposed to 0.57 percent, 0.25 percent, and 0.14 percent of migrants on the western Mediterranean, western Balkan, and eastern Mediterranean routes, respectively. In absolute terms, 941 migrants died on the central Mediterranean route, compared with 557, 231, and 118 along the western Mediterranean, eastern Mediterranean, and western Balkan routes, respectively. For more about the IOM's Missing Migrants Project dataset, see https://missingmigrants.iom.int /downloads.
2. The eastern Mediterranean route leads across the Mediterranean Sea from Turkey to Greece and Cyprus.
3. Kafala is a system of working and residency visa sponsorship that has been used in Bahrain, Jordan, Kuwait, Lebanon, Oman, Qatar, Saudi Arabia, and the United Arab Emirates. The system gives private persons and companies the right to sponsor visas for migrant workers and to provide housing and food for the worker. Because visas are linked to specific employers under this system, migrants' legal status also entirely depends on them, leading at times to abusive practices toward migrant workers in the region (Andrees, Nasri, and Swiniarski 2015).
4. Saudi Arabia ended its kafala program, which has been in place since the 1970s, in March 2021. Other countries such as the United Arab Emirates are slowly moving away from this system as well (Ratha et al. 2021a).
5. In Denmark, only foreigners from low-income countries and their native-born children are included in this count.
6. Generally, refugees and migrants are more likely than the native population to die from communicable diseases. This phenomenon arises because they often live in overcrowded conditions and because public transportation and new living environments leave them more vulnerable and exposed to diseases (against which they may not have built immunity). It is also well established that population groups with socioeconomic disadvantages are more likely to have serious health conditions and suffer more from chronic diseases, which can increase their comorbidity risks in the context of COVID-19. Immigrants in most OECD countries are overrepresented among these vulnerable groups (Aldridge et al. 2018).
7. For more about the methodology used to define these jobs, see annex 2A.
8. A review of Lafleur and Vintila (2020) and the interpretation of that report's findings led to the development of table 2.1, to facilitate visualization and comparison.
9. A review of UN ESCWA (2020) and the interpretation of that report's findings led to the development of table 2.2, to facilitate visualization and comparison.
10. The IOM regional definition of Middle East and North Africa includes Algeria, Bahrain, the Arab Republic of Egypt, Iraq, Jordan, Kuwait, Lebanon, Libya, Morocco, Oman, Qatar, Saudi Arabia, Sudan, the Syrian Arab Republic, Tunisia, the United Arab Emirates, West Bank and Gaza, and the Republic of Yemen. The IOM regional definition of Southeastern Europe, Eastern Europe, and Central Asia includes Albania, Armenia, Azerbaijan, Belarus, Bosnia and Herzegovina, Georgia, Israel, Kazakhstan, Kosovo, the Kyrgyz Republic, North Macedonia, Moldova, Montenegro, the Russian Federation, Serbia, Tajikistan, Turkey, Turkmenistan, Ukraine, and Uzbekistan. The graphs include countries and economies for which data are available.
11. According to the ILO's classification, the Arab states include Bahrain, Iraq, Jordan, Kuwait, Lebanon, Oman, Qatar, Saudi Arabia, Syria, the United Arab Emirates, West Bank and Gaza, and the Republic of Yemen.
12. Statistical Office of the European Union (Eurostat) database (https://ec.europa.eu/eurostat).
13. This analysis is based on data from Eurostat's Labour Force Survey (LFS) database: https://ec.europa .eu/eurostat/web/lfs/data/database.

14. In Croatia, Cyprus, France, Greece, Italy, Malta, Slovenia, and Spain, the 2019/2021 (first quarter) employment gap for natives was 0.002, –0.002, 0.010, –0.023, –0.018, 0.011, –0.032, and –0.009, respectively. The 2019/2021 (second quarter) employment gap for natives was 0.02, –0.006, 0.016, –0.002, –0.009, 0.013, –0.005, and –0.007, respectively. As for foreigners, the 2019/2021 (first quarter) employment gap for foreigners was unavailable (for Croatia), –0.021, 0.018, –0.032, –0.053, 0.007, –0.033, and –0.058, respectively. The 2019/2021 (second quarter) employment gap for foreigners was unavailable (for Croatia), –0.032, –0.001, 0.003, –0.040, 0.021, –0.019, and –0.032, respectively.

15. The trends in the extended Mediterranean region are consistent with findings from the United States that migrants, especially undocumented migrants, were more likely than the host population to lose their jobs during the COVID-19 pandemic (Borjas and Cassidy 2020; Cowan 2020) and to be unemployed (Rahman 2020). From February to April 2020, while the number of overall business owners in the United States dropped by 22 percent overall, immigrant business owners were disproportionally hit, their numbers falling by 36 percent (Fairlie 2020). In Norway, migrants were more likely to be laid off in the first months of the crisis (Alstadsæter et al. 2020). Evidence from Sweden shows that young third-country nationals, especially those in low-income occupations, were most at risk of becoming unemployed (Campa, Roine, and Strömberg 2021). Despite the immediate shock, in some cases migrant employment recovered relatively quickly. For instance, in the United States, despite being hit hard at the beginning of the pandemic, migrant employment rebounded by the first quarter of 2021. Migrant employment in the United States fell by 21 percent between February and April 2020—differentially more than natives—but steadily recovered over the following year (Ratha et al. 2021b).

16. A review of Lafleur and Vintila (2020) and the interpretation of that report's findings led to the development of table 2.3, to facilitate visualization and comparison.

17. In 2020, Egypt, France, Italy, and Spain were among the top 20 recipients of remittances worldwide. Mediterranean and GCC countries such as (in this order) the United Arab Emirates, Saudi Arabia, France, Qatar, and Italy are also among the top 20 remittance senders worldwide. (Remittances to Monaco are included in remittances to France.) These remittance flow rankings are based on World Bank Annual Remittances Data (updated as of May 2021): https://www.worldbank.org/en/topic /migrationremittancesdiasporaissues/brief/migration-remittances-data.

18. For additional information on costs of remittances in the region, by corridor, see box 2.4.

19. Data on remittances, especially in Sub-Saharan Africa, are sparse and have varying standards of quality and measurement. Furthermore, during the pandemic, because of border closures, many migrants shifted from informal to formal channels of sending money. For example, despite a recorded 89.3 percent increase in remittances to The Gambia during the second and third quarters of 2020, 84.6 percent of households reported a decrease in international remittances in a survey conducted between March and August 2020 (Ratha et al. 2021a).

References

Abraído-Lanza, A. F., B. P. Dohrenwend, D. S. Ng-Mak, and J. B. Turner. 1999. "The Latino Mortality Paradox: A Test of the 'Salmon Bias' and Healthy Migrant Hypotheses." *American Journal of Public Health* 89 (10): 1543–48.

Abu-Raddad, L. J., H. Chemaitelly, H. H. Ayoub, Z. Al Kanaani, A. Al Khal, E. Al Kuwari, A. A. Butt, P. Coyle et al. 2021. "Characterizing the Qatar Advanced-Phase SARS-CoV-2 Epidemic." *Scientific Reports* 11 (1): 6233.

Adams, R. H. Jr. 2011. "Evaluating the Economic Impact of International Remittances on Developing Countries Using Household Surveys: A Literature Review." Journal of Development Studies 47 (6): 809–28.

Adams, R. H. Jr., and J. Page. 2005. "Poverty, Inequality and Growth in Selected Middle East and North Africa Countries, 1980–2000." World Development 31 (12): 2027–48.

Ahmed, H., N. Aoun, N. Kaloustian, F. Asfahani, R. Suarez, and S. Varkey. 2021. "Vaccinating Refugees: Lessons from the Inclusive Lebanon Vaccine Roll-Out Experience." Online feature, June 18, World Bank, Washington, DC. https://www.worldbank.org/en/news/feature/2021/06/18/vaccinating-refugees-lessons-from-the-inclusive-lebanon-vaccine-roll-out-experience.

Alabdulla, M., S. M. Reagu, A. Al-Khal, M. Elzain, and R. M. Jones. 2021. "COVID-19 Vaccine Hesitancy and Attitudes in Qatar: A National Cross-Sectional Survey of a Migrant-Majority Population." Influenza and Other Respiratory Viruses 15 (3): 361–70.

Aldridge, R. W., L. B. Nellumbs, S. Bartlett, A. L. Barr, P. Patel, and R. Burns. 2018. "Global Patterns of Mortality in International Migrants: A Systematic Review and Meta-Analysis." The Lancet 392 (10164): 2553–66.

Alkhamis, A., A. Hassan, and P. Cosgrove. 2014. "Financing Healthcare in Gulf Cooperation Council Countries: A Focus on Saudi Arabia." International Journal of Health Planning and Management 29 (1): e64–e82.

Almagro, M., and A. Orane-Hutchinson. 2022. "The Determinants of the Differential Exposure to COVID-19 in New York City and Their Evolution Over Time." Journal of Urban Economics 127: 103293.

Alstadsæter, A., B. Brasberg, G. Eielsen, W. Kopczuk, S. Markussen, O. Raaum, and K. Røed. 2020. "The First Weeks of the Coronavirus Crisis: Who Got Hit, When and Why? Evidence from Norway." Working Paper No. 27131, National Bureau of Economic Research, Cambridge, MA.

Andrees, B., A. Nasri, and P. Swiniarski. 2015. "Regulating Labour Recruitment to Prevent Human Trafficking and to Foster Fair Migration: Models, Challenges and Opportunities." Working Paper No. 1/2015, International Labour Organization, Geneva.

Aoun, R. 2020. "COVID-19 Impact of Female Migrant Domestic Workers in the Middle East." Gender-Based Violence Area of Responsibility (GBV AoR) HelpDesk Research Query, United Nations Population Fund, Geneva.

Apedo-Amah, M., B. Avdiu, X. Cirera, M. Cruz, E. Davies, A. Grover, L. Iacovone et al. 2020. "Unmasking the Impact of COVID-19 on Businesses: Firm Level Evidence from Across the World." Policy Research Working Paper 9434. World Bank, Washington, DC.

Asi, Y. M. 2020. "Migrant Workers' Health and COVID-19 in GCC Countries." Online article, July 7, Arab Center, Washington, DC.

Bah, T. L., C. Batista, F. Gubert, and D. McKenzie. 2021. "How Has COVID-19 Affected the Intention to Migration via the Backway to Europe and to a Neighboring African Country? Survey Evidence and a Salience Experiment in The Gambia." Policy Research Working Paper 9658, World Bank, Washington, DC.

Barker, N., C. Davis, P. López-Peña, H. Mitchell, A. Mobarak, K. Naguib, M. Reimão, A. Shenoy, and C. Vernot. 2020. "Migration and the Labour Market Impacts of COVID-19." WIDER Working Paper No. 2020/139, United Nations University World Institute for Development Economics Research (UNU-WIDER), Helsinki.

Basso, G., T. Boeri, A. Caiumi, and M. Paccagnella. 2020. "The New Hazardous Jobs and Worker Reallocation." OECD Social, Employment and Migration Working Papers No. 247, Organisation for Economic Co-operation and Development, Paris.

Benitez, J., C. Courtemanche, and A. Yelowitz. 2020. "Racial and Ethnic Disparities in COVID-19: Evidence from Six Large Cities." Working Paper No. 27592, National Bureau of Economic Research, Cambridge, MA.

Betcherman, G., and M. Testaverde. 2020. "COVID-19 Can Teach Us a Lot about Social Protection and Jobs: Reflections based on the Greek Experience." *Jobs and Development* (blog), August 12. World Bank. https://blogs.worldbank.org/jobs/covid-19-can-teach-us-lot -about-social-protection-and-jobs-reflections-based-greek-experience.

Borjas, G. 2020. "Demographic Determinants of Testing Incidence and COVID-19 Infections in New York City Neighborhoods." Discussion Paper No. 13115, IZA Institute of Labor Economics, Bonn.

Borjas, G., and H. Cassidy. 2020. "The Adverse Effect of the COVID-19 Labor Market Shock on Immigrant Employment." Working Paper No. 27243, National Bureau of Economic Research, Cambridge, MA.

Bossavie, L., D. Sanchez, M. Makovec, and Ç. Özden. 2020. "Do Immigrants Shield the Locals: Exposure to COVID-Related Risks in the European Union." Policy Research Working Paper 9500, World Bank, Washington, DC.

Caballero, M., B. Cadena, and B. Kovak. 2021. "The International Transmission of Local Economic Shocks through Migrant Networks." Working Paper No. 28696, National Bureau of Economic Research, Cambridge, MA.

Campa, P., J. Roine, and S. Strömberg. 2021. "Unemployment Inequality in the Pandemic: Evidence from Sweden." *Covid Economics* 83: 1–24.

Constant, A. F., T. García-Muñoz, S. Neuman, and T. Neuman. 2018. "A 'Healthy Immigrant Effect' or a 'Sick Immigrant Effect'? Selection and Policies Matter." *European Journal of Health Economics* 19 (1): 103–21.

Cowan, B. 2020. "Short-Run Effects of COVID-19 on U.S. Worker Transitions." Working Paper No. 27315, National Bureau of Economic Research, Cambridge, MA.

Dajani Consulting. 2018. "Health Access and Utilization Survey: Access to Healthcare Services among Syrian Refugees in Jordan, December 2018." Report for the United Nations High Commissioner for Refugees prepared by Dajani Consulting, Amman, Jordan.

Dempster, H., T. Ginn, J. Graham, M. Guerrero-Ble, D. Jayasinche, and B. Shorey. 2020. "Locked Down and Left Behind: The Impact of COVID-19 on Refugees' Economic Inclusion." Policy Paper No. 179, Center for Global Development, Washington, DC.

Dingel, J. I., and B. Neiman. 2020. "How Many Jobs Can be Done at Home?" Working Paper No. 26948, National Bureau of Economic Research, Cambridge, MA.

ECDC (European Centre for Disease Prevention and Control). 2021. "Reducing COVID-19 Transmission and Strengthening Vaccine Uptake among Migrant Populations in the EU/EEA." Technical report, ECDC, Solna, Sweden.

ERF (Economic Research Foundation). 2021. "COVID-19 MENA Monitor Household Survey (CMMHH)." Version 1.0 of the licensed data files, CMMHH-Nov-2020. Open Access Data Initiative (OAMDI) of ERF, Giza, Arab Republic of Egypt. http://erf.org.eg/data-portal/.

Fairlie, R. 2020. "The Impact of Covid-19 on Small Business Owners: Evidence of Early Stage Losses from the April 2020 Current Population Survey." Working Paper No. 27309, National Bureau of Economic Research, Cambridge, MA.

Fallah, B., C. Krafft, and J. Wahba. 2019. "The Impact of Refugees on Employment and Wages in Jordan." *Journal of Development Economics* 139: 203–16.

Garcés, I. C., I. C. Scarinci, and L. Harrison. 2006. "An Examination of Sociocultural Factors Associated with Health and Health Care Seeking among Latina Immigrants." *Journal of Immigrant and Minority Health* 8 (4): 377–85.

Garrote Sanchez, D., N. Gomez Parra, Ç. Özden, B. Rijkers, M. Viollaz, and H. Winkler. 2021. "Who on Earth Can Work from Home?" *The World Bank Research Observer* 36 (1): 67–100.

GFMD (Global Forum on Migration and Development). 2020. "Inventory of Social Protection Provisions for Temporary Migrant Workers in GCC Countries." Data tables, GFMD, https://www .gfmd.org/inventory-social-protection-provisions-temporary-migrant-workers-gcc-countries.

Giammarinaro, M. 2020. "The Impact and Consequences of the COVID-19 Pandemic on Trafficked and Exploited Persons." COVID-19 position paper, United Nations Office of the High Commissioner for Human Rights, Geneva.

Grove, N. J., and A. B. Zwi. 2006. "Our Health and Theirs: Forced Migration, Othering, and Public Health." *Social Science and Medicine* 62 (8): 1931–42.

Guintella, O., and F. Mazzonna. 2014. "Do Immigrants Bring Good Health?" Discussion Paper No. 8073, IZA Institute of Labor Economics, Bonn.

Horwood, C., and B. Frouws, eds. 2021. "Mixed Migration Review 2021: Reframing Human Mobility in a Changing World." Annual publication, Mixed Migration Centre, Geneva.

IFRC and TRC (International Federation of Red Cross and Red Crescent Societies and Turkish Red Crescent Society). 2020. "Impact of COVID-19 on Refugee Populations Benefitting from the Emergency Social Safety Net (ESSN) Programme." Rapid assessment, IFRC, Geneva; and TRC, Ankara.

ILO (International Labour Organization). 2021a. "ILO Monitor: COVID-19 and the World of Work. Seventh Edition. Updated Estimates and Analysis." Briefing note, ILO, Geneva.

ILO (International Labour Organization). 2021b. "ILO Monitor: COVID-19 and the World of Work. Eighth Edition. Updated Estimates and Analysis." Briefing note, ILO, Geneva.

INDICATORS, IBC, and WATAN (INDICATORS, International Blue Crescent Relief and Development Foundation, and WATAN Foundation). 2020. "Syrian Refugees Needs during COVID-19 Outbreak – Turkey." Needs assessment, INDICATORS, Gaziantep, Turkey; IBC, Istanbul; and WATAN, Gaziantep, Turkey.

IOM (International Organization for Migration). 2021a. "Alarming Loss of Life on Way to Canaries Worsens in 2021." IOM News, September 24.

IOM (International Organization for Migration). 2021b. "Migrant Inclusion in COVID-19 Vaccination Campaigns: IOM Country Office Review." Report, IOM, Geneva.

IOM (International Organization for Migration). 2021c. *World Migration Report 2022.* Geneva: IOM.

IOM and WFP (International Organization for Migration and World Food Programme). 2020. "Populations at Risk: Implications of COVID-19 for Hunger, Migration and Displacement." Joint report, IOM, Geneva; WFP, Rome.

IsDB (Islamic Development Bank). 2021. "The Impact of Covid-19 on Forced Displacement and Economic Migration in Fragile Contexts." Assessment report, IsDB, Jeddah, Saudi Arabia.

Jasso, G., D. S. Massey, M. R. Rosenzweig, and J. P. Smith. 2004. "Immigrant Health: Selectivity and Acculturation." In *Critical Perspectives on Racial and Ethnic Differences in Health and in Late Life*, edited by N. B. Anderson, R. A. Bulatao, and B. Cohen, 227–66. Washington, DC: National Academies Press.

Kennedy, S., J. McDonald, and N. Biddle. 2006. "The Healthy Immigrant Effect and Immigrant Selection: Evidence from Four Countries." Social and Economic Dimensions of an Aging Population Research Papers No. 164, McMaster University, Ontario.

Kokas, D., G. Lopez-Acevdo, A. R. El Lahga, and V. Mendiratta. 2021. "Impacts of COVID-19 on Household Welfare in Tunisia." Policy Research Working Paper 9503, World Bank, Washington, DC.

Kondilis, E., D. Papamichail, S. McCann, E. Carruthers, A. Veizis, M. Orcutt, and S. Hargreaves. 2021. "The Impact of the COVID-19 Pandemic on Refugees and Asylum Seekers in Greece: A Retrospective Analysis of National Surveillance Data from 2020." *The Lancet eClinicalMedicine* 37: 100958.

Lafleur, J.-M., and D. Vintila, eds. 2020. *Migration and Social Protection in Europe and Beyond (Volume 1): Comparing Access to Welfare Entitlements*. International Migration, Integration and Social Cohesion in Europe (IMISCOE) Research Series. Cham, Switzerland: Springer.

Lebano, A., S. Hamed, H. Bradby, A. Gil-Salmerón, E. Durá-Ferrandis, J. Garcés-Ferrer, F. Azzedine et al. 2020. "Migrants' and Refugees' Health Status and Healthcare in Europe: A Scoping Literature Review." *BMC Public Health* 20 (1): 1039.

López-Peña, P., C. Davis, A. Mobarak, and S. Raihan. 2020. "Prevalence of COVID-19 Symptoms, Risk Factors, and Health Behaviors in Host and Refugee Communities in Cox's Bazar: A Representative Panel Study." *Bulletin of the World Health Organization*. E-pub: May 11, 2020. doi:10.2471/BLT.20.265173.

McLaren, J. 2020. "Racial Disparity in COVID-19 Deaths: Seeking Economic Roots with Census Data." Working Paper No. 27407, National Bureau of Economic Research, Cambridge, MA.

MMC (Mixed Migration Centre). 2020. "Impact of COVID-19 on Migrant Smuggling." COVID-19 Global Thematic Update #1, MMC, Brussels.

Nauk, G., and V. Steinmayer. 2014. "Integrated Social Policy Report V: Towards a New Welfare Mix? Rethinking the Role of the State, the Market and Civil Society in the Provision of Social Protection and Social Services." Report, United Nations Economic and Social Commission for Western Asia, Beirut, Lebanon.

Neuman, S. 2014. "Are Immigrants Healthier than Native Residents?" *IZA World of Labor* 108.

OECD (Organisation for Economic Co-operation and Development). 2020. "What Is the Impact of the COVID-19 Pandemic on Immigrants and Their Children?" Policy brief, OECD, Paris.

OECD (Organisation for Economic Co-operation and Development). 2021. *International Migration Outlook 2021*. Paris: OECD Publishing.

OECD and EU (Organisation for Economic Co-operation and Development and European Union). 2018. *Settling In 2018: Indicators of Immigrant Integration.* Paris: OECD Publishing; Brussels: EU.

Orrenius, P., and M. Zavodny. 2009. "Do Immigrants Work in Riskier Jobs?" *Demography* 46 (3): 535–51.

Özvarış, Ş. B., İ. Kayı, D. Mardin, S. Sakarya, A. Ekzayez, K. Meagher, and P. Patel. 2020. "COVID-19 Barriers and Response Strategies for Refugees and Undocumented Migrants in Turkey." *Journal of Migration and Health* 1–2: 100012.

Palloni, A., and E. Arias. 2004. "Paradox Lost: Explaining the Hispanic Adult Mortality Advantage." *Demography* 41 (3): 385–415.

Papon, S., and I. Robert-Bobée. 2020. "The Number of Deaths Rose Twice as High for People Born Abroad as for Those Born in France during the COVID-19 Health Crisis." Technical Report No. 198, National Institute of Statistics and Economic Studies (Insee), Paris.

Rahman, A. 2020. "Why Can't Everybody Work Remotely? Blame the Robots." *COVID Economics* 36: 105–28.

Ratha, D., S. De, E. J. Kim, S. Plaza, G. Seshan, and N. D. Yameogo. 2020. "Phase II: COVID-19 Crisis through a Migration Lens." Migration and Development Brief No. 33. Global Knowledge Partnership on Migration and Development (KNOMAD), World Bank, Washington, DC.

Ratha, D., E. J. Kim, S. Plaza, and G. Seshan. 2021a. "Resilience: COVID-19 Crisis through a Migration Lens." Migration and Development Brief No. 34. Global Knowledge Partnership on Migration and Development (KNOMAD), World Bank, Washington, DC.

Ratha, D., E. J. Kim, S. Plaza, G. Seshan, E. J. Riordan, and Vandana Chandra. 2021b. "Recovery: COVID-19 Crisis through a Migration Lens." Migration and Development Brief No. 35, Global Knowledge Partnership on Migration and Development (KNOMAD), World Bank, Washington, DC.

RI (Relief International). 2020. "Impact of the COVID-19 Outbreak on Syrian Refugees in Turkey." Results from rapid needs assessment, RI, Washington, DC.

Sanchez, G., and L. Achilli. 2020. *Stranded: The Impacts of COVID-19 on Irregular Migration and Migrant Smuggling.* Migration Policy Centre Brief No. 2020/20. Florence: European University Institute.

Sorkar, M. N. I. 2020. "COVID-19 Pandemic Profoundly Affects Bangladeshi Workers Abroad with Consequences for Origin Communities." Feature article, Migration Policy Institute, Washington, DC.

Tanner, J., H. Mugera, D. Tabasso, J. Lazić, and B. Gillsäter. 2021. "Answering the Call: Forcibly Displaced during the Pandemic." Paper Series on Forced Displacement No. 2, World Bank–UNHCR Joint Data Center on Forced Displacement, Copenhagen.

Teppert, T., and L. Rossi. 2020. "Migration in Libya Post-2016: Recently Arrived Migrants and Migrants Who Have Been in Libya for at Least One Year." In *Migration in West and North Africa and across the Mediterranean: Trends, Risks, Development and Governance,* 54–76. Geneva: International Organization for Migration.

3RP (Regional Refugee and Resilience Plan in Response to the Syria Crisis). 2020. "3RP Turkey Consolidated: 2020 Appeal Overview." Financial appeal consolidation document, 3RP Turkey Chapter.

TRC (Turkish Red Crescent). 2020. "COVID-19 Needs Assessment Report." Report, TRC, Ankara.

UN (United Nations). 2019. "Global Compact for Safe, Orderly and Regular Migration." UN General Assembly Resolution A/RES/73/195 (December 19, 2018).

UNDP (United Nations Development Programme). 2020. "Survey on Impact of COVID-19 on Enterprises in Turkey: Report on Results of Second Survey (11-12 May 2020)." Report of Business for Goals (B4G) survey administered by TÜRKONFED and TÜSİAD, Istanbul; UNDP, New York.

UNDP (United Nations Development Programme). 2021. "The Socio-Economic Impact of COVID-19 and Low Oil Prices on Migrants and Remittances in the Arab Region." Working paper, UNDP, New York.

UN ESCWA (United Nations Economic and Social Commission for Western Asia). 2020. "Situation Report on International Migration 2019: The Global Compact for Safe, Orderly and Regular Migration in the Context of the Arab Region." Publication E/ESCWA/ SDD/2019/3, UN ESCWA, Beirut, Lebanon.

UNHCR (United Nations High Commissioner for Refugees). 2021. "Turkey: Inter-Agency Protection Sector Needs Assessment Analysis Round 4 - June 2021." Needs assessment, Inter-Agency Coordination Unit, UNHCR, Geneva.

UNODC (United Nations Office on Drugs and Crime). 2020. "How COVID-19 Restrictions and the Economic Consequences Are Likely to Impact Migrant Smuggling and Cross-Border Trafficking in Persons to Europe and North America." Research brief, UNODC, Vienna.

UNODC (United Nations Office on Drugs and Crime). 2021. "West Africa, North Africa and the Central Mediterranean: Key Findings on the Characteristics of Migrant Smuggling in West Africa, North Africa and the Central Mediterranean." Research report, UNODC Observatory on Smuggling of Migrants, Vienna.

UN Women (United Nations Entity for Gender Equality and the Empowerment of Women). 2020a. "Addressing the Impacts of the COVID-19 Pandemic on Women Migrant Workers." Guidance note, UN Women, New York.

UN Women (United Nations Entity for Gender Equality and the Empowerment of Women). 2020b. "Amid COVID-19 Lockdown in Turkey, UN Women Runs Campaign to Curb Violence against Women and Promote Gender Equality at Home." UN Women News, May 4. https://eca.unwomen.org/en/news/stories/2020/5/amid-covid19-lockdown-in-turkey -un-women-runs-campaign-to-curb-vaw-and-promote-gender-equality.

Wenham, C., J. Smith, S. E. Davies, H. Feng, K. A. Grépin, S. Harman, A. Herten-Crabb, and R. Morgan. 2020. "Women Are Most Affected by Pandemics—Lessons from Past Outbreaks." *Nature* 583: 194–98.

WFP (World Food Programme). 2017. "WFP Turkey Country Brief, June 2017." Brief, WFP Turkey Country Office, Ankara.

WFP (World Food Programme). 2020. "Comprehensive Vulnerability Monitoring Exercise (CVME), Round 4." Report, WFP Turkey Country Office, Ankara.

WHO (World Health Organization). 2018. *Report on the Health of Refugees and Migrants in the WHO European Region: No Public Health without Refugee and Migrant Health – Summary.* Copenhagen: WHO Regional Office for Europe.

WHO (World Health Organization). 2020. "*Report of the WHO-China Joint Mission on Coronavirus Disease 2019 (COVID-19).*" WHO, Geneva.

World Bank and UNHCR (United Nations Refugee Agency). 2020. "Compounding Misfortunes: Changes in Poverty since the onset of COVID-19 on Syrian Refugees and Host Communities in Jordan, the Kurdistan Region of Iraq and Lebanon." World Bank, Washington, DC; UNHCR, Geneva; World Bank–UNHCR Joint Data Center on Forced Displacement, Copenhagen.

CHAPTER 3

Mobility-Related Implications of COVID-19 for Receiving Countries

Introduction

Migrants play an essential role in filling labor shortages in their destination countries. During the COVID-19 pandemic, mobility restrictions only exacerbated these labor shortages—for example, by preventing or delaying the entry of key workers. Migrants are often necessary to fill, and are overrepresented in, essential occupations such as health care and agriculture.

The disruptions caused by the COVID-19 crisis may also have repercussions on migration that will manifest in the longer term. For instance, the disruptions to learning and lack of peer interactions caused by the pandemic may have halted the integration process of migrants and refugees, with potential long-lasting scarring effects and the perpetuation of preexisting inequalities. The fear of contagion and the social distancing measures imposed since the COVID-19 outbreak may have also triggered less openness to foreigners and deteriorated attitudes toward migrants.

This chapter presents detailed evidence on these short-term impacts and longer-term implications of the COVID-19–related mobility restrictions from a receiving country's perspective.

Labor disruptions in receiving countries

Migrants account for a large share of workers in key occupations in Mediterranean countries and economies. Fasani and Mazza (2020) identify "key occupations" as those that the European Commission deemed exempt from COVID-19–related mobility restrictions during the first half of 2020. Several of these occupations, from low- to high-skill jobs, rely heavily on migrant labor.

In the European Union (EU) countries of the northern Mediterranean, migrants make up 8–37 percent of the workforce in key low-skill jobs, including cleaners, construction workers, machine operators, and personal care workers. In the key high-skill occupations, they account for more than 6 percent of the workforce in information and communication technology (ICT), science and engineering, health, and teaching (figure 3.1).

Labor shortages and migrants: the prepandemic picture

In Europe, the COVID-19 crisis might have exacerbated preexisting labor shortages in both high- and low-skill occupations. Before the pandemic, there was a

Figure 3.1   Share of foreigners in key occupations, by place of birth, in selected northern Mediterranean EU countries, 2018

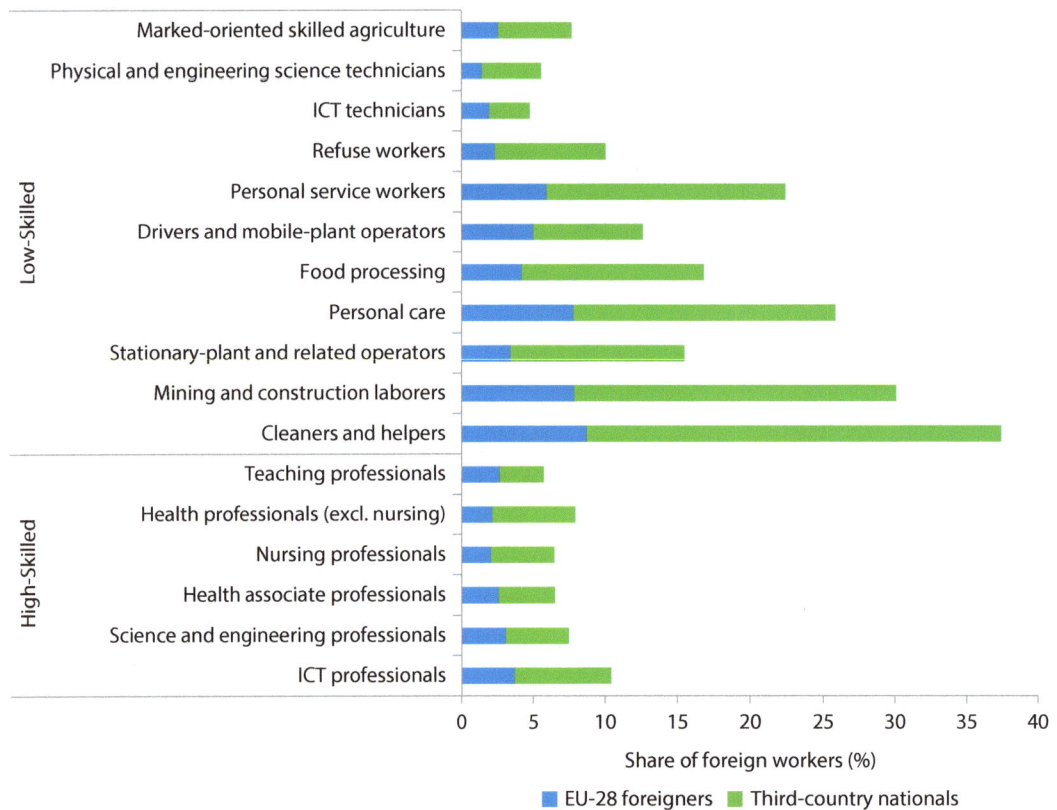

Source: European Union Labor Force Survey (EU-LFS) 2018 data from Eurostat (https://ec.europa.eu/eurostat).
Note: The northern Mediterranean European Union (EU) countries include Cyprus, Croatia, France, Greece, Italy, Malta, Slovenia, and Spain. EU-28 countries include the United Kingdom, which subsequently withdrew from EU on January 31, 2020. Following Fasani and Mazza (2020), "high-skill" occupations are defined as those in which the workforce's median education level is above International Standard Classification of Education (ISCED) level 3 (upper secondary education), while "low-skill" occupations are those in which the median education level is equal to or below ISCED level 3. ICT = information and communication technology.

positive correlation between the share of foreigners in an occupation and the share of European countries that reported labor shortages in that occupation, with the most extreme shortage being of nursing professionals (figure 3.2).

Among the high-skill professions with Europe's largest labor shortages (including software developers, civil engineers, and systems analysts), foreigners make up 12–19 percent of the workforce. In the low-skill professions with reported shortages, foreigners account for even larger shares—for example, over a quarter of cooks and waiters.

As for the medical professions, 15 percent of the nursing professionals in European countries in 2018 were foreign-born,[1] and 18 of the 30 European countries or regions reported having shortages of nursing professionals in the second half of 2019 (figure 3.2). Similarly, in 2018, more than 6 percent of all health care professionals (excluding nurses) and health associate professionals across eight northern Mediterranean EU countries were foreigners, with more than half of those being third-country nationals (figure 3.1). Overall, the shortage of health workers in the EU, an estimated 1.6 million in 2013, is projected to reach 4.1 million by 2030 (0.6 million physicians, 2.3 million nurses, and 1.3 million other health professionals) (Michel and Ecarnot 2020).

Figure 3.2   Share of European countries with labor shortages, by occupation, and share of foreigners in those occupations, 2018 to 2019

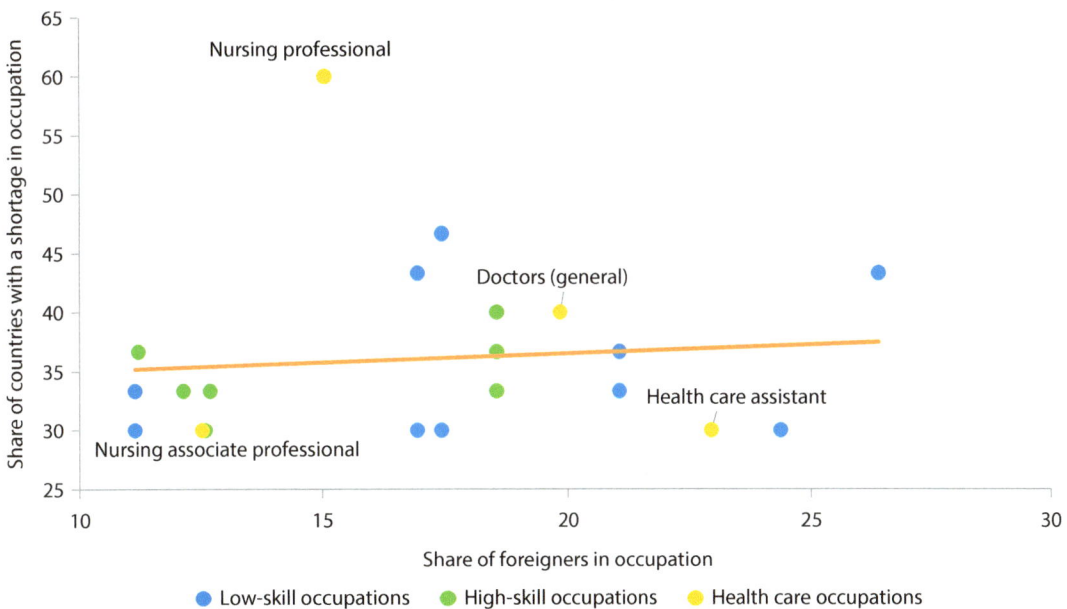

Sources: European Union Labour Force Survey (EU-LFS) 2018 data, Eurostat (https://ec.europa.eu/eurostat); EC 2020.
Note: The x-axis is the 2018 share of foreigners in each occupation in the EU-28 (pre-Brexit) countries plus Iceland, Norway, and Switzerland, according to the EU-LFS. Shares are calculated using survey weights. The y-axis is the share of EU-28 countries (plus Norway and Switzerland but excluding Austria and France, which did not submit data) that reported having a shortage in each occupation in the second half of 2019, according to EC (2020). Outliers across all occupations in the EU-LFS with a share of foreigners more than three standard deviations from the mean are excluded.

Migrants are also an essential source of labor for the Gulf Cooperation Council (GCC) countries,[2] where they account for large shares of the population but are allowed entry only on a temporary basis and for a specific and prearranged job with an employer. As a result, GCC countries have some of the world's highest shares of foreign labor in the workforce—ranging from 79 to 96 percent of the employed population depending on the country (De Bel-Air 2017, 2018a, 2018b, 2018c, 2019a, 2019b).[3]

In Saudi Arabia, for instance, migrants account for three-quarters of the workforce, with almost two-thirds employed in the private sector, one-third working as domestic workers, and very few working in the public sector. Approximately 2.2 million workers in Saudi Arabia are employed in construction, representing a vital source of labor without which the sector would face severe challenges (World Bank 2020). Migrants' contributions in the construction sector have also been crucial to support the development of infrastructure needed for megaprojects in other GCC countries, such as the Expo 2020 in the United Arab Emirates and FIFA World Cup Qatar 2022™ (ILO 2017).

Pandemic's impact on the agriculture sector

Given the essential role of foreigners in the agricultural labor forces of many Mediterranean countries, the COVID-19–related mobility restrictions could affect the food supply chain. In Turkey, for example, 20 percent of the 552,000 agricultural workers are refugees (3RP 2020). In Italy, approximately 27 percent of the formal agricultural workforce, or 370,000 workers, are foreigners (box 3.1). France and Spain also rely on foreign agricultural workers, employing approximately 276,000 and 150,000 seasonal workers per year, respectively (EPRS 2021).

Concerns about shortages of migrant workers emerged during Europe's planting and harvesting seasons in 2020, particularly for labor-intensive crops, such as tomatoes, cucumbers, peppers, strawberries, cherries, potatoes, and asparagus. In April 2020, the Food and Agriculture Organization of the United Nations (FAO) warned that COVID-19–related labor shortages could disrupt global food production, processing, and distribution (FAO 2020). European farmers' unions estimated a shortfall of about 1 million seasonal agricultural workers in the first half of 2020: 200,000 in France, 300,000 in Germany, 370,000 in Italy, and a 40 percent drop in the agricultural workforce in Spain, where most seasonal workers come from Morocco and Tunisia (Mitaritonna and Ragot 2020).

Between January 2020 and June 2021, global food prices rose by 40 percent owing to pandemic-related uncertainty, macroeconomic conditions, and disrupted supply chains. The World Food Programme estimated that because of the COVID-19 pandemic, 272 million people were already in, or were at risk of, acute food insecurity (WFP 2020; World Bank 2021).

BOX 3.1   The agriculture industry in Italy

BOX 3.1   The agriculture industry in Italy

Foreigners are necessary to fill labor shortages in Italy's agriculture industry. Many of these workers come from other Mediterranean countries. In 2017, Moroco, Albania, and Tunisia were among the top countries of origin for agricultural workers in Italy (figure B3.1.1).

Figure B3.1.1   Top providers of agricultural workers to Italy, by country of origin, 2017

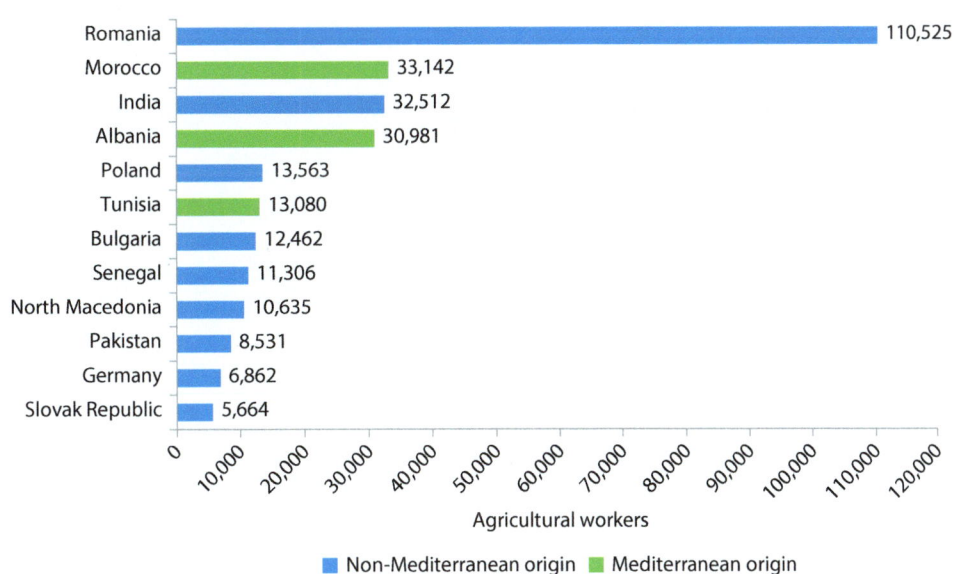

Source: Macrì 2019, using National Institute for Social Security (INPS) data.

The employment of foreigners in Italy's agriculture industry has been increasing in recent years. Between 2008 and 2017, the number of seasonal agricultural workers from Morocco increased by 62 percent, from Albania by 44 percent, and from Tunisia by 40 percent (figure B3.1.2).

A large percentage of the agricultural workers work in Italy's agriculture industry on temporary contracts (less than 100 days). This percentage is as high as 93 percent for Gambian agricultural workers. More than a third of the Albanian and Tunisian agricultural workers and nearly half of the Moroccan and North Macedonian agricultural workers in Italy come on these short-term contracts.

(continued on next page)

BOX 3.1   *continued*

Figure B3.1.2   **Percentage change in migrant agricultural workers in Italy, by country of origin, 2008 to 2017**

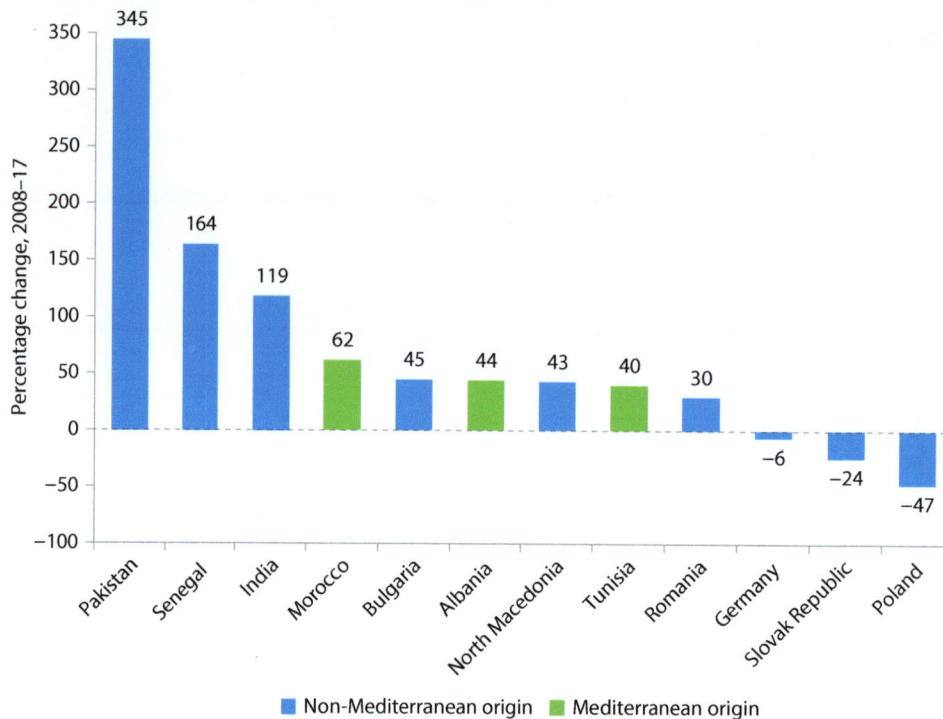

■ Non-Mediterranean origin   ■ Mediterranean origin

Source: Macrì 2019, using National Institute for Social Security (INPS) data.
Note: In 2016, foreigners made up only 9 percent of the Italian population but 36 percent of temporary and 23 percent of permanent agricultural contracts.

A "telemigrant" trend in nonagricultural jobs?

A shift toward remote work may accelerate offshoring for some jobs—a trend already in motion long before the COVID-19 pandemic. A 2005 study by the McKinsey Global Institute predicted that 11 percent of all service jobs in the 2008 global economy "could in theory be carried out remotely" (Farrell et al. 2005).[4] Just a few years later, Blinder (2009) predicted that 22–29 percent of all US jobs were, or would be, potentially offshorable within a decade or two. Indeed, before the pandemic, based on labor force survey data, the International Labour Organization (ILO) estimated that 7.9 percent of the world's workforce (approximately 260 million workers) already worked from home on a permanent basis (Berg, Bonnet, and Soares 2020).[5]

During the pandemic, however, teleworking may have risen as many companies invested in digital infrastructure and otherwise facilitated remote-work options to keep their operations going. An estimated 30–62 percent of workers in Europe and the United States had jobs that could be performed remotely (Berg, Bonnet, and Soares 2020; Brenan 2020; Dingel and Neiman 2020).

Now that the technological barriers to remote working have been lessened or removed, companies may shift toward hiring workers, or "telemigrants," in low-wage countries (Baldwin 2020). This phenomenon may reduce the need for people to physically move to fill certain jobs, reducing the push-pull factors driving migration (Ottaviano, Peri, and Wright 2013). However, the possibility of offshoring a job depends upon the extent to which the job's tasks require "soft skills"—such as verbal and written communication, persuasion, and social perceptiveness—that are generally more difficult to offshore. In some cases, domestic and international workers may not be interchangeable (Baldwin and Dingel 2021).

Although the shift toward a digital workplace and technology adoption induced by the pandemic may have affected migration patterns in some cases, in other cases, in-person human labor is needed and cannot be automated away (box 3.2).

BOX 3.2 COVID-19, automation, and migration

COVID-19 may have changed how firms and people think about business processes, potentially making investments in automation less risky. However, there is evidence that jobs lost because of the pandemic may be permanently lost and replaced by technology.

Looking at data on the fraction of jobs with routine tasks, combined with worker exposure indexes, Blit, Skuterud, and Veall (2020) show that the retail, construction, manufacturing, wholesale, and transportation industries are more likely to experience a postpandemic increase in automation. In a McKinsey Global Institute survey of executives in July 2020, 35 percent of respondents reported their companies were accelerating investment in automation and artificial intelligence in their supply chains (Lund et al. 2021). Autor and Reynolds (2020), too, find that the COVID-19 pandemic will lead to increased automation, translating in turn into economic hardship for those with less job security, particularly in the low-paid personal services sector.

Sedik and Yoo (2021) confirm that concerns are warranted about "the rise of robots" and corresponding worker job losses in the aftermath of the COVID-19 pandemic. They find that pandemics over the past two decades, although much smaller in scale than COVID-19, accelerated robot adoption, which can in turn result in the displacement of low-skilled workers and hence can increase inequality as well.

(continued on next page)

BOX 3.2   *continued*

However, migration and automation are not necessarily substitutable alternatives to dealing with labor shortages. Although a proposed alternative to filling jobs with immigrants is automation, robots and immigrants do not always fill the same roles. Furthermore, migrants often fill labor shortages in positions that are unattractive to native workers.

In the United States, greater automation in a region is associated with a lower ability of workers in that region to work remotely, and low-skilled migrants are overrepresented in those areas (Rahman 2020). Similarly, Basso, Peri, and Rahman (2020) show that openness to immigration attenuated the job and wage polarization faced by native-born workers owing to technological change, suggesting that whereas natives and robots may be substitutable, immigrants and natives are often complementary. They also show that automation generates more migration. This may be partially because "routine-substituting" technological progress has attracted immigrants who increasingly specialize in manual service occupations that *cannot be* automated away. According to an alternative explanation, this may be in part because firms often have trouble recruiting natives for routine-substituting jobs that *are* at risk to be automated away, because they will likely be temporary positions, and thus firms may end up recruiting workers from abroad (Baruah et al. 2021).

In sum, the relationship between automation and migration and how they are used to respond to labor shortages is not straightforward. More research is needed to disentangle the relationship between automation, migration, and the COVID-19 pandemic.

Implications of COVID-19 for long-term migrant integration

Lost schooling, lost learning

The COVID-19 crisis led many countries to close schools and transition to online learning. In April 2020, schools were closed in more than 180 countries, affecting approximately 1.6 billion students (Azevedo et al. 2020). By May 2021, it was estimated that more than 80 days of schooling were lost in Italy, 60 in Greece, 50 in France, and more than 40 in Spain (OECD 2021). Countries have tried different strategies to implement remote learning, but their effectiveness has varied widely (Azevedo et al. 2020).

The effects of short-term school closures can persist long into the future and be particularly detrimental for vulnerable groups. Hanushek and Woessmann (2020) show that if one-third of a school year was lost, the average current student might expect something on the order of 2.5–4 percent lower future career earnings if schools immediately returned to 2019 performance levels. They also emphasize that these losses will be permanent unless the schools return to *better* performance levels than those in 2019. Similarly, Azevedo et al. (2020) predict that a five-month school closure could lead nearly 7 million students to drop out of school and result in a 2–8 percent reduction in the yearly future earnings of the average student from today's cohort in primary or secondary school.

Greater impacts on migrants' children

Language barriers. Although these learning and potential earning losses are universal for all students during the COVID-19 pandemic, the impacts are even more severe for migrants and refugees, who face several additional barriers. For example, students from households that speak a language at home other than the language of instruction in school have seen larger learning losses. Large shares of foreign-born 15-year-old students do not speak the language of instruction at home. In some Mediterranean countries, this share is as large as one quarter of all foreign-born students (figure 3.3).

Students who speak a different language at home are already approximately one year of schooling behind their peers (OECD 2015). Those students who immigrated at a later age face even more difficulty catching up. Maldonado and de Witte (2020) find that while primary school students in the Dutch-speaking Flemish region of Belgium, on the whole, experienced learning losses because of pandemic-related school closures, schools with higher shares of students who do not speak the language of instruction (Dutch) at home saw larger learning losses in their language arts classes.

Socioeconomic disadvantages. Immigrant students are more likely to come from socioeconomically disadvantaged homes—another factor that makes them more vulnerable to falling behind (figure 3.4). Furthermore, in Organisation for Economic Co-operation and Development (OECD) countries, immigrant parents are 17 percentage points less likely than native-born parents to be involved in their child's school community, and this lower parental engagement is associated with lower levels of academic performance and belonging at school (OECD 2018). In Israel, more than half of all foreign-born students come from disadvantaged homes, as opposed to just over a third of native-born students.

Several studies have shown that the learning losses caused by pandemic-related school closures are even more extreme for these students. In Australia, following an eight-week school closure, students from disadvantaged schools achieved the equivalent of two months' less improvement in mathematics test scores

Figure 3.3   Share of 15-year-old students whose mother tongue differs from the language of instruction at school in selected Mediterranean countries, 2018

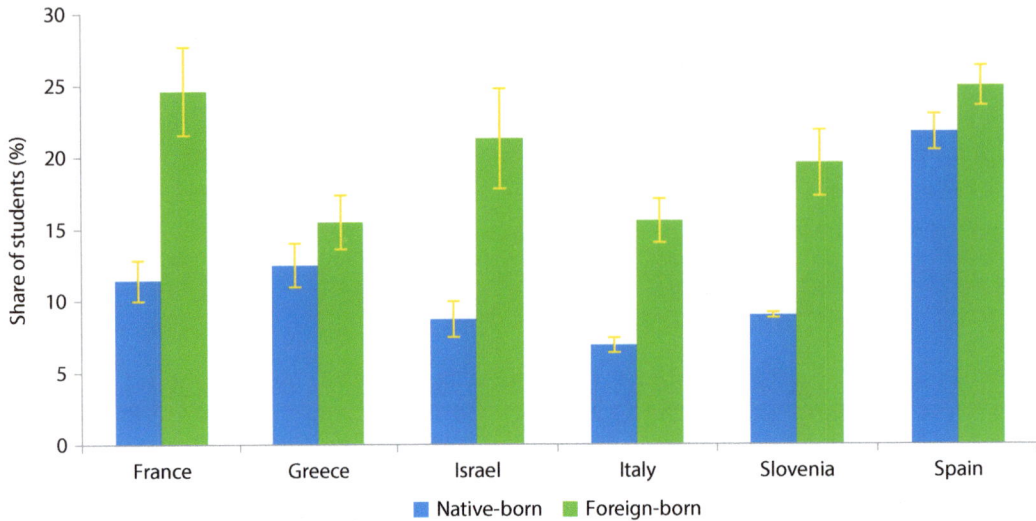

Source: Organisation for Economic Co-operation and Development (OECD) Programme for International Student Assessment (PISA) 2018 database (https://www.oecd.org/pisa/data/2018database/).
Note: The "native-born" group does not include second-generation immigrants. The results do not differ significantly when second-generation immigrants are included in the native-born group. The gold error bars indicate the standard error. Foreign-born students with at least one native-born parent are also excluded from the analysis.

Figure 3.4   Share of 15-year-old students who are socioeconomically disadvantaged in selected Mediterranean countries, 2018

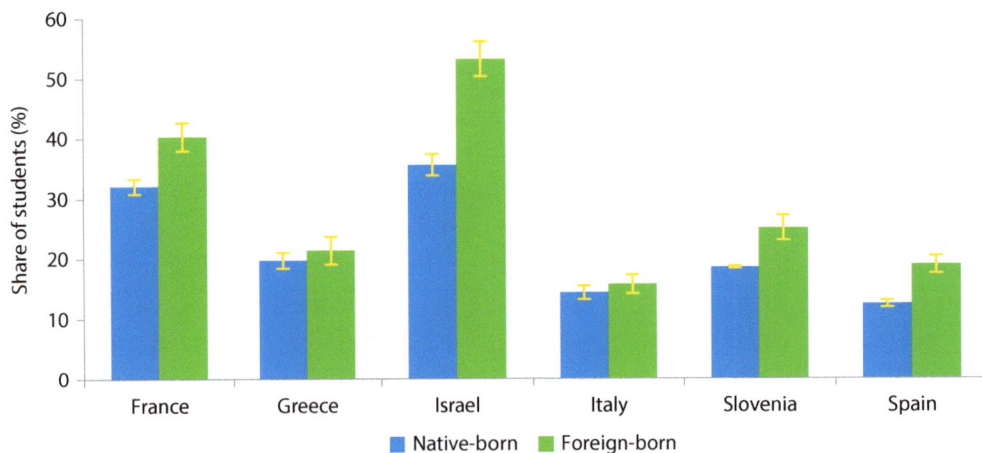

Source: Organisation for Economic Co-operation and Development (OECD) Programme for International Student Assessment (PISA) 2018 database (https://www.oecd.org/pisa/data/2018database/).
Note: The "native-born" group does not include second-generation immigrants. The results do not differ significantly when second-generation immigrants are included in the native-born group. The gold error bars indicate the standard error. Foreign-born students with at least one native-born parent are also excluded from the analysis.

than students from other schools (Gore et al. 2021). Looking at other countries and regions, Maldonado and de Witte (2020) and Hanushek and Woessmann (2020) similarly find the pandemic-related effects were worse for disadvantaged students.

Less access to remote-learning technology. In addition to socioeconomic barriers and limited parental education and involvement, foreign-born students are less likely to have technology available at home, making remote learning more difficult. Across several OECD Mediterranean countries, a PISA-OECD "index of availability" shows, foreign-born children have less access to technology at home (figure 3.5).

And in an April 2020 survey in Turkey, although 93 percent of refugee children reported being enrolled in school, 31 percent reported not having access to online learning because they lacked the remote learning TV channel, internet access, or understanding of how to follow remote-learning programs (IFRC and TRC 2020). Similarly, a June 2021 needs assessment in Turkey shows that 45 percent of refugee respondents reported difficulty in gaining remote access to services because of a lack of digital tools such as computers, tablets, cell phones, and Wi-Fi service (UNHCR 2021). Furthermore, only 43 percent of respondents claimed to be able to use digital platforms such as Zoom or others easily or very easily, 36 percent claimed to be able to use these platforms with some or many difficulties, and 21 percent said they could not use them at all.

Figure 3.5 ICT availability at home for 15-year-old students in selected Mediterranean countries, 2018

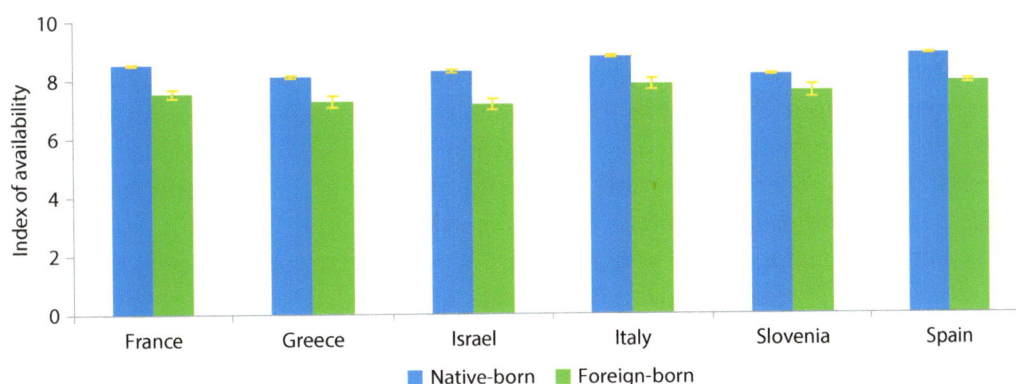

Source: Organisation for Economic Co-operation and Development (OECD) Programme for International Student Assessment (PISA) 2018 database (https://www.oecd.org/pisa/data/2018database/).

Note: The "native-born" group does not include second-generation immigrants. The results do not differ significantly when second-generation immigrants are included in the "native-born" group. The gold error bars indicate the standard error. The "index of availability" is a sum of how many of 10 specified information and communication technology (ICT) devices or connections the student has available at home. Foreign-born students with at least one native-born parent are also excluded from the analysis.

Impacts on adult integration programs

A variety of integration courses for adult migrants and refugees have also been suspended or delivered only online. For many migrants, in particular recent arrivals, the near-global lockdown caused by COVID-19 meant a disruption to language courses they were receiving (OECD 2020b). Most countries were also forced to end other in-person integration courses as restrictions were imposed.

Recognizing that deferring classes altogether likely results in learning losses and potential dropouts, many countries turned to novel digital tools or ramped up existing offerings. Although online courses were somewhat successful—providing a flexible alternative to in-person classes for some subgroups of migrants, such as recent arrivals with little or no host-country language knowledge or women with childcare responsibilities—the transition to distance learning poses particular challenges. In Germany, only 38 percent of eligible migrants in the first months of the pandemic moved into the online integration courses offered as a substitute for in-person courses (OECD 2020b). Germany also considered these courses extra learning and did not subtract these online courses from immigrants' course entitlement. In France, because basic French literacy and access to technology was required for online integration courses, such courses could be provided only to those immigrants with at least a basic proficiency in the French language (OECD 2020b).

These pandemic-driven trends may have significant impacts on long-term integration. Several studies show that language acquisition plays an important role in the economic as well as sociocultural integration of migrants and refugees:

- In a review of studies that measure the effects of language on earnings, Chiswick and Miller (2014) show that knowledge of the host country's language can increase immigrants' earnings by 5–35 percent.
- Comparing Moroccan and Turkish immigrants with Surinamese immigrants in the Netherlands, Zorlu and Hartog (2018) show that knowledge of the host country's language can increase the probability of employment by 30 percentage points, feelings of inclusion by 50 percentage points, and household income by €500 per month.
- Summarizing the literature on migrants and refugees in Europe and the United States, Özden and Wagner (2020) and Schuettler and Caron (2020) confirm the importance of language acquisition for economic integration and stress the importance of language training, particularly when combined with other integration courses.
- Finally, OECD (2020b) notes that program shutdowns may hinder migrants' employability and social integration, emphasizing that (a) the five-year period after arrival is critical; (b) discontinuity of language learning can limit progress in language courses, resulting in demotivation; and (c) social isolation from host-country natives who could help with informal learning is also a concern.

Openness toward migration, before and after COVID-19

Drivers of attitudes toward migrants

The literature on attitudes toward migrants identifies two main economic determinants: labor market competition and fiscal redistribution. Low-skilled workers are more likely to favor lower immigration because an influx of migrants may reduce their wages through increased competition (Scheve and Slaughter 2001). Conversely, in countries where natives are relatively more skilled than immigrants, high-skilled natives are more likely to be pro-immigration (Mayda 2006). In North and West Africa, people who see their country's labor market to be doing well are 15 percent more likely to have a positive view of immigrants than those who see the labor market as doing poorly (Borgnäs and Acostamadiedo 2020).

However, a large body of evidence suggests that natives consider not only labor market outcomes but also the fiscal costs of immigration when taking a stance on immigration policy (Dustmann and Preston 2006, 2007; Facchini and Mayda 2009, 2012; Hanson, Scheve, and Slaughter 2007).

Noneconomic factors such as concerns about cultural identity have also been shown to affect natives' attitudes toward migration. Hainmueller and Hiscox (2007) find that anti-immigration views are more strongly correlated with cultural values related to national identity than with personal economic circumstances. Reviewing findings from the political economy and political psychology literature, Hainmueller and Hopkins (2014) conclude that these patterns hold for Canada, the United States, and Western Europe.

In the economics literature, Dustmann and Preston (2007); Mayda (2006); Card, Dustmann, and Preston (2012); and O'Rourke and Sinnott (2006) find similar results in support of the important role of cultural concerns in determining attitudes toward migrants. In a more recent investigation, Tabellini (2020) focuses on migration to the United States during the early half of the twentieth century. The study shows that opposition to migration was particularly severe against migrants with more-different cultural backgrounds in terms of religion and linguistic distance from English.

Perceived health threats are an additional noneconomic factor affecting attitudes toward migration. A body of literature shows that such perceptions may foster negative attitudes. In a psychological experiment, Faulkner et al. (2004) conclude that when presented with the threat of disease, people react more negatively toward subjectively *foreign* outsiders but not subjectively *familiar* outsiders. Schaller and Neuberg (2012) explain that propaganda is partially to blame for fostering negative attitudes that link subjectively foreign people with disease. Looking at the Ebola epidemic, Kim, Sherman, and Updegraff (2016) find that American survey participants who felt less able to protect themselves from Ebola were more likely to respond negatively to the survey questions about foreigners.

Attitudes since the onset of COVID-19

The experiences of past health crises suggest that COVID-19 may lead to scapegoating of minorities. In an experimental study in the United States, O'Shea et al. (2020) find that priming participants with disease-related images increased pro-white sentiments, especially among the most germ-averse, which can partially explain increased racism during public health crises. Reviewing social responses to 11 past health crises, Jedwab et al. (2020) conclude that epidemics and pandemics may be more likely to lead to social conflict where intergroup tensions are already high and where governments and other public officials promote or permit scapegoating and policies that lower public trust. The characteristics of the COVID-19 pandemic suggest a mild scapegoating scenario, which could turn into a violent scapegoating scenario in cases where tensions are already high.

An emerging number of studies point to the link between COVID-19 and antiforeigner sentiment:

- A Eurobarometer survey shows that at the beginning of the pandemic between March and June 2020, public opinion toward immigrants turned more negative (Ratha et al. 2021).
- In Ireland and the United Kingdom, people exhibited more nationalism and anti-immigrant sentiments when the perceived threat of the pandemic spreading was high (Hartman et al. 2021).
- As the spread of COVID-19 increased, so did exclusionary attitudes toward foreigners. However, when people had more contact with foreigners, these effects were mitigated (Yamagata, Teraguchi, and Miura 2021).
- In the United States, COVID-19 sparked racial animus against Asians, as measured by the share of Google searches and tweets that included an anti-Asian racial slur (Lu and Sheng 2020). The authors use spatial-temporal variation in the timing of the first local COVID-19 diagnosis and find that racist online language increased in the week after COVID-19 arrived in an area. However, the severity of the pandemic in an area did not lead to more racist language.

Some experimental evidence also shows that COVID-19 fuels harmful behaviors against foreigners (Bartoš et al. 2020). In a large-scale experiment in the Czech Republic in March to April 2020 (when the entire population was under lockdown), more than 2,000 participants were asked to increase or decrease rewards to different sets of people at no monetary costs to themselves. During this period, there were decreases in the amounts of money participants chose to give to people living abroad as well as to migrants (although the latter decrease was not statistically significant). Making this decision shortly after answering a set of questions about COVID-19 magnified the average extent of this nation-based discrimination, the authors find.

Return migrants have also faced discrimination from people in their countries of origin. In Ethiopia, for instance, because of the quarantine measures put in place for return migrants (among other reasons), many Ethiopians believed returnees were carrying the virus, stigmatizing those reentering the country (Bizuwerk 2020; OCHA 2021). In Bangladesh, migrants who returned home during the pandemic, many of whom were female domestic workers abroad, expressed feeling shunned and feared by their communities as potential carriers of the virus upon return (UN Women 2020).

However, migrants' important role in responding to the crisis may also positively affect attitudes toward migration. In European subregions with higher shares of immigrant workers (particularly workers from outside of the EU), natives are more likely to move into occupations with less exposure to COVID-19 risks (Bossavie et al. 2020), as shown in figure 3.6. These types of jobs are more amenable to working from home or have less face-to-face interaction.

Figure 3.6   Correlation between share of telework jobs among natives and share of immigrants across NUTS2 regions of EU countries, 2018

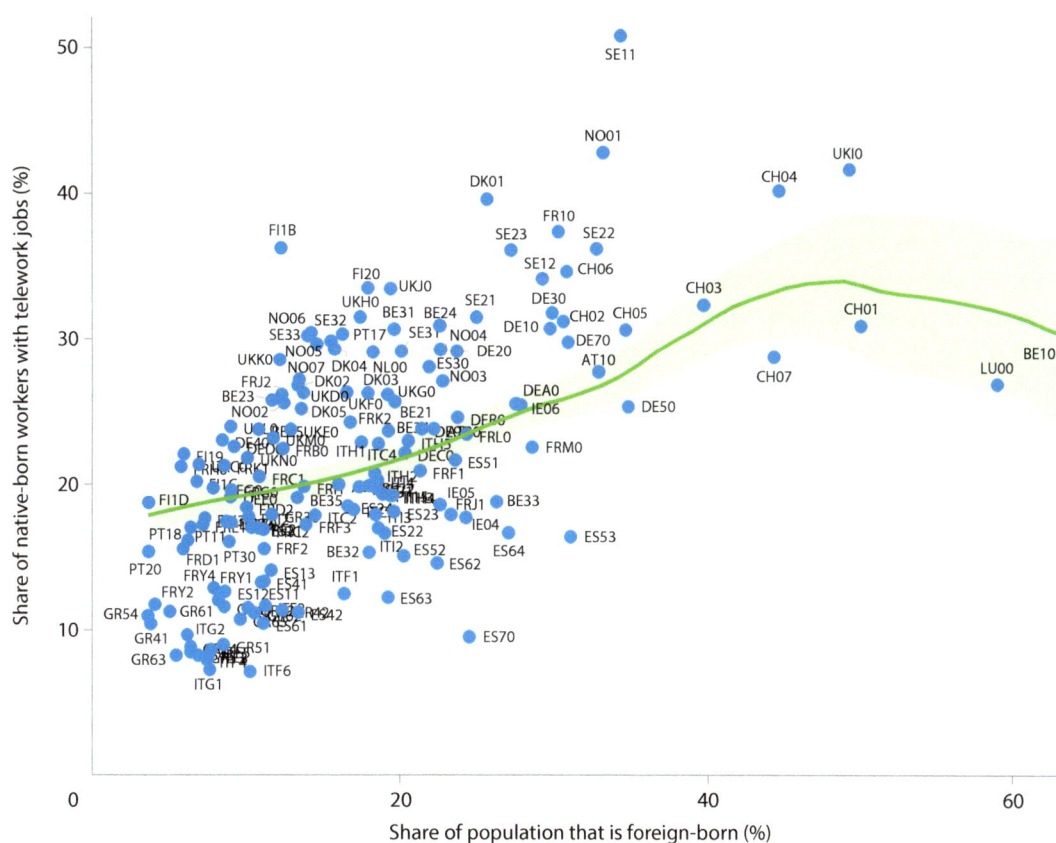

Source: Bossavie et al. 2021.
Note: NUTS = Nomenclature of Territorial Units for Statistics. NUTS2 refers to second-level subdivisions of countries for statistical purposes. Locations are labeled by NUTS2 code. The green line designates the kernel density, and the shaded area, the 95 percent confidence interval.

In general, past research indicated that natives—regardless of their own education and income—prefer high-skilled immigrant workers to low-skilled workers (Hainmueller and Hiscox 2010; Hainmueller and Hopkins 2015; Naumann, Stoetzer, and Pietrantuono 2018). However, during the pandemic, immigrants have been crucial in filling several essential roles, including in health care and low-skill occupations, highlighting the value of various types of migration (Fernández-Reino, Sumption, and Vargas-Silva 2020).

Although crises do not inevitably mean that natives will view migrants more negatively, countries may become less open if migration becomes a more salient issue in the wake of the COVID-19 crisis. Dennison and Geddes (2020) note that the 2008–09 Global Financial Crisis and the 2015 European migrant crisis did not invert the positive trends in attitudes toward migration observable in the European Social Survey in the past 20 years. In the EU Mediterranean countries, attitudes toward migrants have remained relatively stable since 2002 (figure 3.7).

According to the Gallup World Poll, opinions toward migrants are generally more negative in North Africa than in West Africa, but the trends in opinion over time vary by country. Between 2011 and 2017, public opinion toward immigration improved in Libya and the Arab Republic of Egypt but worsened in Algeria, Morocco, and Tunisia (Borgnäs and Acostamadiedo 2020). However, even when attitudes toward migrants do not change, opposition to migration can increase if natives perceive migration as a more salient problem for receiving countries to address (Dennison and Geddes 2020).

Figure 3.7   Public opinion toward immigration in EU Mediterranean countries, by type of immigrant, 2002 to 2018

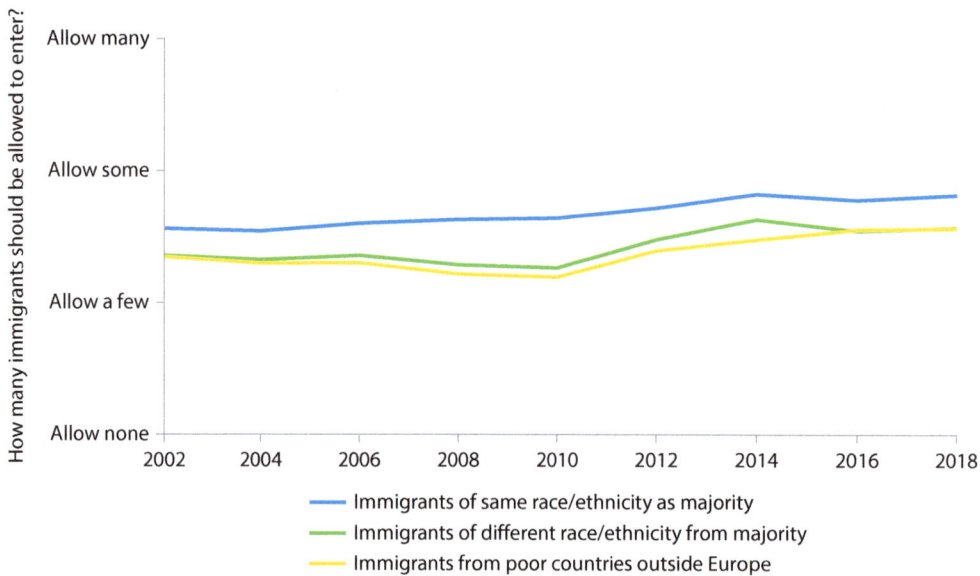

Source: European Social Survey data (https://www.europeansocialsurvey.org/data/).
Note: European Union (EU) countries included are Croatia, Cyprus, France, Greece, Italy, Slovenia, and Spain.

Notes

1. Data on foreign-born health care professionals are from the European Union Labour Force Survey (EU-LFS) 2018, obtained from Eurostat (https://ec.europa.eu/eurostat).
2. The GCC countries include Bahrain, Kuwait, Oman, Qatar, Saudi Arabia, and the United Arab Emirates.
3. Data for the United Arab Emirates cover only Dubai.
4. The report noted that the "11 percent theoretical maximum" represented "an average across all industries in the global economy" and that individual sectors would vary widely in their potential shares of remote employment, depending largely on how many customer-facing functions a sector has (Farrell et al. 2005).
5. Although some of these workers were "teleworkers," most were not. The share includes a wide range of occupations including industrial outworkers (for example, embroidery stitchers, beedi rollers), artisans, self-employed business owners, and freelancers in addition to employees. Employees accounted for 18.8 percent of the total number of home-based workers worldwide, but this number is as high as 55.1 percent in high-income countries. Globally, among employees, 2.9 percent were working exclusively or mainly from their homes before the COVID-19 pandemic (Berg, Bonnet, and Soares 2020).

References

Autor, D., and E. Reynolds. 2020. "The Nature of Work after the COVID Crisis: Too Few Low-Wage Jobs." Essay 2020-14, The Hamilton Project of the Brookings Institution, Washington, DC.

Azevedo, J., A. Hasan, D. Goldemberg, S. Iqbal, and K. Geven. 2020. "Simulating the Potential Impacts of COVID-19 School Closures on Schooling and Learning Outcomes: A Set of Global Estimates." Policy Research Working Paper 9284, World Bank, Washington, DC.

Baldwin, R. 2020. "COVID, Hysteresis, and the Future of Work." VoxEU.org, May 29. https://voxeu.org/article/covid-hysteresis-and-future-work.

Baldwin, R., and J. Dingel. 2021. "Telemigration and Development: On the Offshorability of Teleworkable Jobs." Discussion Paper Series No. 16641, Center for Economic and Policy Research, Washington, DC.

Bartŏs, V., M. Bauer, J. Cahlíková, and J. Chytilová. 2020. "COVID-19 Crisis Fuels Hostility against Foreigners." Discussion Paper No. 13250, IZA Institute of Labor Economics, Bonn.

Baruah, N., J. Chaloff, J.-C. Dumont, and R. Kawasaki. 2021. "The Future of Labor Migration in Asia: Post-COVID-19 Pandemic." In *Labor Migration in Asia: Impacts of the COVID-19 Crisis and the Post-Pandemic Future*, 38–59. Tokyo: Asian Development Bank Institute; Paris: Organisation for Economic Co-operation and Development; Bangkok: International Labour Organization.

Basso, G., G. Peri, and A. S. Rahman. 2020. "Computerization and Immigration: Theory and Evidence from the United States." *Canadian Journal of Economics* 53 (4): 1457–94.

Berg, J., F. Bonnet, and S. Soares. 2020. "Working from Home: Estimating the Worldwide Potential." Policy Brief, International Labour Organization, Geneva.

Bizuwerk, D. 2020. "As Migrants Return to Ethiopia, Social Workers Show They're Essential to COVID-19 Response." Article, May 21, United Nations Children's Fund (UNICEF), https://www.unicef.org/coronavirus/migrants-return-ethiopia-social-workers-show-theyre-essential-covid-19-response.

Blinder, A. 2009. "How Many US Jobs Might be Offshorable?" *World Economics* 10 (2): 41–78.

Blit, J., M. Skuterud, and M. R. Veall. 2020. "The Pandemic and Short-Run Changes in Output, Hours Worked and Labour Productivity: Canadian Evidence by Industry." *International Productivity Monitor* 39: 16–32.

Borgnäs, E., and E. Acostamadiedo. 2020. "Public Opinion on Immigration in North and West Africa: An Exploration of the Available Evidence." In *Migration in West and North Africa and across the Mediterranean: Trends, Risks, Development and Governance*, 406–17. Geneva: International Organization for Migration.

Bossavie, L., D. Sanchez, M. Makovec, and Ç. Özden. 2020. "Do Immigrants Shield the Locals: Exposure to COVID-Related Risks in the European Union," Policy Research Working Paper 9500, World Bank, Washington, DC.

Bossavie, L., D. Garrote Sanchez, M. Makovec, and Ç. Özden. 2021. "Immigration and Natives' Exposure to COVID-Related Risks in the EU." VoxEU.org, September 1. https://voxeu.org /article/immigration-and-natives-exposure-covid-related-risks-eu.

Brenan, M. 2020. "US Workers Discovering Affinity for Remote Work." Gallup Poll report, April 3. https://news.gallup.com/poll/306695/workers-discovering-affinity-remote-work .aspx.

Card, D., C. Dustmann, and I. Preston. 2012. "Immigration, Wages, and Compositional Amenities." *Journal of the European Economic Association* 10 (1): 78–119.

Chiswick, B., and P. Miller. 2014. "International Migration and the Economics of Language." Discussion Paper No. 7880, IZA Institute of Labor Economics, Bonn.

De Bel-Air, F. 2017. "Demography, Migration, and Labour Market in Qatar." Gulf Labour Markets and Migration (GLMM) Explanatory Note No. 3/2017, Migration Policy Centre, European University Institute, Florence.

De Bel-Air, F. 2018a. "Demography, Migration, and the Labour Market in Oman." Gulf Labour Markets and Migration (GLMM) Explanatory Note No. 7/2018, Migration Policy Centre, European University Institute, Florence.

De Bel-Air, F. 2018b. "Demography, Migration and Labour Market in Saudi Arabia." Gulf Labour Markets and Migration (GLMM) Explanatory Note No. 5/2018, Migration Policy Centre, European University Institute, Florence.

De Bel-Air, F. 2018c. "Demography, Migration, and the Labour Market in the UAE." Gulf Labour Markets and Migration (GLMM) Explanatory Note No. 1/2018, Migration Policy Centre, European University Institute, Florence.

De Bel-Air, F. 2019a. "Demography, Migration, and the Labour Market in Bahrain." Gulf Labour Markets and Migration (GLMM) Explanatory Note No. 1/2019, Migration Policy Centre, European University Institute, Florence.

De Bel-Air, F. 2019b. "Demography, Migration, and the Labour Market in Kuwait." Gulf Labour Markets and Migration (GLMM) Explanatory Note No. 3/2019, Migration Policy Centre, European University Institute, Florence.

Dennison, J., and A. Geddes. 2020. "Why COVID-19 Does Not Necessarily Mean that Attitudes Towards Immigration Will Become More Negative." International Organization for Migration Policy Paper, Migration Policy Centre, European University Institute, Florence.

Dingel, J. I., and B. Neiman. 2020. "How Many Jobs Can be Done at Home?" Working Paper No. 26948, National Bureau of Economic Research, Cambridge, MA.

Dustmann, C., and I. Preston. 2006. "Is Immigration Good or Bad for the Economy? Analysis of Attitudinal Responses."(Discussion Paper No. 06/04, Centre for Research and Analysis of Migration (CReAM), Department of Economics, University College London.

Dustmann, C., and I. P. Preston. 2007. "Racial and Economic Factors in Attitudes to Immigration." *B.E. Journal of Economic Analysis & Policy* 7 (1): 1–41.

EC (European Commission). 2020. *Analysis of Shortage and Surplus Occupations 2020.* Luxembourg: Publications Office of the European Union.

EPRS (European Parliamentary Research Service). 2021. "Migrant Seasonal Workers in the European Agricultural Sector." Briefing for the European Parliament, European Union, Luxembourg.

Facchini, G., and A. M. Mayda. 2009. "Does the Welfare State Affect Individual Attitudes toward Immigrants? Evidence across Countries." *Review of Economics and Statistics* 91 (2): 295–314.

Facchini, G., and A. M. Mayda. 2012. "Individual Attitudes Towards Skilled Migration: An Empirical Analysis across Countries." *The World Economy* 35 (2): 183–96.

FAO (Food and Agriculture Organization of the United Nations). 2020. "Migrant Workers and the COVID-19 Pandemic." Policy brief, FAO, Rome.

Farrell, D., M. Laboissière, R. Pascal, C. de Segundo, J. Rosenfeld, S. Stürze, and F. Umezawa. 2005. "The Emerging Global Labor Market." Three-part report, McKinsey Global Institute, Washington, DC.

Fasani, F., and J. Mazza. 2020. "Immigrant Key Workers: Their Contribution to Europe's COVID-19 Response." Policy Paper No. 155, IZA Institute of Labor Economics, Bonn.

Faulkner, J., M. Schaller, J. H. Park, and L. A. Duncan. 2004. "Evolved Disease-Avoidance Mechanisms and Contemporary Xenophobic Attitudes." *Group Processes & Intergroup Relations* 7 (4): 333–53.

Fernández-Reino, M., M. Sumption, and C. Vargas-Silva. 2020. "From Low-Skilled to Key Workers: The Implications of Emergencies for Immigration Policy." *Oxford Review of Economic Policy* 36 (Suppl1): S382–S396.

Gore, J., L. Fray, A. Miller, J. Harris, and W. Taggart. 2021. "The Impact of COVID-19 on Student Learning in New South Wales Primary Schools: An Empirical Study." *Australian Educational Researcher* 48 (4): 605–37.

Hainmueller, J., and M. J. Hiscox. 2007. "Educated Preferences: Explaining Attitudes Toward Immigration in Europe." *International Organization* 61 (2): 399–442.

Hainmueller, J., and M. J. Hiscox. 2010. "Attitudes toward Highly Skilled and Low-Skilled Immigration: Evidence from a Survey Experiment." *American Political Science Review* 104 (1): 61–84.

Hainmueller, J., and D. J. Hopkins. 2014. "Public Attitudes toward Immigration." *Annual Review of Political Science* 17 (1): 225–49.

Hainmueller, J., and D. J. Hopkins. 2015. "The Hidden American Immigration Consensus: A Conjoint Analysis of Attitudes toward Immigrants." *American Journal of Political Science* 59 (3): 529–48.

Hanson, G. H., K. Scheve, and M. J. Slaughter. 2007. "Public Finance and Individual Preferences over Globalization Strategies." *Economics & Politics* 19 (1): 1–33.

Hanushek, E. A., and J. Woessmann. 2020. "The Economic Impacts of Learning Losses." Report, Organisation for Economic Co-operation and Development, Paris.

Hartman, T. K., T. V. A. Stocks, R. McKay, J. Gibson-Miller, L. Levita, A. P. Martinez, L. Mason, et al. 2021. "The Authoritarian Dynamic during the COVID-19 Pandemic: Effects on Nationalism and Anti-Immigrant Sentiment." *Social Psychological and Personality Science* 12 (7): 1274–85.

IFRC and TRC (International Federation of Red Cross and Red Crescent Societies and Turkish Red Crescent Society). 2020. "Impact of COVID-19 on Refugee Populations Benefitting from the Emergency Social Safety Net (ESSN) Programme." Rapid assessment, IFRC, Geneva; and TRC, Ankara.

ILO (International Labour Organization). 2017. *Employer-Migrant Worker Relationships in the Middle East: Exploring Scope for Internal Labour Market Mobility and Fair Migration.* Beirut: ILO Regional Office for Arab States.

Jedwab, R., A. M. Khan, R. Damania, J. Russ, and E. D. Zaveri. 2020. "Epidemics, Poverty, and Social Cohesion: Lessons from the Past and Possible Scenarios for COVID-19." COVID Economics 48: 171–209.

Kim, H. S., D. K. Sherman, and J. A. Updegraff. 2016. "Fear of Ebola: The Influence of Collectivism on Xenophobic Threat Responses." *Psychological Science* 27 (7): 935–44.

Lu, R., and Y. Sheng. 2020. "From Fear to Hate: How the COVID-19 Pandemic Sparks Racial Animus in the United States." *COVID Economics* 39: 72–108.

Lund, S., A. Madgavkar, J. Manyika, S. Smit, K. Ellingrud, M. Meaney, and O. Robinson. 2021. "The Future of Work after COVID-19." Postpandemic economy report, McKinsey Global Institute, Washington, DC.

Macrì, M. C. 2019. "Il Contributo dei Lavoratori Stranieri all'Agricoltura Italiana" [The Contribution of Foreign Workers to Italian Agriculture]. Council for Agricultural Research and Economics, Rome.

Maldonado, J. E., and K. de Witte. 2020. "The Effect of School Closures on Standardised Student Test Outcomes." Discussion Paper Series DPS20.17, Department of Economics, KU Leuven, Belgium.

Mayda, A. M. 2006. "Who Is Against Immigration? A Cross-Country Investigation of Individual Attitudes toward Immigrants." *Review of Economics and Statistics* 88 (3): 510–30.

Michel, J.-P., and F. Ecarnot. 2020. "The Shortage of Skilled Workers in Europe: Its Impact on Geriatric Medicine." *European Geriatric Medicine* 11 (3): 345–47.

Mitaritonna, C., and L. Ragot. 2020. "After COVID-19, Will Migrant Agricultural Workers in Europe Be Replaced by Robots?" Policy Brief No. 2020-33, Institute for Research on the International Economy (CEPII), Paris.

Naumann, E., L. F. Stoetzer, and G. Pietrantuono. 2018. "Attitudes towards Highly Skilled and Low-Skilled Immigration in Europe: A Survey Experiment in 15 European Countries." *European Journal of Political Research* 57 (4): 1009–30.

OCHA (United Nations Office for Coordination of Humanitarian Affairs). 2021. "Humanitarian Needs Overview: Ethiopia." Needs assessment, OCHA, New York.

OECD (Organisation for Economic Co-operation and Development). 2015. *Immigrant Students at School: Easing the Journey towards Integration*. Paris: OECD Publishing.

OECD (Organisation for Economic Co-operation and Development). 2018. *The Resilience of Students with an Immigrant Background: Factors that Shape Well-Being*. Paris: OECD Publishing.

OECD (Organisation for Economic Co-operation and Development). 2020a. "Towards 2035– Strategic Foresight: Making Migration and Integration Policies Future Ready." Report, OECD, Paris.

OECD (Organisation for Economic Co-operation and Development). 2020b. "What Is the Impact of the COVID-19 Pandemic on Immigrants and Their Children?" Policy brief, OECD, Paris.

OECD (Organisation for Economic Co-operation and Development). 2021. "The State of Global Education: 18 Months into the Pandemic." Report, OECD, Paris.

O'Rourke, K. H., and R. Sinnott. 2006. "The Determinants of Individual Attitudes Towards Immigration." *European Journal of Political Economy* 22 (4): 838–61.

O'Shea, B. A., D. G. Watson, G. D. A. Brown, and C. L. Fincher. 2020. "Infectious Disease Prevalence, Not Race Exposure, Predicts Both Implicit and Explicit Racial Prejudice across the United States." *Social Psychological and Personality Science* 11 (3): 345–55.

Ottaviano, G. I. P., G. Peri, and G. C. Wright. 2013. "Immigration, Offshoring, and American Jobs." *American Economic Review* 103 (5): 1925–59.

Özden, Ç., and M. Wagner. 2020. *Moving for Prosperity: Global Migration and Labor Markets*. Policy Research Report. Washington, DC: World Bank.

Rahman, A. 2020. "Why Can't Everybody Work Remotely? Blame the Robots." *COVID Economics* 36: 105–28.

Ratha, D., E. J. Kim, S. Plaza, and G. Seshan. 2021. "Resilience: COVID-19 Crisis through a Migration Lens." Migration and Development Brief No. 34, Global Knowledge Partnership on Migration and Development (KNOMAD), World Bank, Washington, DC.

Schaller, M., and S. L. Neuberg. 2012. "Danger, Disease, and the Nature of Prejudice(s)." In *Advances in Experimental Social Psychology* Vol. 46, edited by M. P. Zanna and J. M. Olson, 1–54. Burlington, MA: Academic Press.

Scheve, K. F., and M. J. Slaughter. 2001. "Labor Market Competition and Individual Preferences over Immigration Policy." *Review of Economics and Statistics* 83 (1): 133–45.

Schuettler, K., and L. Caron. 2020. "Jobs Interventions for Refugees and Internally Displaced Persons." Jobs Working Paper No. 47, World Bank, Washington, DC.

Sedik, T. S., and J. Yoo. 2021. "Pandemics and Automation: Will the Lost Jobs Come Back?" Working Paper No. 21/11, International Monetary Fund, Washington, DC.

Tabellini, M. 2020. "Gifts of the Immigrants, Woes of the Natives: Lessons from the Age of Mass Migration." *Review of Economic Studies* 87 (1): 454–86.

3RP (Regional Refugee and Resilience Plan in Response to the Syria Crisis). 2020. "3RP Turkey Consolidated: 2020 Appeal Overview." Financial appeal consolidation document, 3RP Turkey Chapter.

UNHCR (United Nations High Commissioner for Refugees). 2021. "Turkey: Inter-Agency Protection Sector Needs Assessment Analysis Round 4 - June 2021." Needs assessment, Inter-Agency Coordination Unit, UNHCR, Geneva.

UN Women (United Nations Entity for Gender Equality and the Empowerment of Women). 2020. "Far from the Spotlight, Women Workers are among the Hardest Hit by COVID-19 in Bangladesh." UN Women News, April 27. https://www.unwomen.org/en/news/stories/2020/4/feature-women-workers-hardest-hit-by-covid-19-in-bangladesh.

WFP (World Food Programme). 2020. "WFP Global Update on COVID-19: November 2020—Growing Needs, Response to Date and What's to Come in 2021." Report, WFP, Rome.

World Bank. 2020. "MoMRA's Low Income Labor Housing Strategy." Internal report, World Bank, Washington, DC.

World Bank. 2021. "Food Security and COVID-19." Food Security Brief (last updated July 14), https://reliefweb.int/report/world/brief-food-security-and-covid-19.

Yamagata, M., T. Teraguchi, and A. Miura. 2021. "The Relationship between Infection-Avoidance Tendencies and Exclusionary Attitudes toward Foreigners: A Panel Study of the COVID-19 Outbreak in Japan." Working paper. doi:10.31234/osf.io/x5emj.

Zorlu, A., and J. Hartog. 2018. "The Impact of Language on Socioeconomic Integration of Immigrants." Discussion Paper No. 11485, IZA Institute of Labor Economics, Bonn.

CHAPTER 4
Policy Directions

From findings to policy directions

As this report has shown, the pandemic has not only had short-run implications specific to the COVID-19 crisis but also made more visible the structural problems related to mobility in the extended Mediterranean region. Mobility restrictions increased risks for people on the move. Worker shortages threatened economic recovery. Concentrated COVID-19 outbreaks among migrants increased the risk of transmission to local populations. Some of these challenges emerged as a result of new risks posed by the COVID-19 pandemic. Others resulted from preexisting issues in migration systems, suggesting that going back to a pre–COVID-19 equilibrium may not be the solution.

The report also shows that migration can and should continue safely during public health crises. To address the mobility-related challenges emerging during the pandemic, many countries fast-tracked migration procedures and extended coverage of key services. These efforts show that migration can continue safely during the pandemic and that doing so is beneficial for migrants as well as for the receiving and sending countries and economies. The next section, on policy proposals, includes numerous specific examples of actions taken by countries within and outside the region.

The findings of the report also draw attention to the importance of building migration systems that can promptly respond to a variety of shocks. Resilient migration systems are shock-responsive. The underlying components of shock-responsive migration systems—from admission channels to provision of various services in receiving and sending countries—are built with the flexibility to adapt to unexpected events.

These systems require coordination between sending and receiving countries and economies to ensure that mechanisms are put in place to take actions at different stages of the migration cycle when an unexpected shock occurs.

The unfolding of the COVID-19 pandemic and the policy actions implemented worldwide have generated lessons that could be useful to inform the response to future shocks. Whereas some of the lessons learned focus on challenges typically arising from public health shocks, other lessons apply to a broader set of shocks, including those related to economic, conflict, or climate-related factors. Four main lessons have emerged during the COVID-19 crisis that can inform countries' efforts to develop shock-responsive mobility systems:

1. Travel restrictions may have an impact in delaying contagion, but they are only a temporary solution that comes with non-negligible costs for employers, migrants, and sending countries. When the structural drivers of migration are strong, mobility restrictions do not necessarily halt migration flows, and they are likely to increase the vulnerabilities faced by people on the move.
2. Migrants play an important role in the workforce of many receiving countries and have been shown to be an essential resource in managing the health and economic impacts of the COVID-19 pandemic. Their contributions have been key in helping receiving countries to address shocks associated with high risks and to promptly restart economic activity.
3. Applying human development policies equally to migrants and locals in the wake of large shocks keeps locals "safe," protects migrants, and keeps economies strong. In contrast, limiting migrants' access to health care, social welfare, active labor market programs, and adequate housing may cause them to adopt coping mechanisms that can slow down economic recovery—with severe implications in both the short and the long term. As such, expanding migrants' access to services even during crises, when overall fiscal space might be limited, is an investment with a strong economic rationale.
4. Sudden shocks can put long-term immigrant integration efforts at risk. Although it is important to address the immediate impacts of shocks, attention should also be paid to their potential scarring effects on migrants.

Policy interventions can help migration continue safely in the aftermath of public health shocks such as the COVID-19 outbreak while making migration systems more resilient to different types of shocks. The COVID-19 crisis has shown that action is needed to reduce the risk of transmission posed by the pandemic and to ensure that labor can flow safely where needed. Although the interventions implemented by many countries and economies were key to addressing the pandemic's immediate migration-related impacts, complementary and systematic reforms are also necessary to address the remaining challenges and to better respond to different types of future shocks.

Proposed policy actions

This report suggests a set of policy actions to achieve three broad objectives: (1) safely continue migration and preserve long-term integration efforts in the wake of public health shocks such as the COVID-19 pandemic, (2) make migration systems more ready to respond to different types of future shocks, and (3) address preexisting structural issues exacerbated by the pandemic to ensure the future sustainability of migration. The 10 proposed actions, grouped under three policy objectives with their implementation time frames, are presented in figure 4.1.

The first group of actions focuses on initiatives aimed at continuing migration safely and addressing issues that can put migrants' long-term integration at risk. These actions are particularly relevant in the case of public health crises. Because these interventions are important to prevent challenges specific to the COVID-19

Figure 4.1   Proposed policy objectives and actions

Start immediately and complete as soon as possible

Policy objective 1: Safely continue migration and preserve long-term integration efforts in the wake of public health shocks

1. Establish and follow agreed-upon health protocols such as vaccination certificates, testing, contact tracing, quarantine, and isolation
2. Support migrant learners with access to internet connection, IT equipment, and tutors

Start in the short term and complete in the short and medium term

Policy objective 2: Make migration systems more ready to respond to different types of shocks

3. Put mechanisms in place to automatically simplify procedures and allow timely entry of essential workers in the case of a shock
4. Automatically expand migrants' access to health care and social welfare during crises
5. Extend access to employment retention and promotion policies to migrants during crises

Start in the short term to fully complete in the medium and long term and adjust regularly

Policy objective 3: Address preexisting structural issues exacerbated by the pandemic to ensure the future sustainability of migration

6. Address de facto barriers that may limit migrants' use of key services
7. Ensure that camps and migrants' accommodations meet health and safety requirements
8. Expand and strengthen mobility schemes to fill labor shortages and protect migrants
9. Address misinformation and raise awareness of migrants' contributions
10. Strengthen data capacity to apply an evidence-based approach to migration policy making

Source: Original figure for this publication.
Note: IT = information technology.

pandemic from becoming long-term problems, efforts in these areas should start as soon as possible.

The second group of actions builds on the lessons learned during the COVID-19 pandemic to develop mobility systems that can promptly respond to a broader set of shocks. It is suggested that countries start these reforms in the short term and aim to complete them in the short-to-medium term.

Finally, the last group of actions focuses on prepandemic structural issues that were exacerbated during the COVID-19 crisis. Addressing these challenges is crucial to ensure the sustainability of migration flows in the Mediterranean. Because most of these actions will require significant efforts and commitment from both sending and receiving countries and economies, governments are advised to start these reforms in the short term and aim to fully complete them in the medium-to-long term.

The remainder of this chapter discusses in detail the 10 proposed policy actions. Although some actions are more relevant for certain groups of migrants than for others,[1] the pandemic has shown that the traditional distinctions between low-skilled and high-skilled migrants, and between refugees and economic migrants, may not always be clear-cut in the wake of large shocks. For this reason, the 10 proposed interventions all apply to varying degrees to the different categories of people on the move discussed in the report.

Policy objective 1: Safely continue migration and preserve long-term integration efforts in the wake of public health shocks

Action 1: Establish and follow agreed-upon health protocols such as vaccination certificates, testing, contact tracing, quarantine, and isolation

Establishing and following public health protocols is an important step to safely restart large-scale international travel. Practices such as testing, contact tracing, quarantine, and isolation have been introduced around the world to allow the continuous flows of essential workers during the peak of the crisis.

Quarantine measures. Despite border closures, Austria allowed seasonal agricultural and forestry workers as well as health workers to enter the country, subject to self-quarantine for two weeks, after which they received a COVID-19 medical clearance. The government also provided places to quarantine for those without a space. Germany followed a similar approach. Canada also permitted international students and both permanent and temporary foreign workers to enter the country if they completed 14 days of self-isolation upon entry (Moroz, Shrestha, and Testaverde 2020).

Sending countries also need enhanced testing and support in implementing quarantine measures for returning migrants who may be infected. In Ethiopia, the government partnered with the Ethiopian Public Health Institute to set up quarantine centers and screening procedures for return migrants in addition to providing them with personal protective equipment. Likewise, to facilitate the safe reentry of return migrants from places with vulnerable conditions, the Sri Lankan government reserved quarantine centers for those repatriating who could not pay to self-isolate in hotels (Moroz, Shrestha, and Testaverde 2020).

Vaccination certificates. To safely continue mobility during the pandemic, several countries have introduced the requirement for travelers to provide a COVID-19 vaccination certificate to travel without having to follow more time-consuming health protocols. However, vaccination efforts are still at an early stage in most countries that send migrants to the extended Mediterranean region (EIU 2021), and booster doses of the vaccine seem to be required to guarantee continued high protection from the virus over time. For this reason, further actions might be needed to ensure that vaccination certificates do not put migrants at a disadvantage if they are from sending countries where vaccines are not easily accessible (Lau, Hooper, and Zard 2021).

Experience with the European Union (EU) Digital COVID Certificate (Green Pass) can provide a useful model for other countries, although it mainly applies to travel within the EU (box 4.1).

BOX 4.1   The EU Digital COVID Certificate, or Green Pass

The European Union (EU) Digital COVID Certificate (Green Pass) is free of charge and can be obtained in any EU country by any EU citizen, resident, or their family members and companions through vaccination, negative tests, or proof of recovery. The certificate is also equipped with a quick response (QR) code that can be printed or carried in a smartphone or tablet. It can be used to facilitate mobility inside and among all EU countries. What makes this possible is a centralized digital system that can verify EU COVID certificates no matter where they have been issued.

The European Commission is currently working on making this system interoperable with other existing ones. Meanwhile, several non-EU countries in the extended Mediterranean region have also adopted the system (for example, Israel, Lebanon, Morocco, Turkey, and the United Arab Emirates).

For an updated list of countries currently adhering to this system, see the "EU Digital COVID Certificate" page of the European Commission website: https://ec.europa.eu/info/live-work-travel-eu/coronavirus-response/safe-covid-19-vaccines-europeans/eu-digital-covid-certificate_en.

Source: EC 2021b.

Multilateral coordination. A coordinated public health approach between sending and receiving countries is essential to limit the spread of the virus and guarantee the safety of migration flows. Lack of such coordination may result in delays and missed opportunities for migration when the sending countries' health protocols are not recognized by the receiving countries. For this reason, countries beyond the EU have also strengthened their coordination on this matter (box 4.2).

This type of coordinated approach will also be essential to ensure that vaccine passports can meet their intended objectives without imposing long waiting times and numerous additional steps on travelers and enforcers (*Economist* 2021). In parallel, receiving countries' support would also be needed to ensure that vaccination campaigns in sending countries are sufficiently funded, vaccine infrastructure and distribution capacity are strengthened, regulatory processes are harmonized, and public trust in health systems and vaccines is boosted (Lau, Hooper, and Zard 2021).

BOX 4.2   Multilateral public health efforts in Africa

Several examples of multilateral coordination have emerged in the African continent since the start of the COVID-19 crisis. For instance, the Africa Centres for Disease Control and Prevention (Africa CDC) has attempted to streamline cross-border travel during the pandemic by providing a centralized database for information on mobility restrictions, travel requirements, and authorized testing laboratories through the Trusted Travel portal and MyCOVIDPass app. This technology has also allowed for digital verification and the collection of travel and testing information from passengers.

Furthermore, the East African Community (EAC), with help from the Africa CDC, has created a system to facilitate the testing of truck drivers in the region. The system includes COVID testing before departure and upon arrival to a border—often at rapid-processing or mobile clinics—and a common database and app to share and certify the results and to track the drivers. Despite concerns regarding corruption or unreliability in the testing infrastructure, as well as occasional border delays, the system as a whole aims to enable the safe and transparent mobility of drivers throughout the region.

The Economic Community of West African States (ECOWAS) has also been trying to develop a harmonized approach to managing COVID-19 in the region. For instance, at the beginning of 2021, ECOWAS set a regional cap on testing prices and created a unified vaccine procurement approach.

Sources: EC 2021b; Lau, Hooper, and Zard 2021.

Action 2: Support migrant learners with access to internet connection, information technology equipment, and tutors

Supporting migrants and refugees with internet access can help them address the additional barriers to skills acquisition imposed by COVID-19. Investing in education infrastructure—especially school facilities in areas with large inflows of migrant students—is considered an investment with potentially high economic returns (Özden and Wagner 2020). The transition to online learning has allowed many countries to continue delivering important education and integration services while at the same time providing flexibility to migrants with competing schedules and introducing a format that can also be useful after the end of the pandemic (OECD 2020). However, this new delivery method may also create additional challenges for migrants and refugees with limited access to a reliable internet connection.

To make connection available to refugees, the United Nations High Commissioner for Refugees (UNHCR) suggests different connection solutions depending on factors such as target population, digital literacy, access to smartphones versus computers, existing infrastructure, dispersion of refugees across city areas, and type of settlement, among others (UNHCR 2020). The suggested solutions range from Subscriber Identity Module (SIM) cards with third- or fourth-generation (3G or 4G) connections (for migrants with access to smartphones and scattered in different parts of urban centers) to Wi-Fi hot spots for those concentrated in certain areas and with access to the necessary information technology (IT) equipment. For migrants without access to computers or smartphones, a proposed solution is the installation of physically distanced computers in a well-ventilated area where refugees could book and use the equipment needed to access online services.

Additional challenges posed by the transition to online services could be attenuated by making the support of tutors or the necessary IT equipment available. Even once an internet connection is available, some challenges remain in providing online education, training, and employment services; these include low digital literacy, language barriers, and limited access to the necessary equipment. Mobility restrictions may have also further exacerbated barriers such as childcare responsibilities that may prevent women from attending training classes.

Some countries already had a framework in place that facilitated the transition to online activities. Other countries tackled language and digital literacy barriers by trying to improve the learning delivery and by making tutors available to address migrants' difficulties. Yet other strategies tackled the connectivity problem by simply providing the necessary equipment directly to students (OECD 2021).

For instance, Germany's Federal Office for Migration and Refugees invested close to €40 million in 2020 to transfer integration and language courses to online formats (Bathke 2020). As a result, lessons were delivered via videoconference by virtual classrooms or by online tutorials. France adopted a virtual classroom format to ensure the continuity of language classes to those who had already started them under their integration contract, especially for those in beginner levels, when language is most crucial. To avoid creating disadvantages for migrants with no access to technology or to an internet connection or who had low computer literacy, Finland (a) provided the necessary equipment to learners at the beginning of the course, and (b) had in place a mail option for receiving and delivering course materials and assignments. Belgium has also opted to provide the necessary equipment to migrants who lack access to it (OECD 2021). Finally, to avoid disruption in language learning and to encourage social interactions, Estonia started a program that matches migrants willing to learn the local language with volunteer tutors via online channels.

Policy objective 2: Make migration systems more ready to respond to different types of shocks

Action 3: Put mechanisms in place to automatically simplify procedures and allow timely entry of essential workers in the case of a shock

Even before the pandemic, various factors significantly prolonged hiring processes for foreign workers. For instance, bottlenecks in the system—including complex and duplicative bureaucratic steps, human resource constraints, and suboptimal IT infrastructure—often cause delays to employers in many receiving countries wanting to hire foreign workers (SVR Research Unit and MPI Europe 2019).

The COVID-19 crisis has further shown the importance of establishing and implementing mechanisms to automatically simplify procedures and avoid unnecessary delays in recruiting foreign workers needed in essential occupations. Such mechanisms, which can be automatically triggered in response to a shock, would be important to ensure that complex procedures do not prevent countries from accessing essential workers when they are particularly needed.

To make sure that migrants were available to help address the health and economic impacts of the pandemic, several countries have simplified administrative procedures and loosened requirements, as in the following ways (further discussed in box 4.3):

- Identifying essential sectors and allowing entry to workers in these sectors
- Waiving specific visa requirements
- Simplifying procedures for recognition of foreign qualifications
- Extending the duration of work permits of existing workers
- Allowing employment to different groups of foreigners already in the country.

Ensuring that these actions can be automatically executed in response to future shocks could help countries address the labor shortages that these shocks may create.

BOX 4.3 Interventions introduced during the pandemic to simplify hiring procedures for essential workers

European countries have introduced exemptions to ensure a continued supply of workers in certain categories. Despite the general restrictions, most European Union (EU) countries identified sectors as essential that justified continued admission during the COVID-19 crisis. Occupations that were typically considered key were (a) health care professionals, health researchers, and eldercare professionals; (b) transport personnel engaged in haulage of goods and other transport staff; and (c) seasonal agricultural workers (EC 2020a).

The pandemic further exposed the need for health workers and the possibility for migrants to fill those positions. For example, a 2001 Italian law permits only nationals, EU citizens, permanent residents, or recognized refugees to work in public hospitals. However, in early 2020, the government issued a new decree (the Cura Italia Decree)[a] that opened these public medical jobs to any regular foreigner with a work permit (Gostoli 2020). Similarly, Spain sped up the processes of recognizing foreign doctors' and nurses' professional qualifications and of granting visas for immigrants—including asylum seekers with pending cases—in these health care professions.

Countries worldwide took additional actions to quickly fill emerging shortages with foreign workers already in or outside the country. Germany, for example, expedited the procedure for hiring high-skilled workers. Particularly, young people finishing vocational training programs and university could be hired more quickly and stay in the country amid mobility restrictions. Likewise, the United States waived the in-person interview requirement for seasonal guest workers and extended the length of time these workers are allowed to remain in the country. Similarly, aware of potential labor shortages, Finland increased the number of third-country nationals admitted to work in agricultural jobs and opened those opportunities to asylum seekers with minimal bureaucratic delays.

Source: Moroz, Shrestha, and Testaverde 2020.
a. Italian Law Decree No. 18 of 2020.

Action 4: Automatically expand migrants' access to health care and social welfare during crises

Including migrants in new programs introduced during crises or waiving eligibility requirements in existing programs are effective strategies to improve access to health care and social protection in the midst of crises. The report shows that some but not all receiving countries in the extended Mediterranean region give migrants access to health care and social welfare services (as detailed in chapter 2). Even where access is granted, some eligibility requirements and bureaucratic procedures may leave a portion of the migrant population uncovered or discourage timely use of key services.

For this reason, establishing mechanisms to allow easy access to health care and social welfare programs to all migrants during crises is important to limit risks for all. Automatically covering migrants in new programs introduced during crisis periods is a first strategy to reach this objective. Waiving eligibility requirements that prevent migrants from accessing standard health care and social welfare programs is another option that could be implemented in case of unexpected shocks.

Various restrictions could be automatically lifted during crises. One such restriction is the "minimum stay" requirement that limits migrants who arrived recently in a country from accessing social welfare and other services. Similar waivers could be considered for undocumented migrants, who have often limited access to health care and social welfare in the extended Mediterranean region. Examples of specific initiatives to include migrants in health and social welfare responses during the COVID-19 pandemic are presented in box 4.4. Ensuring that these initiatives are automatically triggered in response to shocks could help countries react quickly and limit the negative repercussions that crises may have on both migrants and local communities.

Action 5: Extend access to employment retention and promotion policies to migrants during crises

Employment retention and promotion policies could mitigate the negative health and economic impacts of crises by helping migrants stay employed and helping employers to resume full production more rapidly. Employment retention policies incentivize employers to keep their existing workforces, while employment promotion policies help job seekers to find jobs and employers to find workers.

Extending employment retention and promotion policies to migrants during crises would be important for two reasons: First, these measures can protect migrants from economic shocks that could result in health risks. Second, extending these measures to migrants would allow employers to restore production more quickly because they would reduce turnover and allow employers to benefit from the contributions of migrants who have already developed firm-specific experience and skills.

Emerging evidence suggests that in countries with job retention and training schemes, young migrants experienced lower increases in unemployment and inactivity (OECD 2021). Employment retention policies that could be effective during times of crisis include deductions in social insurance contributions or employment subsidies. Job matching and job search programs are relevant employment promotion policies that can help migrant workers displaced during crises to fill labor shortages resulting from mobility disruptions. Box 4.5 provides examples of initiatives implemented during the COVID-19 pandemic.

BOX 4.4 Measures to expand migrants' access to health care and social welfare during the COVID-19 crisis

Many countries have taken important steps to expand access to health care to migrants and refugees during the pandemic. Most European countries, within and outside the Mediterranean region, expanded health care for migrants, irrespective of their legal status, to provide free treatment in case of COVID-19 contagion. Measures were also taken to temporarily waive eligibility requirements that could limit access to health care. For instance, Portugal undertook a temporary regularization program to ensure full access to health care to undocumented migrants. Spain waived the requirement for migrants to have regular documents to qualify for basic support (OECD 2020).

Other countries in the extended Mediterranean region undertook similar efforts. For instance, Saudi Arabia provided COVID-19 testing and treatment to migrants free of charge. Similarly, Qatar has made COVID-related medical as well as quarantine services freely available to all (Moroz, Shrestha, and Testaverde 2020). Turkey required COVID-19 testing and provision of care for migrants regardless of legal status, though decisions to treat undocumented patients often varied between health providers or faced delays (Özvarış et al. 2020).

Still other countries have taken measures to include migrants in social protection schemes during the pandemic. Migrant workers with permits could apply for the federal stimulus payment introduced in Italy during the pandemic. France and Spain reduced the minimum duration of employment needed to access unemployment benefits. And in the Netherlands, temporary access to social funds was granted to some categories of residence permit holders who are normally not eligible (Moroz, Shrestha, and Testaverde 2020; OECD 2020).

Certain countries in the extended Mediterranean region also introduced interventions specifically targeted to refugees. During June and July 2020, additional transfers were made to refugees in Turkey through the existing cash transfer program funded by the European Union to help them cope with the negative impacts of the pandemic (IFRC and TRC 2021). In Jordan, the government together with the United Nations Children's Fund (UNICEF) provided emergency cash transfers to refugee daily-wage workers who were vulnerable to income losses because of the pandemic and lockdown measures (Hagen-Zanker and Both 2021). In Morocco, the United Nations High Commissioner for Refugees (UNHCR) created a cash transfer program for refugees similar to that implemented by the government to reach those affected by COVID-19–related shocks (Hagen-Zanker and Both 2021).

BOX 4.5 Employment retention and promotion policies open to migrants during the COVID-19 crisis

Countries in the extended Mediterranean region and beyond have acted to retain employment opportunities for migrants during the crisis. The United Arab Emirates created a new decree that listed ways firms could cut costs as an alternative to laying off workers. For example, if mutually agreed upon between employers and workers, firms could allow migrants to work remotely, take leave, or accept temporary or permanent salary reductions instead of losing their employment. If migrant workers were laid off, firms could register their names in an online job-matching platform. Qatar has required and provided funds for companies to pay migrant workers in full who are in quarantine or receiving treatment. Similarly, in New Zealand, seasonal workers under a recognized employer who were self-isolating because of illness or a COVID-19 contact were eligible for the government wage subsidy.

Numerous employment promotion policies were also introduced worldwide during the COVID-19 crisis. Both the German and the French employment agencies offered matching services, including to foreigners living in the country, to fill shortages in the agriculture sector. In the Republic of Korea, the government created initiatives to help fill shortages in the agriculture sector with foreigners already present in the country to compensate for the lack of arrival of new seasonal workers. India introduced a rural public work scheme for internal migrants returning to their home state, focused on the construction of necessary infrastructure in rural regions.

Source: Moroz, Shrestha, and Testaverde 2020.

Employment promotion policies in sending countries could also provide important assistance to returning migrants affected by the COVID-19 outbreak. Reintegration programs can help returning migrants address some of the barriers they face when looking for jobs in their home countries. These programs are common in the Philippines, including for people in situations of distress. In particular, the Assist WELL (Welfare, Employment, Legal, Livelihood) program provides a mix of benefits and services to migrants returning from emergency situations, ranging from transportation and accommodation assistance to employment intermediation, skills certification, and training (DOLE 2021).

Following the COVID-19 outbreak, through a World Bank-funded project, Bangladesh introduced a range of employment services, including recognition of experience acquired abroad, to support returning migrants (Moroz, Shrestha, and Testaverde 2020). Since 2020, the Arab Republic of Egypt has also introduced new initiatives to support the reintegration of returnees and, in some cases, even their re-emigration (UNDP 2021).

Even before the pandemic, several countries within and outside the extended Mediterranean region have increasingly focused on the potential contributions of their citizens living abroad, leveraging technology to support the reintegration process (box 4.6) or trying to strengthen their diaspora engagements (box 4.7).

BOX 4.6   Digital tools to support migrants' reintegration

Various countries are supporting labor market reinsertion of returnees by leveraging technological tools. For example, in Ethiopia, the SIRA app (developed by the International Labour Organization in collaboration with the Ministry of Labour and Social Affairs) helps connect employers and employees. This app particularly helps those who are low-skilled or semiskilled in industries such as hospitality, retail, manufacturing, construction, and agriculture, among others. The app allows job seekers to create a profile and receive job alerts from vacancies posted by firms. It is designed to work in the Ethiopian context, providing information in both English and Amharic and functioning even with limited internet connectivity together with an accompanying website and call center (Kikkawa, Justo, and Sirivunnabood 2021). This app takes users' education level into account and has been especially targeted at and used by returnees to facilitate reintegration into the home labor market (ILO 2018).

India has developed a digital platform to support reintegration. The Skilled Workers Arrival Database for Employment Support (SWADES) helps match returnees with jobs. The initiative was started by the Ministries of Skill Development and Entrepreneurship, Civil Aviation, and External Affairs. While still abroad, Indian migrants may create an online skill card with their information and skill sets to be entered into a database, which companies may then use to fill vacancies. More than 30,500 Indians abroad created these skill cards, of whom 24,500 returned to India from Gulf Cooperation Council (GCC) countries as of January 2021 (Baruah et al. 2021; Kikkawa, Justo, and Sirivunnabood 2021).

BOX 4.7   Can diaspora engagements be strengthened in the aftermath of the pandemic?

The COVID-19 crisis may have offered an opportunity to strengthen diaspora engagements, which could encourage flows of knowledge and investments to home countries. Workplace closures and the increase in teleworking during the pandemic has triggered the temporary return of large numbers of professionals to their home countries, where they could perform their work remotely. Although it is still early to assess the extent to which these temporary flows may turn into longer-term returns, the closer connection between high-skilled diasporas and their home countries during the crisis may offer space to strengthen diaspora engagement policies to encourage development at home.

Several countries have implemented programs to reverse the phenomenon of brain drain—including the Network of Argentine Researchers and Scientists Abroad (RAICES), the Philippines' Brain Gain Network, the Mapping Jamaica's Diaspora Project, Network Colombia (RedEs Colombia), and Bosnia and Herzegovina's Who Is Who in BiH Diasporus Project (Del Carpio et al. 2016; Dickerson and Özden 2018; McKenzie and Yang 2015). These programs create detailed databases of the countries' high-skilled diaspora, including their locations and skill sets, to help domestic firms identify and perhaps provide opportunities to talent abroad, enabling them to return home. Though evidence of the programs' effectiveness is mixed and limited, other programs provide incentives for migrants to return, such as tax benefits, citizenship of residency for their family members, or professional skills recognition.

Even before the pandemic, many sending countries along the central Mediterranean migration route have increasingly put efforts toward actively engaging with the diaspora living abroad. North and West African countries are primary senders of emigrants along this relatively dangerous route. Their governments, seeking to use diaspora networks in the development of their countries, have tried to create polices to connect emigrants to their home countries economically, culturally, and politically:

- *Economic policies* include monetary policies to attract remittances and direct investment from emigrants.
- *Cultural policies* include campaigns to renew a sense of homeland identity in expatriates or their children.
- *Political policies* target measures to allow voting from abroad to encourage the political participation of nationals living outside of the country.

(continued on next page)

BOX 4.7 *continued*

To make the policies more effective, it is crucial to maintain up-to-date databases on emigrants abroad, though few countries (Nigeria and Senegal) collect this data through online registries and other channels.

The Gambia, Guinea, and Senegal have created investment programs and banks targeted at expatriates for local and national development. With such programs the governments hope to maximize the benefits from remittances beyond individual households' use to additionally benefit the whole country. For example, the Senegalese government created the Support Fund for Investments of Senegalese Abroad (FAISE) to encourage investments from expatriates in national development projects (Quartey, Setrana, and Tagoe 2020). This fund includes a program to encourage female entrepreneurship. The Housing Bank of Senegal's Pack Diaspora financial product has similar goals.

West African emigrants have created associations to contribute to the development of their home countries through return migration, cash contributions, human capital development, and infrastructure development. For example, emigrant scholars based at institutions in the global North participate in knowledge transfers to institutions in their home countries. The Senegalese Diaspora Association in France helps found vocational training centers in Senegal to equip their home communities with technical and entrepreneurial skills (Moser 2018). Furthermore, emigrants from Benin, Ghana, and Togo help develop their home communities both economically and culturally through the Council of Ewe Associations of North America.[a]

a. "Ewe" refers to the Ewe people inhabiting parts of those three countries.

Policy objective 3: Address preexisting structural issues exacerbated by the pandemic to ensure the future sustainability of migration

Action 6: Address de facto barriers that may limit migrants' use of key services

Involving local organizations and conducting awareness campaigns in migrants' native languages could be helpful to address some de facto barriers faced by migrants and increase their use of important services. Even when migrants can access services on paper, the existence of various de facto barriers implies that migrants' use of health and other social welfare services remains limited. In fact, targeting migrants for assistance might be challenging given the potential disincentives—such as being identified by country authorities, especially in the case of undocumented migrants.

To ensure that all migrants and refugees have access to and use services that can help them protect themselves and others, the involvement of local organizations and the use of communications material in languages that migrants and refugees understand could be considered. Specific outreach techniques could ensure that women are encouraged to use key services. For instance, messages could be tailored to the needs and possible concerns of female migrants.

Several initiatives in this direction have been introduced since the start of the pandemic. For instance, to improve targeting of people in need who have been excluded from other public assistance, all Italian municipalities received funds to allocate to people in need through vouchers, without distinctions of nationality. Municipalities were in charge of identifying suitable criteria and the amounts to distribute (Moroz, Shrestha, and Testaverde 2020). The German government disseminated COVID-19–related information in multiple languages, leveraging web and social media platforms commonly used by migrants. Similar efforts were undertaken in Denmark, Finland, and France (OECD 2021).

The International Organization for Migration (IOM) and UNHCR also introduced communication campaigns to inform migrants and refugees about the risks associated with COVID-19 as well as about transmission prevention measures and support services available during the crisis. These campaigns produced material, including videos, in different languages and often involved current and returning migrants to increase the legitimacy of these messages among migrant communities.

Action 7: Ensure that camps and migrants' accommodations meet health and safety requirements

The pandemic has drawn attention to the need to improve the standard of housing and accommodations provided to people on the move. Following the emergence of COVID-19 hot spots in dormitories and camps in several countries, governments around the world have introduced short-term measures to address these challenges. For instance, Saudi Arabia allocated more than 3,000 public schools to accommodate migrant workers from densely populated areas. The country also provided food and shelter for migrants in self-isolation. In Bahrain, the government provided a set of guidelines for both private employers and their employees to minimize health risks, including reducing the number of people per room in labor camps and accommodations, practicing social distancing, increasing waste sanitation facilities, designating spaces for people with COVID-19 to self-isolate, and conducting regular inspections to ensure compliance with these rules (Moroz, Shrestha, and Testaverde 2020).

Several European countries also took action to improve housing standards. For instance, Spain introduced guidelines for farmers employing seasonal workers to ensure that workplaces and accommodations were adapted to prevent and control risks. In Germany, employers hiring migrants during the pandemic were mandated to follow specific instructions on the separation of different teams of workers across separated living areas (OECD 2021).

In addition to important short-term emergency actions, a longer-term approach would be needed to sustainably improve the living conditions of migrant workers. The pandemic highlighted that labor accommodation conditions in many places were substandard and could present a public health risk at any time. Certain countries have acted to improve migrant workers' living conditions more permanently. Saudi Arabia has proposed policies regulating the location, amenities, occupancy, and level of private sector involvement in the development of low-income labor housing. More specifically, the Ministry of Municipal and Rural Affairs' planned policy agenda includes the following action areas: increasing awareness of health and safety in group homes, ensuring a sufficient housing supply to meet laborers' demand, creating procedures to register and license this housing, reducing overcrowding, balancing public and private sector involvement in group housing development, and developing financing solutions for these housing developers (World Bank 2020).

Action 8: Expand and strengthen mobility schemes to fill labor shortages and protect migrants

Expanding and strengthening mobility schemes can help countries fill labor shortages while at the same time reducing the risks faced by people on the move. Multilateral or bilateral mobility schemes are examples of pathways for safe and regular migration. These schemes are agreements between sending and receiving countries that can cover seasonal needs in specific sectors as well as broader and longer-term economic needs in destination countries.

The flexibility of this instrument allows receiving and sending countries to tailor their agreements to the specific characteristics and needs of each migration corridor while also giving migrants access to a safer migration channel. In fact, in addition to opening a path to regular migration, mobility agreements usually protect migrants by defining clear terms of employment (wages, duration of contracts, and accommodation arrangements) and often include the provision of predeparture and postarrival services to protect migrants from potential risks and to increase awareness of their roles, responsibilities, and rights while living and working abroad.

To ensure the circularity of migration flows, some bilateral schemes also include measures to facilitate return and reintegration in sending countries and to promote the portability of skills and welfare (Testaverde et al. 2017; Triandafyllidou, Bartolini, and Guidi 2019). Among other factors, the EU's 2020 New Pact on Migration and Asylum emphasizes stronger coordination among countries as an important element to strengthen legal pathways for migration to the EU (box 4.8).

Current schemes in the region. Selected existing schemes in the extended Mediterranean region could provide ideas for the development and adaptation of new programs. The Seasonal Workers Directive adopted by EU member states

BOX 4.8   The EU's New Pact on Migration and Asylum

In September 2020, the European Commission proposed a New Pact on Migration and Asylum with the final objective to maximize the benefits and address the challenges related to migration in the region. The Pact lays out a comprehensive approach to migration, stressing the importance of (a) improved and faster procedures, (b) fair sharing of responsibility and solidarity, and (c) trust between European Union (EU) member states as well as confidence in the system. As part of the proposed holistic approach aimed at building a predictable and reliable migration management system, the Pact emphasizes the importance of improving cooperation with the countries of origin and transit, ensuring effective procedures, successfully integrating refugees, and returning of those with no right to stay.

Several strategies are proposed to accelerate asylum decisions, discourage irregular migration, strengthen legal pathways, and enhance returns. These strategies include (a) a proposed "one-stop asylum" system to speed up the asylum decision process, (b) establishment of a solidarity system to allow EU member states to choose between relocating refugees or sponsoring returns, (c) enhanced border control; (d) strengthened returns processes, and (e) stronger partnerships with third countries to prevent smuggling while at the same time promoting legal pathways and strengthening readmission agreements and arrangements.

The Pact highlights the importance for the EU of attracting foreign talent to address emerging labor shortages due to a shrinking and aging population. The establishment of an EU Talent Pool is one of the actions suggested to match workers to employers' needs. The Pact also suggests the establishment of Talent Partnerships as an example of collaborations with third countries to create better job opportunities in sending countries and legal paths to the EU. These partnerships would have four key elements:

- Supporting legal migration with key partners, scaling up existing cooperation
- Establishing work and training mobility schemes with EU funding and matching EU vacancies and skills
- Building capacity for vocational training and reintegration of returning migrants
- Working together with ministries, employers, and social partners as well as education and diaspora groups.

(continued on next page)

As of November 2021, the Pact was not yet in effect, and negotiations between the EU member states remained deadlocked. The European Commission's detailed "Report on Migration and Asylum" stated that, one year since the New Pact's presentation, "There has been good progress at [a] technical level, but political agreement on some key elements is still distant."

Sources: EC 2020b, 2020c, 2021a; Hein 2021.

in 2014 sets common standards for the entry, residence, and protections of seasonal workers. However, member states still have full control of the total number of yearly admissions and flexibility on various parameters such as maximum duration of stay, reentry, and changes of employers (SVR Research Unit and MPI Europe 2019).

The bilateral agreement between Spain and Morocco, implemented since 2005, focused on employment opportunities for Moroccan seasonal workers in the Spanish agriculture sector. Under this agreement, Moroccan workers have been allowed to work in Spain for a maximum of six months per year, with the potential to be employed again in following years if complying with the terms of the agreement. While not allowing a path to permanent residence, this agreement has been an important instrument to fill labor shortages in Spain while at the same time ensuring a secure source of income for Moroccan seasonal workers without exposing them to the risks of undocumented migration.

Switzerland has also been particularly active in developing bilateral mobility schemes with sending countries (such as Bosnia and Herzegovina, Kosovo, Nigeria, Serbia, and Tunisia) to promote circular migration and curb undocumented flows. Similarly, Poland entered into bilateral agreements (first with Ukraine and later with Georgia and Moldova) with a focus on domestic services, nursing, cleaning, construction, and agriculture (Triandafyllidou, Bartolini, and Guidi 2019). Germany's Western Balkan Regulation (box 4.9) and the Triple Win Program (box 4.10) are other examples of mobility schemes that offer useful insights for the design of legal pathways for migration in the extended Mediterranean region.

Lessons learned. The lessons learned from agreements implemented so far could inform the negotiation of future schemes. Schemes that provide future visa-based incentives have proven more effective than mere compulsory return policies. For example, when the Spanish government required seasonal workers in Spain to return to Morocco, 60 percent of the workers overstayed their visas. However, when the

BOX 4.9 The Western Balkan Regulation

Germany's Western Balkan Regulation is an interesting example of a temporary mobility scheme designed to reroute irregular migration into regular channels. The Western Balkan Regulation (currently extended through 2023) represents an exception among the channels available for third-country nationals to work in the European Union, because it allows nationals from Albania, Bosnia and Herzegovina, Kosovo, Montenegro, North Macedonia, and Serbia to be employed in Germany without any skills or qualification requirements as long as they have a job offer for which no eligible person in Germany can be found.

The regulation was introduced in response to the steadily increasing inflows of Western Balkan citizens arriving in Germany and filing for asylum even though barely 1 percent of them would normally qualify for protection (Bither and Ziebarth 2018). As the number of applications from these migrants reached over 120,000 in 2015, and recognizing the limited alternatives for them to apply for work visas, the German government introduced this directive in 2016 to decongest the asylum system while at the same time addressing employers' needs.

The demand from employers and potential migrants has been significant. As of May 2020, more than 300,000 applications were submitted, with over 244,000 being approved (Brücker et al. 2020). In the 2016–17 period, almost 40 percent of the approved applications resulted in visas being issued, with over 44,000 Western Balkan workers benefiting from the regulation. Although the contemporaneous drop in the number of first-time asylum seekers from the Western Balkan region may suggest that the regulation has contributed to rerouting migrants from the asylum channel to the economic channel of admission, it is difficult to assess the causality of this relationship given the many asylum policy measures introduced by the German government at the same time (Bither and Ziebarth 2018).

Several lessons can be drawn from the first five years of implementation of the Western Balkans Regulation. A recent study by the Institute for Employment Research (IAB) of Germany's Federal Employment Agency highlights that although no specific skills or qualification levels were required as part of the directive, more than 50 percent of the work visas issued were related to skilled jobs (Brücker et al. 2020). Overall, the skills of selected workers were a good match for the jobs they were hired to perform, and their labor market integration was successful when considering employment

(continued on next page)

BOX 4.9   *continued*

stability and earnings. These findings were consistent for both high- and low-skilled workers compared with other migrant groups and German job entrants. As such, the study concludes that "the Western Balkans regulation has achieved the goal of the legislation, namely, to facilitate labor migration and to ensure successful labor market integration. At the same time, this brought about economic benefits and additional revenue for the state and the social insurance systems" (Brücker et al. 2020, 11).

The regulation's success notwithstanding, some important lessons can also be learned from areas of the regulation that would benefit from improvements. Particularly when these programs are designed, attention needs to be paid to potential capacity bottlenecks and administrative restrictions that could cause significant delays, thus preventing employers from filling labor shortages in a timely manner. A clear communication strategy also needs to be developed to ensure that both employers in receiving countries and potential migrants in sending countries are aware of these new legal migration channels. Finally, strict verification of employers' compliance is also an important element to ensure that the rights of migrants are not violated and that this channel is not used at the expense of local workers (Bither and Ziebarth 2018).

government instead made the next year's work visa conditional on having returned home the previous year, only 8 percent of workers overstayed their visas (González-Enríquez and Reynès-Ramón 2011). Such policies, which promote circular and temporary migration, also ease natives' worries about the potential negative impacts of immigrant arrivals on the labor market.

To maximize the efficiency gains from migrants, policy makers could consider tailoring bilateral labor agreements to the needs of their labor markets, targeting occupations in which the host countries face labor shortages or rising labor demand. However, linking migrants' legal status to employment with only one specific employer could give firms too much power over workers and result in negative outcomes for both migrants and natives (Norlander 2021). Because migrants are filling essential labor gaps, the agreements could explicitly include certain protections for migrants, including direct-deposit mechanisms to prevent wage theft, gender-specific protections, and a fair and transparent implementation of the agreement contents about working conditions and rights (Testaverde, Moroz, and Dutta 2020).

BOX 4.10   The German "Triple Win" program

The heavy involvement of, and financing by, employers is a success factor of the German "Triple Win" program. As part of this program, Germany has identified countries with a surplus of professional nurses who cannot find employment in their home countries and whose qualifications can be recognized in Germany. The predeparture phase in the home countries involves language and cultural orientation training, while the recognition of professional certificates takes place in receiving countries.

Bosnia and Herzegovina, the Philippines, Serbia, and Tunisia are the partner countries for this project. The program's sustainability derives from the heavy involvement of employers and a variety of other actors at different stages of the program. Employers provide the funds to finance this initiative, which in less than 10 years has given labor market access to over 5,000 workers from the four partner countries.

Source: SVR Research Unit and MPI Europe 2019.

Action 9: Address misinformation and raise awareness of migrants' contributions

The COVID-19 pandemic brought health risks that triggered various antimigration episodes, but long-term international travel restrictions have been shown to be not only ineffective in stopping the pandemic but also severely costly for both receiving and sending countries (as further discussed in the previous chapters). For this reason, addressing misinformation and ensuring that people are aware of the key role played by migrants in receiving and sending societies will be crucial to address the potential rise of antimigration sentiments.

For these interventions to be successful, the choice of content and channels used to share information matters. A large-scale randomized experiment in Japan finds promising evidence on the role that information sharing can play in countering negative attitudes toward migration. A large national sample of citizens who participated in a text-assessment study were randomly exposed to information about potential social and economic benefits from immigration, and "this exposure led to a substantial increase in support for a more open immigration policy (Facchini, Margalit, and Nakata 2016). Communication efforts that engage the audience in perspective-taking exercises and draw parallels between migrants' lives and natives' personal experiences have also shown to be promising in increasing trust toward migrants (Rodríguez Chatruc and Rozo 2021).

Many initiatives introduced across the Mediterranean region since the start of the pandemic provide examples of actions to combat the misinformation that stigmatizes migrants and refugees. France, Germany, Italy, and Spain were active in this area in 2020 and 2021, in partnership with nongovernmental organizations (NGOs) and local organizations (OECD 2021). In line with these efforts, some countries also rewarded the contributions of essential foreign workers during the pandemic. For example, France has fast-tracked citizenship for a number of foreign frontline workers (Moroz, Shresta, and Testaverde 2020).

International organizations have also addressed misinformation. For instance, the UN's "Verified" initiative invited influencers, civil society members, and business and media organizations to be "digital first responders" or "information volunteers" to share only verified, trusted content and to combat misinformation (UN 2020). With similar intentions, Irish Aid and the IOM founded the Global Migration Media Academy to give journalism and communications students worldwide the tools, contextual knowledge, and ethical standards needed to report factually on migration (IOM 2021). The IOM has implemented similar initiatives in North and West African countries over the past few years (box 4.11).

BOX 4.11   Improving the accuracy of migration coverage in North and West Africa

Over the past three years, as part of the European Union–International Organization for Migration (EU-IOM) Regional Development Protection Programme, the IOM together with other journalists has trained more than 300 media students, journalists, and editors in Algeria, Libya, Morocco, and Tunisia. The training program aims to help these media professionals cover the topic of migration in a more factual and accurate way. For instance, it teaches them how to use proper terminology in covering key migration topics such as the difference between irregular migration, trafficking, and smuggling. The initiative grew out of a master's program in media and migration developed with Morocco's Higher Institute of Information and Communication.

In 2018, the IOM also conducted several workshops in West and Central Africa for media practitioners, attracting more than 600 participants. Similarly, the objective of these workshops was to train these professionals on proper ways of reporting on migration, including learning about local, regional, and global migration contexts; the use of language; and the legal implications of the terminology used when speaking about migration. Participants were then encouraged to change and improve the conversation about migration in the press in their home countries.

Source: Pace, Zayed, and Borgnäs 2020.

Action 10: Strengthen data capacity to apply an evidence-based approach to migration policy making

Even before the COVID-19 outbreak, the United Nations (UN) Global Compact for Safe, Orderly and Regular Migration identified the collection of accurate data on international migrants as an important gap to fill. The Migration Global Compact mentions the need to "collect and utilize accurate and disaggregated data" as an important objective to inform evidence-based policies (UN 2019). For instance, assessing labor market needs and whether the existing supply of workers is sufficient to meet the demand is crucial to inform decisions on the quantity and skill mix of migrants to admit in a country, thus helping employers fill gaps that cannot be filled by local workers. Similarly, information about nationals abroad and about returnees is important to allow sending countries to design potential policies in support of these groups and the families they leave behind.

Currently, when available, migration data mainly come from national statistics based on population censuses, household surveys, and administrative data sources. Although these data sources are useful to provide a general picture of overall migration trends over time, each of them comes with pros and cons, which need to be carefully considered before using them for migration-related analysis. The need to include more detailed questions on migration in regular household surveys and to potentially carry out ad hoc surveys to fill any remaining information gaps is a priority common to many countries and economies in the extended Mediterranean region, to varying extents. Furthermore, when relevant data are collected, ensuring that they are accessible to carry out policy-relevant analysis is fundamental to promote an evidence-based approach.

A combination of ad hoc migration and standard household surveys, together with census and administrative data, can be useful for receiving countries in the Mediterranean to gain useful insights on the migrant populations living within their borders. Standard labor force surveys can provide useful information on migrants as long as information on country of birth or citizenship has been collected from respondents. However, because these surveys are not specifically designed to capture information on migrants, small sample sizes and potential biases in the sample of the foreign population may limit the extent to which these data can be used to inform policy. Census data, given their universal coverage, are an ideal source to address the small sample size issue; however, their reduced frequency and relatively limited amount of labor market and migration information do not always allow for a detailed analysis of migration patterns. To address this issue, some receiving countries have carried out ad hoc surveys targeting the migrant population. The Spanish National Immigrant Survey conducted in 2007–09 is an example of these efforts.

Longitudinal surveys—surveys that track respondents over time—are the most powerful sources of data to better understand migrants' trajectories in host countries' labor markets and societies. France's Longitudinal Survey of the Integration of First-Time Arrivals (launched in 2010) and the Survey of Refugees in Germany (launched in 2016) are examples of good practices that can effectively inform migration policy making.[2]

Finally, administrative data from government agencies can also be used to gain interesting insights on the impacts of migrants on the local labor market (Garrote Sanchez 2019). For instance, Foged and Peri (2016) use administrative longitudinal data for Denmark to examine how an increased inflow of low-skilled refugee immigrants would affect the market for low-skilled labor. They find that "an increase in the supply of refugee-country immigrants pushed less educated native workers (especially the young and low-tenured ones) to pursue less manual-intensive occupations. As a result immigration had positive effects on native unskilled wages, employment, and occupational mobility" (Foged and Peri 2016, 1).

Sending countries face significant limitations in their ability to collect information about their citizens living abroad as well as returnees, but some promising practices have emerged in the region. Surveys that include questions about family members residing abroad are helpful to gather partial information on current migrants, but these questions do not capture migrants who have moved abroad with all members of their households. The identification of returnees in survey or census data is, in principle, easier, because data collection tools could include detailed questions about migration history. However, many sending countries and economies in the Mediterranean region do not include these questions in household surveys or census data, implying that returnees can only be approximately identified by checking whether respondents report having lived abroad in the previous years. To address some of these issues, the EU Labour Force Surveys in 2008 and 2014 included an ad hoc module focused on migration, which yields interesting insights on the characteristics and labor market outcomes of returnees.

Several countries within and outside the Mediterranean region have conducted ad hoc migration surveys. For instance, the 2013 Albania Return Migration Survey and the 2018/19 Bangladesh Return Migrants Survey included questions on migration trajectories, socioeconomic conditions before departure, education and employment abroad, and reintegration in their home country upon return (Garrote Sanchez 2019).

Egypt has also undertaken significant data efforts to better understand the dynamics of outmigration and return migration in the country. For instance, the Egypt Labor Market Panel Survey conducted in 1988, 1998, 2006, 2012, and 2018 included a detailed module on migration and remittances, enabling the collection of detailed data about the characteristics of household members living abroad. This data source has been key to gaining insights on different aspects of return migration in the country (El-Mallakh and Wahba 2021a, 2021b; Wahba 2015). The 2013 Egypt Household International Migration Survey is another example of migration data collected to gain further insights on the drivers and impacts of migration from Egypt.

Administrative data collected at different points of exit from or reentry into sending countries could also provide useful insights. For instance, in Egypt, the Central Agency for Public Mobilization and Statistics produces three useful annual bulletins (CAPMAS 2019): (a) "Egyptians Obtaining Approval to Migrate Abroad and Egyptians Acquiring Foreign Nationality"; (b) "Work Permits Issued for Egyptians to Work Abroad"; and (c) "Foreigners Working in Private and Investment Sectors." The Egyptian Ministry of Foreign Affairs also collects information on Egyptian citizens living abroad.

The COVID-19 crisis has drawn further attention on the importance of accessing timely labor market and migration data to ensure that adequate policy responses can be promptly introduced. The disruptions caused by the pandemic have further complicated access to timely, detailed, and representative labor market statistics, highlighting the shortcomings of traditional data collection methods and labor market definitions in this context (ILO 2020).

To address these challenges, a number of researchers have explored not only the potential use of big data to forecast migration (Zagheni, Weber, and Gummadi 2017) but also the use of online platforms to accurately and cost-effectively target migrants for survey research (Pötzschke and Braun 2017). Initial results based on Google search trends and Facebook data have shown promising results but also suggest that more work is needed to fully understand how to best use these data as complements, and not substitutes, of standard sources (Tjaden 2020).

Closing remarks

The COVID-19 pandemic posed a severe test of migration systems both in the extended Mediterranean region and globally. The region's countries and economies responded to this public health shock but at great economic cost and with results that often revealed gaps in migration systems rather than resilience—the ability to adjust to shocks flexibly, recover quickly, and operate sustainably.

This chapter set forth the policy objectives and actions that could rebuild and even strengthen migration systems in the wake of any large shock that disrupts people's movements, whether from a pandemic or from violent conflict, disaster, or climate change. One of these actions speaks to better developing the evidence basis for addressing new and ongoing migration challenges. Policy makers need more comprehensive, more timely data to respond quickly and effectively to the mobility disruptions, whatever their cause, that are certain to come.

As a whole, these proposed policy actions point toward a vision of migration resilience that, even during crises, can address key labor shortages, keep both migrant and native populations safer, sustain household incomes, and ameliorate blows to economic growth. Despite the COVID-19 pandemic and the resulting travel restrictions, as the documented mobility trends show, the structural drivers of migration remained strong throughout the extended Mediterranean region. Whether this crisis can illuminate the way toward better adapting migration systems to future crises will depend on learning its lessons.

Notes

1. For instance, Action 2 is most relevant to refugees and long-term economic migrants, Action 3 to economic migrants across the skills spectrum, and Action 7 to refugees and low-skilled temporary migrants.
2. The Survey of Refugees in Germany is a collaboration of the Institute for Employment Research (IAB) of Germany's Federal Employment Agency; the Federal Office for Migration and Refugees (BAMF) Research Centre; and the Socio-Economic Panel (SOEP) at the German Institute for Economic Research in Berlin.

References

Baruah, N., J. Chaloff, J.-C. Dumont, and R. Kawasaki. 2021. "The Future of Labor Migration in Asia: Post-COVID-19 Pandemic." In *Labor Migration in Asia: Impacts of the COVID-19 Crisis and the Post-Pandemic Future*, 38–59. Tokyo: Asian Development Bank Institute; Paris: Organisation for Economic Co-operation and Development; Bangkok: International Labour Organization.

Bathke, B. 2020. "Germany Invests in E-Learning after 220,000 Migrants Had to Interrupt Integration Courses." InfoMigrants report, May 19.

Bither, J., and A. Ziebarth. 2018. "Creating Legal Pathways to Reduce Irregular Migration? What We Can Learn from Germany's 'Western Balkan Regulation'." Paper, Migration Strategy Group on International Cooperation and Development, German Marshall Fund of the United States, Washington, DC.

Brücker, H., M. Falkenhain, T. Fendel, M. Promberger, and M. Raab. 2020. "Strong Demand and Sound Labour Market Integration: Labour Migration to Germany based on the Western Balkans Regulation." Brief Report No. 16|2020, Institute for Employment Research (IAB), Nuremberg, Germany.

CAPMAS (Central Agency for Public Mobilization and Statistics, Arab Republic of Egypt). 2019. "Migration Booklet in Egypt 2018." Booklet, CAPMAS, Cairo.

Del Carpio, X., Ç. Özden, M. Testaverde, and M. Wagner. 2016. "Global Migration of Talent and Tax Incentives: Evidence from Malaysia's Returning Expert Program." Policy Research Working Paper 7875, World Bank, Washington, DC.

Dickerson, S., and Ç. Özden. 2018. "Diaspora Engagement and Return Migration Policies." In *Handbook on Migration and Globalisation*, edited by A. Triandafyllidou, 206–25. Cheltenham, UK: Edward Elgar Publishing.

DOLE (Department of Labor and Employment, Republic of the Philippines). 2021. "Assist WELL (Welfare, Employment, Legal, Livelihood)." Web page, DOLE website: https://www.dole.gov.ph/assist-well-welfare-employment-legal-livelihood/.

EC (European Commission). 2020a. "Council Recommendation 2020/912 of 30 June 2020 on the Temporary Restriction on Non-Essential Travel into the EU and the Possible Lifting of Such Restriction." https://eur-lex.europa.eu/legal-content/EN/TXT/HTML/?uri=CELEX:32 020H0912&from=EN.

EC (European Commission). 2020b. *Migration: New Pact on Migration and Asylum.* Luxembourg: Publications Office of the European Union.

EC (European Commission). 2020c. "A Fresh Start on Migration: Building Confidence and Striking a New Balance between Responsibility and Solidarity." Press release IP/20/1706, September 23, EC, Brussels.

EC (European Commission). 2021a. "Communication from the Commission to the European Parliament, the Council, the European Economic and Social Committee and the Committee of the Regions on the Report on Migration and Asylum." Report COM(2021) 590 final, September 29, EC, Brussels.

EC (European Commission). 2021b. "Report from the Commission to the European Parliament and the Council pursuant to Article 16(1) of Regulation (EU) 2021/953 of the European Parliament and of the Council on a framework for the issuance, verification and acceptance of interoperable COVID-19 vaccination, test and recovery certificates (EU Digital COVID Certificate) to facilitate free movement during the COVID-19 pandemic." Report COM(2021) 649 final, October 18, EC, Brussels.

EIU (Economist Intelligence Unit). 2021. "More than 85 Poor Countries Will Not Have Widespread Access to Coronavirus Vaccines before 2023." EIU Update, January 27, The Economist Group, London.

Economist. 2021. "Why Vaccine Passports are Causing Chaos." *Economist*, October 26.

El-Mallakh, N., and J. Wahba. 2021a. "Return Migrants and the Wage Premium: Does the Legal Status of Migrants Matter?" *Journal of Population Economics.* doi:10.1007 /s00148-021-00872-z.

El-Mallakh, N., and J. Wahba. 2021b. "Upward or Downward: Occupational Mobility and Return Migration." *World Development* 137: 105203.

Facchini, G., Y. Margalit, and H. Nakata. 2016. "Countering Public Opposition to Immigration: The Impact of Information Campaigns." Discussion Paper No. 10420, Institute of Labor Economics, Bonn.

Foged, M., and G. Peri. 2016. "Immigrants' Effect on Native Workers: New Analysis on Longitudinal Data." *American Economic Journal: Applied Economics* 8 (2): 1–34.

Garrote Sanchez, Daniel. 2019. "Data Availability on Migration in Europe and Central Asia." Unpublished manuscript, World Bank, Washington, DC.

González-Enríquez, C., and M. Reynès-Ramón. 2011. "Circular Migration between Spain and Morocco: Something More than Agricultural Work?" Technical report, METOIKOS Research Project, European University Institute, Florence.

Gostoli, Y. 2020. "Coronavirus: Short on Doctors, Italy Looks to Migrants." DW.com, December 1. https://www.dw.com/en/coronavirus-short-on-doctors-italy-looks-to-migrants/a-55789791.

Hagen-Zanker, J., and N. Both. 2021. "Social Protection Provisions to Refugees during the Covid-19 Pandemic: Lessons Learned from Government and Humanitarian Responses."

Working Paper No. 612, Overseas Development Institute (ODI), London; and German Agency for International Cooperation (GIZ), Bonn.

Hein, C. 2021. "Looking for Pact-Makers: The Debate on the Deadlocked EU Migration and Asylum Pact." Analysis, Heinrich-Böll-Stiftung Paris office.

IFRC and TRC (International Federation of Red Cross and Red Crescent Societies and Turkish Red Crescent Society). 2021. "Cash Assistance in Times of COVID-19: Impacts on Refugees Living in Turkey." Survey report, IFRC, Geneva; and TRC, Ankara.

ILO (International Labour Organization). 2018. "SIRA Mobile Application Links Migrant Returnees with Employers." Press release, December 26.

ILO (International Labour Organization). 2020. "COVID-19 Impact on the Collection of Labour Market Statistics." Note, ILO Department of Statistics (ILOSTAT), Geneva.

IOM (International Organization for Migration). 2021. "Global Migration Media Academy Seals Partnership with NUI Galway to Address Anti-Migrant Rhetoric." Press release, April 26.

Kikkawa, A., C. J. Justo, and P. Sirivunnabood. 2021. "Migtech: How Technology Is Reshaping Labor Mobility and the Landscape of International Migration." In *Labor Migration in Asia: Impacts of the COVID-19 Crisis and the Post-Pandemic Future*, 60–102. Tokyo: Asian Development Bank Institute; Paris: Organisation for Economic Co-operation and Development; Bangkok: International Labour Organization.

Lau, L. S., K. Hooper, and M. Zard. 2021. "From Unilateral Response to Coordinated Action: How Can Mobility Systems in Sub-Saharan Africa Adapt to the Public-Health Challenges of COVID-19?" Policy brief, Migration Policy Institute, Washington, DC.

McKenzie, D., and D. Yang. 2015. "Evidence on Policies to Increase the Development Impacts of International Migration." *The World Bank Research Observer* 30 (2): 155–92.

Moroz, H., M. Shrestha, and M. Testaverde. 2020. "Potential Responses to the COVID-19 Outbreak in Support of Migrant Workers." Note, World Bank, Washington, DC.

Moser, C. 2018. "It Takes a Village: Despite Challenges, Migrant Groups Lead Development in Senegal." *Migration Information Source*, October 4. Migration Policy Institute, Washington, DC.

Norlander, P. 2021. "Do Guest Worker Programs Give Firms Too Much Power?" *IZA World of Labor* 484.

OECD (Organisation for Economic Co-operation and Development). 2020. "What Is the Impact of the COVID-19 Pandemic on Immigrants and Their Children?" Policy brief, OECD, Paris.

OECD (Organisation for Economic Co-operation and Development). 2021. *International Migration Outlook 2021*. Paris: OECD Publishing.

Özden, Ç., and M. Wagner. 2020. *Moving for Prosperity: Global Migration and Labor Markets*. Policy Research Report. Washington, DC: World Bank.

Özvarış, Ş. B., İ. Kayı, D. Mardin, S. Sakarya, A. Ekzayez, K. Meagher, and P. Patel. 2020. "COVID-19 Barriers and Response Strategies for Refugees and Undocumented Migrants in Turkey." *Journal of Migration and Health* 1–2: 100012.

Pace, P., S. Zayed, and E. Borgnäs. 2020. "Balancing Migration Narratives through Programming and Media Reporting in North Africa." In *Migration in West and North*

Africa and across the Mediterranean: Trends, Risks, Development and Governance, 418–25. Geneva: International Organization for Migration.

Pötzschke, S., and M. Braun. 2017. "Migrant Sampling Using Facebook Advertisements: A Case Study of Polish Migrants in Four European Countries." *Social Science Computer Review* 35 (5): 633–53.

Quartey, P., M. B. Setrana, and C. A. Tagoe. 2020. "Migration across West Africa: Development-Related Aspects." In *Migration in West and North Africa and across the Mediterranean: Trends, Risks, Development and Governance*, 270–78. Geneva: International Organization for Migration.

Rodríguez Chatruc, M., and S. V. Rozo. 2021. "In Someone Else's Shoes: Promoting Prosocial Behavior through Perspective Taking." Policy Research Working Paper 9866, World Bank, Washington, DC.

SVR Research Unit and MPI Europe (Research Unit, Expert Council of German Foundations on Integration and Migration and Migration Policy Institute Europe). 2019. "Legal Migration for Work and Training: Mobility Options to Europe for Those Not in Need of Protection." Study 2019-2, SVR Research Unit, Berlin.

Testaverde, M., H. Moroz, and P. Dutta. 2020. "Labor Mobility as a Jobs Strategy for Myanmar: Strengthening Active Labor Market Policies to Enhance the Benefits of Mobility." Report, World Bank, Washington, DC.

Testaverde, M., H. Moroz, C. H. Hollweg, and A. Schmillen. 2017. *Migrating to Opportunity: Overcoming Barriers to Labor Mobility in Southeast Asia*. Washington, DC: World Bank.

Tjaden, J. 2020. "Assessing the Impact of Awareness-Raising Campaigns on Potential Migrants: What We Have Learned So Far." In *Migration in West and North Africa and across the Mediterranean: Trends, Risks, Development and Governance*, 426–34. Geneva: International Organization for Migration.

Triandafyllidou, A., L. Bartolini, and C. Guidi. 2019. *Exploring the Links Between Enhancing Regular Pathways and Discouraging Irregular Migration: A Discussion Paper to Inform Future Policy Deliberations*. Geneva: International Organization for Migration.

UN (United Nations). 2019. "Global Compact for Safe, Orderly and Regular Migration." UN General Assembly Resolution A/RES/73/195 (December 19, 2018).

UN (United Nations). 2020. "United Nations Launches Global Initiative to Combat Misinformation, Led by Department of Global Communications." Press release PI/2285, May 21.

UNDP (United Nations Development Programme). 2021. "The Socio-Economic Impact of COVID-19 and Low Oil Prices on Migrants and Remittances in the Arab Region." Working paper, UNDP, New York.

UNHCR (United Nations High Commissioner for Refugees). 2020. "Internet Governance in Displacement." Digital Access, Inclusion and Participation research brief, UNHCR Innovation Service, Geneva.

Wahba, J. 2015. "Selection, Selection, Selection: The Impact of Return Migration." *Journal of Population Economics* 28 (3): 535–63.

World Bank. 2020. "MoMRA's Low Income Labor Housing Strategy." Internal report, World Bank, Washington, DC.

Zagheni, E., I. Weber, and K. Gummadi. 2017. "Leveraging Facebook's Advertising Platform to Monitor Stocks of Migrants." *Population and Development Review* 43 (4): 721–34.

www.ingramcontent.com/pod-product-compliance
Lightning Source LLC
Chambersburg PA
CBHW050907210326
41597CB00002B/56